Covert Radio Agents, 1939–1945

Covert Radio Agents, 1939–1945

Signals From Behind Enemy Lines

David Hebditch

Pen & Sword
MILITARY

First published in Great Britain in 2021 by
Pen & Sword Military
An imprint of
Pen & Sword Books Ltd
Yorkshire – Philadelphia

ISBN 978 1 52679 494 9

A CIP catalogue record for this book is
available from the British Library.

Typeset by Mac Style
Printed and bound in the UK by TJ Books Ltd,
Padstow, Cornwall.

Pen & Sword Books Limited incorporates the imprints of Atlas,
Archaeology, Aviation, Discovery, Family History, Fiction, History,
Maritime, Military, Military Classics, Politics, Select, Transport,
True Crime, Air World, Frontline Publishing, Leo Cooper, Remember
When, Seaforth Publishing, The Praetorian Press, Wharncliffe
Local History, Wharncliffe Transport, Wharncliffe True Crime
and White Owl.

For a complete list of Pen & Sword titles please contact

PEN & SWORD BOOKS LIMITED
47 Church Street, Barnsley, South Yorkshire, S70 2AS, England
E-mail: enquiries@pen-and-sword.co.uk
Website: www.pen-and-sword.co.uk

Or

PEN AND SWORD BOOKS
1950 Lawrence Rd, Havertown, PA 19083, USA
E-mail: Uspen-and-sword@casematepublishers.com
Website: www.penandswordbooks.com

Contents

Acknowledgements

Dr Ian Herrington provided an invaluable guiding hand through his remarkable research into the activities of the Special Operations Executive in Norway. My friend, historian and author Ola Flyum on Sula Island, Trøndelag made sure the Scandinavian perspective was kept in focus. I am grateful to veteran radio-interceptors Geoffrey Pidgeon and Bob King for trying to locate a legible version of the Radio Security Service's plotting map. I am indebted to Henry Wilson of Pen & Sword for his wise advice on the development of the book. And many thanks to military historian Dan Hebditch for his guidance on the key events of the Second World War, especially in Australia and the South Pacific. In all cases any errors are entirely of my own making.

Unless otherwise credited, all images used are freely available in the public domain.

Four 'Technical Briefings' are included in Chapter 8. These are tutorials covering: (8.1) the radios and how they worked; (8.2) how enemy radio intelligence could monitor and locate wireless transmissions; (8.3) the use of Morse code and the format of messages and (8.4) how messages were encrypted by the agent and the home station to make them as difficult as possible for the enemy to read. If you are confident in your knowledge of these topics, it is fine to skip the briefings selectively. Otherwise you might even consider reading them first – they include many more accounts of the exploits of the Second World War's radio agents.

Indigenous content warning

Aboriginal and Torres Strait Islander peoples should be aware this book contains the images and names of people who have passed away.

Introduction: Unsung Heroes?

Radio agents, who appeared for the first time during World War II, decisively influenced the entire course of the unhappy struggle.
Wilhelm F. Flicke, cryptanalyst, German High Command

A short-wave radio's rate of fire was agonisingly slow. There was no nose-art on the transmitter, no swastikas bragging of each kill. But a single message of a few words from these boxes could obliterate hundreds of the enemy. A different signal at another time might ensure fighters on your side would get home to their families, alive and well.

'Wireless operator' was a perilous occupation; at times, life expectancy behind enemy lines was six weeks. The truth was bleak: to do their job they had to announce their whereabouts to the enemy.

These are the actions a well-trained radio agent would undertake in order to transmit a message. First, he or she would extend the correct length of wire aerial up a nearby tree or other structure. Then they would double check the planned time of contact and tune to the next scheduled frequency. After connecting the battery, headphones would be pulled on and the Morse key plugged in. Turning the set on and flipping a switch to 'transmit' was the instant the agent effectively announced 'Hello, I'm here' to an enemy impatient to shoot them dead with machine-pistols.

Next to the radio would be the messages ready for transmission. They would consist of neat arrays of seemingly random combinations of letters in 'five-letter groups': KXJEY, UREBA, ZWNHE, and so on. The first message might be a report on the movement of warships not far off the coast. It had been enciphered as carefully as possible; if it couldn't be read at home base the operator would be asked to transmit it again, giving the Funkabwehr (Radio Intelligence) a second chance to locate them. Other messages might be sent on behalf of a network whose radio had given up the ghost; these still had to be sent with 100 per cent accuracy.

Agents were urged to keep transmission times below five minutes. Instructors taught that the enemy's signals intelligence units – the 'direction-finders' (D/F) – would orientate their antennae to pin the transmitter's location down to a radius of 30–50km (18–30 miles). Each station would send via teletype the bearing in degrees to a central location, where it would be plotted on a map. Mobile D/F trucks, boats and aircraft in the vicinity would then become active, narrowing the triangulation down to one or two kilometres. Each extra bearing made the radius smaller; the agent was at the centre of a noose tightening remorselessly around their neck.

Once the radio's location had been pinpointed, military units and civilian police would be alerted. If the wireless was still transmitting, the operator's fate would be sealed. Infantry sweeping the area would look out for likely hiding places, poorly concealed aerials, unattended bicycles or cars.

In urban areas they used D/F sets that could be carried in suitcases or strapped to their bodies under a topcoat as they walked the streets trying to narrow their focus to an individual building that could be stormed by soldiers. If the target was an apartment block, one of the assault team would enter and disconnect the electricity supply to each floor, one at a time, until the signal stopped. Then, fingers on triggers, they would start kicking doors in.

Pushing such threats from their mind, agents watched the seconds tick down. At a predetermined interval before the scheduled time they switched the radio on; the set needed to warm up before it could operate at full power. The agent adjusted the headphones and pulled the Morse key a little closer.

The instant the second hand reached twelve, a short sequence was transmitted: 'Hello, this is AJR, AJR. I have three messages. Over.' A hiss of noise took over the radio channel. It seemed an eternity, but the frequency came to life in seconds: 'This is NDE. Go ahead.' 'NDE' was home-base call sign for the day. (See Chapter 8.3)

The agent's thumb and forefinger gripped the top of the Morse key again, and they began sending the first message. Each letter had to be correct, with no transpositions; getting *anything* wrong could require the whole message to be sent again. The delay of a signal about the movements of an enemy submarine could result in the death of scores of merchant mariners. After sending the last five-letter group the agent signalled the message was finished. After the third it was time to move.

The radio, aerial, headset and Morse key went into a metal box to be returned to their hiding-place – everything except the battery; that needed to be recharged. The agent put the heavy unit into a backpack and surveyed the surrounding landscape. Nothing moved, but was that the engine of a distant car?

A woman who lived a nearby village regularly recharged batteries from the mains electricity supply. It took an hour to reach her house, and the agent sat exhausted behind the dwelling, watching and waiting. Caution was dictated not merely by the danger of being spotted by enemy patrols but by concern about the woman. Just 24 hours earlier, her husband had been seen talking to an enemy intelligence officer. It could have been innocent; he might have been stopped randomly in the street. However, the depressing fact was that *nobody* could be trusted.

*   *   *

The notional covert radio operator portrayed in this sketch could have been located anywhere in the world. The stresses under which he – or she – had to work were universal, defined by the job itself. Some of the pressures, especially the technical problems, agents could tackle themselves, but others, the cold-blooded determination of the enemy to track their location and the risk of betrayal by the local population, were in the hands of the gods.

This book tells the stories of the remarkably courageous radio operators whose work was indispensable to the circuits of agents who operated covertly behind enemy lines throughout the Second World War. The radio specialists were the first in, the first out and, if caught with their equipment, the first to be killed.

Les Marguerites Fleuriront Ce Soir ('The Daisies Will Flower Tonight'). A CIA artist's post-war romanticized imagining of an OSS radio operator at work.

Chapter 1

How to Make a Radio Agent

Espionage has always played a great role in wartime. The difficulty in carrying it on successfully lay less in the procurement of information than in passing the information in good season to the military or political leaders of the country involved.
Wilhelm F. Flicke, cryptanalyst, German High Command

1.1 Infiltration: unusual arrangements

Compared with the First World War, the conflict of 1939–45 was far more global. But its defining characteristic was the way in which so many countries were *occupied* by the enemy, in terms of their geography, natural resources, infrastructure, economic assets and those members of the population who could not or would not flee. Every square kilometre seized was available for exploitation and plunder. In Europe the main occupying power was Germany; its change of name in 1943 from 'Deutsches Reich' to 'Großdeutsches Reich' ('German Realm' to 'Greater German Realm') reflected the scale of its territorial expansion. In the Far East, Imperial Japan added some twenty-eight countries to the domain it occupied in 1939. Italy did its bit by taking over only marginally important Abyssinia and Albania.

The situation in lands occupied by the enemy was of vital significance to the Allies' conduct of the war. France's Atlantic coast, especially Brittany, provided the Kriegsmarine with a fine choice of lairs for the U-boat 'wolf-packs' which, during the early years, wrought havoc on merchant shipping supplying an isolated Britain. Northern France, Belgium and the Netherlands offered excellent ground for airfields which put Luftwaffe bombers within easy range of southern England and London. This was an advantage denied to the Royal Air Force and, from 1942, the United States Army Air Corps targeting Hitler's industrial centres and, later, his major cities. Taking a longer view, the geographical deployment of ground forces influenced where and when the Allies would start the lengthy and bloody undertaking of liberating continental Europe.

The islands and fjords of Norway's 2,650km (1,650 mile) coastline – especially the stretch facing the North Atlantic – could have been designed to meet the German Navy's requirements. A total of 239,057 islands and some 1,200 fjords gave unlimited – but not impenetrable – cover to warships being repaired and provisioned before striking out west above the British Isles to the North Atlantic and up around Nordkapp (North Cape) towards the Soviet Union. The disadvantage of Norway was its mountainous terrain; Galdhøpiggen is, at 2,469m (8,100ft), the tallest European peak north of the Alps. Consequently, roads have to follow the difficult, twisty contours of this landscape. Even in the twenty-first century Norway boasts only 500km (310 miles) of motorway (freeway), and almost all of this is in the east, serving the capital of Oslo. For the German occupying forces this logistical nightmare could be solved only by sending troops and materiel up and down the country by train or sea.

When Japan extended its reach south through Indo-China, Indonesia and the islands of the South Pacific towards Australia and New Zealand, its logistics inevitably became stretched and totally dependent on sea-borne

CHIFFCHAFF RED W/T.
Operator.

CHIFFCHAFF was an SOE operation in Norway in early 1945 to support the arming and training of Milorg resistance fighters.

support and supplies. On some islands, the jungle was so impenetrable that distances were measured in days of travel rather than miles or kilometres. There, even a Norwegian road would have been viewed as an extravagant luxury.

* * *

Co-operation between Allied special operations units was a marked feature of the clandestine effort in this war. The first nine hundred Office of Strategic Services (OSS) agents were trained at SOE's Camp X (Special Training Station 103) on the shores of Lake Ontario in Canada, just 48 km (30 miles) from the border with the United States. Even more American radio operators were taught in the UK at a dedicated school (STS 53c) in Poundon, Buckinghamshire.

The scale of this co-operation – and, indeed, the indebtedness of OSS to the SOE – may come as a surprise to many readers on both sides of the Atlantic. Most Hollywood screenwriters and, less forgivably, some military historians must shoulder the responsibility for this, having depicted major events like Operation OVERLORD as all-American actions without mentioning the presence on the Normandy battlefields of Canadian or British forces. In 2006 the balance was redressed a little when the US Army Special Operations Command (USASOC) History Office published a biography of one of its most distinguished and long-serving officers, Herbert R. Brucker.[1] This is of interest in the immediate context of this book because Brucker was a W/T operator who was trained by SOE for Operation JEDBURGH.

Herbert Brucker was born in Newark, New Jersey on 10 October 1921 to a French-American father and a German-American mother, but grew up in the French province of Alsace-Lorraine, which borders Belgium,

Private Herbert R. Brucker aged nineteen, US Army, 1940.

Luxembourg, Germany and Switzerland. He was seventeen when his family brought him back to the US, and two years later, he enlisted in the army as a private soldier, long before America entered the war. Understandably, his English was not very good, but while training as a radio operator he demonstrated considerable skill in Morse code and rose to the rank of Technician/4 (T/4). When the OSS was created, he volunteered for special operations, and the combination of prior military training with fluent Morse and French made him a candidate the new agency could not ignore. In fact, he was recruited at the time of Operation JEDBURGH's gestation, when there was pressure on OSS to find operators they were prepared to serve up to the SOE. Briscoe's 2006 article (written a year before Brucker's death) explains in no uncertain terms why the British were doing the training:

> British SOE had been putting agents into the German-occupied countries of Europe since 1940. This was almost three years before the United States formed the Office of Strategic Services. As such, British field training for special operatives far surpassed anything that the OSS could provide. Colonel Charles Vanderblue, Chief, Special Operations Branch, OSS, knew this because he had detailed one of his training officers, Captain John Tyson, to evaluate SOE instruction. Tyson reported on 30 July 1943: 'The training any prospective SO agent has received in our Washington schools prior to his arrival in this theater is entirely inadequate and no trainees should be considered for field operations until they have had further training in this theater, which in many cases will involve a period of three months.'

On completion of his OSS courses Brucker was sent to New York, where he boarded a troop-transporter (a converted Australian cattle boat) for an unpleasant and hazardous winter voyage across the North Atlantic. He and his fellow passengers landed in Glasgow on 23 December 1943 and headed south by train to London. On the drive to a US Army 'Replacement Center' they were appalled by the sight of the damage the Luftwaffe had inflicted on the capital – but they must also have noticed most of the pubs were still open. Early on 26 December, a car collected Brucker and took him to 'a headquarters' – presumably that of SOE F section, Norseby House, 83 Baker Street. There he was informed he had a few more days off before, on 2 January 1944, he was sent for further training.

Having been told nothing about the exact nature of his deployment, the young American protested he had already been trained by the OSS 'and was ready for combat'. The Commander of F section, Maurice Buckmaster, told him, 'It would simply be murder to send you on an operation with just OSS training.' At the time, Brucker was not happy, but he was just one of sixty-five other OSS operators to endure this indignity. However, on completing the course at Special Training School 7 in Surrey (home to the Students Assessment Board) he was forced to concede that 'SOE training was far superior. It made most of my OSS/SO stateside training seem amateurish.' His next stop was STS 54, the Special Radio and Wireless School at Thame Park in Oxfordshire. He later described the training there in admiring terms:

> The shed [one of many dotted about the grounds] was just big enough for table, chair, electric lamp, and radio transmitter and receiver. Antennas were set up to limit transmissions to a couple hundred yards … 'We transmitted and received using the large Type 3 Mark II suitcase radio (fifty pounds with transformer), the little Type A Mark III radio, and the cigarette pack-sized "Biscuit" receiver with an earplug,' said Brucker.[2]

(See Briefing Chapter 8.1 for more on the radios.)

*   *   *

This co-ordinated transatlantic effort bore fruit when, in the late evening of 5 June 1944 – the day before the D-Day landings in Normandy – Operation HUGH parachuted into central France near Châteauroux on the banks of the River Indre. The three-man team was the first of ninety-three units tasked to rally, train and supply resistance groups in support of the invasion. They operated under the banner of Operation JEDBURGH. Each team's members were carefully selected from the British SOE, the US OSS and the French *Bureau Central de Renseignements et d'Action* (Central Bureau of Intelligence and Operations). One agent would be a British or American officer, a second would be a French interpreter and the third a radio agent, an NCO of any nationality. The wireless operator played an essential role in providing liaison with other units and communications with Special Forces HQ in London to schedule the airdrops of the arms, ammunition and explosives needed to sabotage and delay the German defences against Operation OVERLORD.

JEDBURGH teams also operated in the Low Countries (where they worked in concert with the Special Air Service) and in the Far East.

1.2 Irregular Warfare: cogs in a very large machine

After the failure of the British Expeditionary Force (BEF) and the French Army to repulse Germany's westward onslaught in 1940, Allied commanders looking on nervously from the other side of the Channel needed to get creative.

The Secret Intelligence Service (SIS) was originally established in 1909 with the specific objective of gathering and analysing foreign human intelligence (HUMINT). It took its present formal name after the First World War; 'MI6' became one of its cover names in the Second World War and stuck. SIS contributes another acronym to this story: GC&CS (the Government Code & Cypher School) at Bletchley Park was part of the same organization but specialized in the highly technical field of signals intelligence (SIGINT). It has now been renamed the Government Communications Headquarters (GCHQ).

However, the SOE and the SAS were responses to the immediate circumstances of 1940. SOE was formed specifically to implement Winston Churchill's edict to put the torch to occupied Europe. It set up shop in London's Baker Street in 1940, and the SAS began its behind-the-lines attacks on the Afrika Korps in the Libyan Desert the following year.

For SOE the disadvantage of starting with no agents was turned into the advantage of being able to train all its recruits in its own evolving doctrine. SOE's training manual sets out the objectives of irregular warfare, specifically: 'to undermine enemy's morale'; 'to raise morale of Occupied Territories'; 'to damage enemy's materiel'; 'to infiltrate weapons, explosives, sabotage equipment'; 'to damage enemy's man-power and communications'; and 'to improve our own man-power and communications by infiltration of "organizers", radio sets and operators'.

The manual goes on to state that:

> All these methods are interdependent. Each one singly has its relation to our fundamental objectives; but, if each is used singly, the objectives can never be attained … You will be a cog in a very large machine whose smooth functioning depends on each separate cog carrying out its part efficiently.[3]

These edicts are clearly directed at students who will graduate to become members of SOE; SIS/MI6 disliked any activities that would draw attention to its spies.

1.3 Recruitment: 'don't want them overburdened'

In the UK, an initial obstacle to the urgent recruitment of agents was the MI6 and MI5* tradition of only employing candidates who were British born and

---

* 'MI5' is more correctly called the Security Service. In the USA its equivalent counter-intelligence role is played by the FBI.

bred (and preferably educated at a Jolly Good School). SOE was expected to do the same. Dual citizenship offered an exception to the rule, but an agreement with General Charles de Gaulle's Free French prohibited the signing up of French nationals, so the hunt for fluent speakers of French tended to focus on people with one British parent or who were raised in France.

A primary source of recruits, especially in the first year, was the stream of refugees arriving in the UK from occupied Europe. All were interrogated to filter out any agents Germany attempted to infiltrate behind *our* lines. Everyone was asked what languages they could read, write and speak, and how well. If the box next to 'Military experience?' was also ticked, they joined a long short list. If questions like 'Special skills?' resulted in answers such as 'Radio amateur' or 'Military signals officer', the short list got even shorter, and they would be earmarked for further screening. But for SIS and SOE the requirement for linguistic fluency was prime: it might take only a few weeks to teach someone how to key Morse code at twenty words per minute; but a convincing rendition of the Bordeaux accent might require a lifetime.

Word soon got around that a new agency was looking for native speakers – exact job specification unknown. Commanders in the armed services became talent-spotters. Someone overheard speaking a foreign language in a café or at a party might then receive an unexpected telephone call.

In some cases it was very difficult to pass off even the most fluent speaker of a language as local. For example, the Atlantic coast of Norway contains a string of settlements, villages and towns where everyone knows everyone else. They also speak dialects that vary from place to place. Only one foreigner was sent into Norway as an agent throughout the whole war.

1.4 Training: 'everything's highly embryonic here'

SOE's training programme is probably the best example of how to turn raw recruits into clandestine agents who could survive behind enemy lines and make a contribution to winning the war as they did so. It remains a model for training plans used in the twenty-first century.

It came in three parts: the preliminary course, sometimes called 'commando' training; specialist courses such as demolition and radio operation; and then the 'finishing school', which taught how to operate in occupied territories secretly and securely – including grim guidance on how to behave if you fell into the hands of the Gestapo. The commando course, which centred on physical fitness, determination and grit, always came first because it was what soldiers call a 'bottle tester': let's see if you've got what it takes before we invest too much time and effort in you. Failure here was the moment at which trainees climbed on to a truck for the ride back to the railway station, without any choice in the matter.

Specialist courses could come before or after finishing school. The acronym 'STS' appears a lot on the contemporary paperwork; it means 'Special Training School' and is followed by a number indicating which school. Sometimes there are references to 'A-Group' and 'B-Group', but this is not the start of a sequence that ran up to 'Z-Group'. B-Group referred to the training schools in and around the Beaulieu estate of Lord Montagu in Hampshire; A-Group comprised the schools around the isolated village of Arisaig on the west coast of Scotland. There were also training establishments in central England, specifically in the counties of Oxfordshire, Gloucestershire, Leicestershire and Buckinghamshire.

A-Group was chosen as the main centre for training in the use of firearms and explosives because it was remote and sparsely populated; locals puzzled by all the noise could be palmed off with stories of 'commando training' and they quickly learned not to ask too many questions. B-Group taught recruits how to work under cover, the courses using the many large country houses in the area; the teaching staff lived in thirteenth century Palace House, the present home of the Montagu family. All W/T operators would have passed

The house at Thame Park, Oxfordshire, home to STS 52, SOE's main training school for wireless telegraphy operators.

through B-Group for 'finishing', some also taking tuition in coding and decoding at STS 34.

Skills in the use of radio were taught at a number of locations away from A- and B-Groups. STS 54a was at Fawley Court, Henley-on-Thames, an impressive house that stands on land once owned by Edward the Confessor. STS 54b was not in the vicinity of 54a but on the other side of Scotland at Belhaven School, Dunbar, East Lothian, 40km (25 miles) from Edinburgh.

The most important school for SOE's wireless operators was STS 52 at Thame Park in Oxfordshire. Historical references to the location date back to 1130 CE, when Alexander de Blois, Bishop of Lincoln, is recorded as

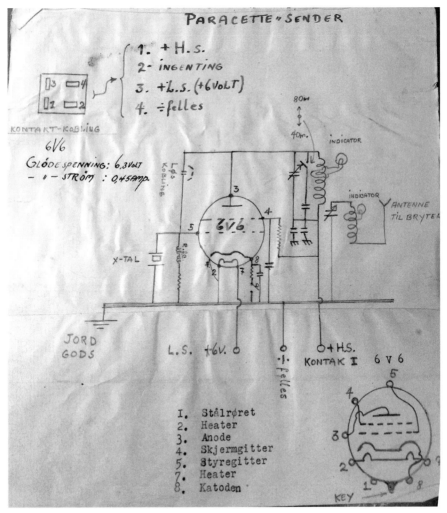

A page of the W/T course notes Finn Berger wrote in Norwegian for fellow agent Eivind Viken, showing part of the transmitter circuit in the Paraset radio.

planning to use the land for hunting deer. The present building dates from the eighteenth century and boasts a crenellated exterior.

It is worth noting that SOE's W/T course was more than a guided tour of the dials and switches on the set's control panel. If you were going to diagnose faults, make repairs when possible and teach operators in the field, *you had to know how it worked*. In the Operation DELIA file in the Norwegian archives are some thirty pages of student notes in Norwegian, some sections hand-written, others typed.[4] A note on the cover in Norwegian dated 6 November 1984, when the 'textbook' was originally archived, states, 'This is an instruction book by Finn Berger written for Eivind Viken during the war.' Eivind Viken was a member of SIS Operation DELIA in Florø during November/December 1943; he may have been struggling to follow the course in English. A glance at one of these pages makes it clear why some trainees preferred to focus on acquiring the skills needed to slit the throats of German sentries.

Station 53c was at Poundon in Buckinghamshire, a brisk walk south through the village from the Sow and Pigs pub. This station was established to train American OSS agents in SOE radio operations. Obviously, this was an activity which needed to expand as the war progressed and, before long, Station 53b was set up in other buildings close nearby. But probably not in the Sow and Pigs.[5]

For the first two years of its existence SOE was totally dependent upon SIS for the supply of portable short-wave radios *and* for the handling and coding of wireless traffic. Given the strained relations between the two organizations, the 'Baker Street Irregulars'* (SOE) could be forgiven for suspecting the 'Bastards of Broadway' (SIS) were reading their communications. It was an unsatisfactory situation, and the divorce came in June 1942. Until that date, all traffic from Scandinavia had been received at an SIS facility in the tiny village of Nash, only 8km (5 miles) west of Bletchley Park. Nash is even closer to Whaddon Hall – 2.5km (1.6 miles) – MI6's base for W/T communications with spies in the field.

It seems the Nash station was set up in February 1940, the same time that SIS Section VIII (radio communications) was moved out of Bletchley Park and into Whaddon Hall. Both Nash and Whaddon communicated with Bletchley via secure telegraph lines. Once messages had been decrypted they were transmitted to SOE in Baker Street by the same means. So, from June 1942, SOE had to set up its own stations for handling radio traffic with agents.

---

* See the Sherlock Holmes books of Sir Arthur Conan-Doyle.

A rare photograph taken inside SIS's radio station in the village of Nash, west of Bletchley Park.

Of the four they commissioned the most important was Grendon Hall, at Grendon Underwood, some 75km (47 miles) north-west of Baker Street. Known as Station 53, it had two operational departments, communications and coding, the latter coming under the protective and nurturing wing of SOE's brilliant young head of cryptology, Leo Marks. Having both

A remarkable photograph taken at STS 51 RAF Ringway during 1944 (the original is in colour). All agents needed to be parachute-trained, and there are probably over 200 of them here. In the background are a number of converted RAF Whitley medium bombers and, to the right, a single-engined STOL Lysander.

FANY Radio Operators sending messages to and receiving messages from agents in the field. They are using Marconi CR100 wireless transceivers. Note the very chunky Morse keys (bottom right).

departments in the same building overcame the time delay inherent in SIS's arrangement of having radio operations in locations like Whaddon and Nash and encryption and decryption at Bletchley Park. Landline telegraphy was only needed to get the traffic to and from London.

Grendon was staffed mostly by young female volunteers from the First Aid Nursing Yeomanry, known as FANYs.* Their work was challenging and demanded unrelenting attention to detail. Thirty-nine of them – those with

German radio operators learning Morse code. The woman at the rear appears to be pedalling a generator. (*Bundesarchiv*)

---
* The FANYs still exist: www.fany.org.uk

language skills to add to their radio and coding experience – were among fifty female agents sent into occupied Europe; of these, thirteen were caught and murdered by the Gestapo.

Of course, the enemy was also training female W/T operators.

1.5 Assessment: steady courage

The evaluation of SOE recruits could be brutal – especially if you were a woman. See for example this report on Noor Inayat Khan. She had just completed a wireless security course (W/X) being run by STS-36 at Boarmans, Beaulieu on 21 May 1943.

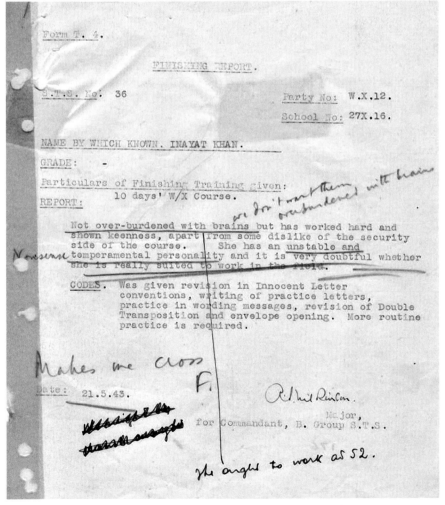

Noor Inayat Khan's W/X course finishing report. (*UK National Archives*)

Signing himself 'F', Buckmaster has angrily underlined passages and scrawled comments. Against 'Not over-burdened with brains' he has written, 'We don't want them overburdened with brains'; next to 'She has an unstable and temperamental personality' he writes, 'Nonsense'; and below the report are the words, 'Makes me cross'. Buckmaster was dead right in his assessment. Noor was the first to break out of the 'courier' straightjacket for women and undertake a dangerous mission in France as a W/T operator. She certainly made mistakes in the field, but that is not why she was caught; she was betrayed by a double agent and arrested on 13 October 1943. The Nazis murdered her and three other agents at Dachau concentration camp at dawn on 13 September 1944. She was posthumously awarded the Military Cross and the Croix de Guerre. In 2020 a blue memorial plaque was added to the front of her former family home in Bloomsbury, London.

A similar negative report was written three months later about 22-year-old Eileen Mary Nearne, known as 'Didi', the daughter of an English father and Spanish mother who was raised in Paris and spoke fluent French. (Her brother and sister were also SOE agents.) Over a period of some twenty-one weeks she sent 105 coded messages from the French capital. Then her luck ran out. On 22 July 1944 the Germans pinpointed her radio. At Gestapo HQ in Rue des Saussaies she was tortured but refused to give up her contacts. After some months in Ravensbrück concentration camp she was transferred to a camp in Poland, from which she escaped. She was awarded the MBE.

Two examples don't exactly make a trend, but women agents were battling the misogyny of the day typified by the remarks of a Lance Corporal Gordon: 'Nice girl, darned the men's socks and would make an excellent wife for an unimaginative man, but not much more than that.' However, the remarkable achievements of female radio agents were finally recognized by the awards they received as the war progressed.

*　*　*

Wireless-telegraphy (W/T) operators of both genders were indispensable members of the 'circuits' or 'networks' of agents deployed behind enemy lines. 'Organizers', usually men, bore the responsibility for the planning and co-ordination of operations. In effect, they were the leaders of the groups, but care was taken not to call them 'commanders' because of the presence of civilians in each team. 'Couriers' were more often female than not.

In 1942, approval was given for women to be sent into France. Since all able-bodied French men were expected to be part of the wartime labour force, the Germans would be suspicious of men moving about the countryside, apparently unemployed. Women, however, would not raise these suspicions, and therefore SOE felt that women would be better able to act as couriers (individuals who carried both information and materials) for the wireless operators, saboteurs and intelligence operatives they sent into France, and to organize regional resistance groups.[6]

'Weapons trainers' were charged with ensuring that the pistols, sub-machine guns and explosives handed out to supporters were kept in working order and put to deadly use. 'Scouts' undertook the hazardous job of observing the location and activities of the enemy. The 'couriers' would ensure their intelligence reached organizers and radio operators.

Often there was overlap in the allocation of jobs. Sometimes the W/T operator would also encrypt and decrypt messages; sometimes the organizer would do it. But the radio man or woman's work was so essential to the success of the circuit that he or she was always first into the field and last out. The initial radio contact was the way in which home base was informed that the group was in place and ready to start operations.

Although SOE was charged with 'setting Europe ablaze', MI6 preferred a quiet life, and not to attract the attention of the enemy. The two organizations squabbled in the corridors of Whitehall and also ran foul of each other operationally. From the start, SIS and SOE agents were forbidden to get in touch directly; this edict, however, was often breached in the field when, for example, common sense dictated that the most likely source of a replacement valve for a radio would be the nearest agent using the same type of set. However, in London, MI6 would routinely veto any SOE operations it thought might compromise its own activities; in at least one case it is thought to have sabotaged an SOE venture, thus earning themselves the sobriquet 'The Bastards of Broadway'.

To achieve Churchill's incendiary edict required SOE to support resistance movements. Indeed, it is evident that SOE's most spectacular successes were operations carried out in close co-operation with partisan groups: Operation ANTHROPOID was the assassination of SS-Obergruppenführer Reinhard Heydrich in Prague, May 1942; Operation HARLING, the November 1942 destruction of a railway viaduct at Gorgopotamos in central Greece; and Operation BRICKLAYER, the kidnapping of Generalmajor Heinrich Kreipe on Crete in February 1944.

All these actions depended on the deployment of W/T operators. The SOE team parachuted into Greece for Operation HARLING comprised three groups of four men: a leader, an interpreter, a combat engineer and a radio operator. In the first group to land was Lieutenant Colonel Eddie

Myers, CO of the mission, Captain Denys Hamson, the interpreter, Captain Tom Barnes (a New Zealander), the sapper, and Sergeants Len Willmott and Frank Hernen as wireless operators. This command group may have had two radio men in order to split the signals burden between calls to HQ in Egypt and calls between the three other groups in the field. Willmott, just twenty-one at the time, was later awarded the Military Medal and the British Empire Medal.

*   *   *

SOE had plenty of problems but, much to the fury of other irregular forces, money was never one of them. Recruiting and training enough W/T operators to support its expanding activities throughout the world was its priority. It wasn't a job for everyone. Not because of the perils associated with the assignment but because of the concentration and attention to detail demanded by the three critical aspects of the training: radio operation, Morse and cryptography. When a semi-qualified candidate fell into SOE's laps, their delight was undisguised:

> *Vita* left Shetland on 10th September [1941] to pick up the Sorlie [Sørli] Gang at a certain point on the Norwegian Coast. This meant a very long trip to latitude 64° 40' [Namsos], from which she returned successfully on 16th September bringing 10 men …
>
> In the meanwhile it was discovered that one of the men with the Sorlie gang is a trained wireless operator. He is being rushed south for ten days intensive training and will then return to Norway.[7]
>
> *Consolidated Progress Report for S Section*
> *(No. 41)b for the week ended 17 September, 1941*

Chapter 2

SIS in Norway

During the raid on Florø there were no boats badly damaged, or sunk. Three private houses and two warehouses slightly damaged. No people were hurt. The inhabitants are disappointed. Much ado about nothing.

Radio message sent by Atle Svardal, 12 January 1942[1]

2.1 Operation ERIC: 'intrepid, sensible, quick'

Atle Svardal was twenty-four years old on 9 April 1940 when Norway surrendered to the Germans. At the time, he was training to be an army officer, but the occupying forces closed the military college, putting an abrupt end to that ambition. His commanding officer wrote on his discharge papers that he was 'intrepid, sensible, quick and immensely persistent'.[2]

Somewhat at a loss, he joined the police, wrongly believing that Norway's civilian force would have some sway over the occupying power and ensure that they acted within the law. Atle's illusions were shattered when the Germans took direct control of the police and made it mandatory for officers to become members of the *Nasjonal Samling* (NS, or 'National Union'), the Nazi-supporting organization led by the notorious Vidkun Quisling. The young man drew the line at swearing allegiance to a political party he despised. He would have to find a different way of resisting the occupiers.

Florø is the westernmost town in Scandinavia. This centre of herring fishing was Atle Svardal's home town, and it was where he headed after bidding farewell to his law enforcement colleagues. There, along with seven other young men, Atle boarded a motorboat called the *Notbas*. The skipper was Dagfinn Ulriksen, a local fisherman very familiar with Florø waters. They left on 29 April 1941 in the dead of night and arrived at Lerwick in the Shetland Islands on 4 May. That's five days, 400km (245 miles) in choppy sea conditions, a constant lookout being maintained for prowling Kriegsmarine warships.

All arrivals from Norway were interviewed by Royal Navy intelligence officers, with the support of their Norwegian opposite numbers. Their primary job was to weed out German spies sent to Britain posing as refugees, but they were also responsible for talent-spotting. Which of the newcomers might play a part in fighting the Nazi occupation of their homeland and thus speed the end of the war?

Atle Svardal, as a former policeman and officer cadet, was an obvious candidate. Dagfinn Ulriksen was also noted to have potential. Such recruits were immediately flown to the Scottish mainland, from where they would take an overnight train to London and report to the War Office in Whitehall. Next stop was the Royal Victoria Patriotic School, a gruesome building on Wandsworth Common, south of the Thames. Originally established as an asylum for girls orphaned during the conflict in Crimea, it had been taken over by the Security Service (MI5) at the outbreak of war. After a round of background checks lasting two or three days, it was decided that Svardal and Ulriksen would join the Secret Intelligence Service (MI6), and they were sent for training.

Barely three months later, they were back in Norway. In that short period MI6 had taught them how to be spies: fluency in Morse code, how to operate a short-wave radio and how to encrypt and decrypt messages. Their mission was initially code-named Operation ERIC (almost certainly as a nod to Commander Eric Welsh, the head of SIS's Norwegian Section) and it was the Service's first 'coast-watching' mission. The name was soon changed to

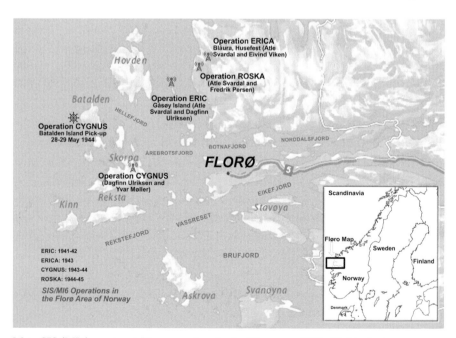

Main SIS (MI6) coast-watching operations in the Florø area, 1941-45. (*Author*)

Operation CRUSOE, probably when Commander Welsh heard his name was being taken in vain.

The two-man team was based on the island of Gåsøy, a sliver of land 1km (1,093 yards) in length and 300m (328 yards) at its widest. But it was perfectly positioned for them to observe all shipping – merchant and naval – sailing north out of or south into the Florø archipelago. They established radio contact with home base on 26 August 1941 and were soon sending regular reports. The messages were terse and the working content followed a predetermined pattern: time and date of sighting; type and size of vessel or vessels; speed and direction of travel, north or south.

```
SECRET.

Royal Norwegian Defence Ministry.

"E" Office.                              N/406.
                                         August 30th, 1941.


Source:  "Crusoe".
Date of information:  1314/27.8.41.

     At 1200 hrs. one tanker 2,000 tons, three trawlers

and one destroyer with two funnels;  direction South.
```

An early radio message from Operation CRUSOE (née ERIC). (*Norges Hjemmefrontmuseum*)

The ability to distinguish between destroyer, tanker and armed trawler was the result of good training. However, determining the size of a vessel and whether a merchantman was carrying cargo or not was more challenging. As a former fisherman, Dagfinn Ulriksen was probably good at this. But Operation CRUSOE had one very marked advantage. Positioned as it was on an island in the middle of a narrow channel, no vessel was ever more than 500m away from their observation post. That was close enough to see through binoculars the Plimsoll line on the bows of a merchant ship and from that to ascertain whether it was loaded. Also, the background of the mainland coast (when looking east) and the island of Hovden (looking west) gave reference points which would help determine the length of vessels.

* * *

The urgency of intelligence for naval forces trying to protect merchant convoys in the North Sea and English Channel soon became obvious. Clearly, the repositioning of three U-boats to the south of Florø would have been of immediate interest to the Royal Navy. The submarines were sighted on 29 September; however, the message wasn't radioed in until 9 October, a delay of ten days.

A 9 Oct 1941 radio message from Operation CRUSOE. (*Norges Hjemmefrontmuseum*)

It could be that this message indicates that Svardal and Ulriksen were having technical problems, but the observation might have been made by one of their support team on the mainland, and the information may not have reached them on Gåsøy until much later, perhaps brought by someone delivering food.

In addition to shipping movements, Svardal and Ulriksen would report on the effect of RAF bombing attacks on German assets in the Florø region. On 12 January 1942 they sent information they had received the previous day:

> During the raid on Floro there were no boats badly damaged, or sunk. Three private houses and two warehouses slightly damaged. No people were hurt. The inhabitants are disappointed. Much ado about nothing. This has been reported to me from one of my connections.[3]

That line from Shakespeare must have hurt back at the squadron's base.

The two SIS agents were to suffer a particularly bleak winter, and their flimsy hut offered little shelter. Dagfinn later joked that the only way they kept warm was by fighting each other. Their sole neighbours, a flock of sheep, did little to raise morale. In fact, the sheep were a problem because they belonged to a farmer on the mainland, and one day, when a young girl arrived by boat to check on the welfare of the animals, she spotted the agents. MI6 could not afford to take a chance on her being friendly, and Svardal and Ulriksen were immediately evacuated back to the UK:

Atle Svardal shortly after meeting King Haakon in London, 26 March 1942.

> In early March 1942, it was found necessary to remove these Agents owing to Gestapo activities in the neighbourhood. The two men were therefore collected in great haste and arrived safely back [in the UK] again on the 20th March 1942.[4]

On 26 March Svardal and Ulriksen were rushed to meet King Haakon in London. They hadn't had a chance to clean up. There was no sauna and no barber's shop on Gåsøy, and on his own admission, Svardal hadn't washed for six months; his hair and beard were infested with lice. The King must have been relieved to see the back of him.

2.2   Operation PI II: 'bravely into action'

While Svardal and Ulriksen were recovering from the rigours of winter on Gåsøy, Eric Welsh was putting together a new team to handle observations at the southern limits of Sunnfjord. Twenty kilometres due south of Florø lies a long, rocky peninsula, at the tip of which the village of Stavenes offers excellent views to the north-west over the open waters of Frøysjøen. MI6 and naval intelligence agreed that this would provide an excellent observation post from which to monitor the movement of German warships.

One of the radio agents was Eivind Viken; more about him later. The other was 25-year-old army officer Ole Hoff Snefjellå.* He had fought the Germans in the far north of the country, and when surrender came in May 1940 he switched to the resistance and continued to fight. Taking his new underground role to heart, Snefjellå even acquired a stencil copying machine and used it to produce illicit flyers containing news he had heard on the BBC. His small unit, made up of a handful of friends, operated in Helgeland independently from other groups. In spite of this isolation, he managed to obtain a shipment of arms and explosives from the UK. In the autumn of 1941 he moved to Ålesund, about halfway between Florø and Trondheim, and continued to serve in the resistance there.

On 1 January 1942 he and some colleagues boarded the fishing boat *Trygve* and set off west, arriving at Lerwick three days later. After passing through the screening process he was recruited by SIS and trained as a radio operator. His first mission as an MI6 agent started in March 1942, when he and Eivind Viken were delivered to Sunnfjord to set up the Operation PI II radio station on Stavenes. The observation post was concealed under a stone slab and gave them an excellent view over Frøysjøen. Commander Eric Welsh's number two at SIS was John M. Turner, a Norwegian-British officer whose grandmother, coincidentally, lived near Stavenes.

Radio reports from PI II were the basis for a number of British air and sea attacks against German vessels, including the 19,000-ton Hipper class *Prinz Eugen* on 17 May 1942. Twelve months earlier, *Prinz Eugen* had accompanied the 40,000-ton battleship *Bismarck* on a breakout into the North Atlantic to attack Allied shipping. Radio played an important part in foiling the attempt of these vessels and their escort of destroyers and minesweepers to sneak undetected out of the Baltic. First they were spotted and followed by the Swedish cruiser HSwMS *Gotland*, which signalled Naval HQ in Stockholm as follows: 'Two large ships, three destroyers, five escort vessels, and 10–12 aircraft passed Marstrand, course 205° 20'.'[5] The Kriegsmarine wasn't too concerned; after all, Sweden was a neutral country. However, within hours of it being received, the signal was on the desk of the British naval attaché at the legation in Stockholm, Captain Henry Denham. Denham had the message urgently recoded and radioed to Naval Intelligence at the Admiralty in London.

In spite of GC&CS at Bletchley Park monitoring German radio traffic (and reconnaissance Spitfires carrying out sorties along the Norwegian coast) *Bismarck* and *Prinz Eugen* reached Bergen unscathed. They sailed again on 21 May 1941 and headed in a wide arc across the Atlantic to the north of

---

* This must be the perfect surname for a Norwegian: *snefjellå* means 'snow mountain'.

Iceland. They were next spotted by the old Kent-class heavy cruiser HMS *Suffolk*, which was on picket duty in the Denmark Strait. What followed is well documented as 'The Battle of the Demark Strait' and vividly depicted in the film *Sink the Bismarck!* In the ensuing engagement the British battleship HMS *Hood* was sunk on 24 May with the tragic loss of 1,415 men. But *Bismarck* was later attacked by the aircraft carrier *Ark Royal*'s slow and obsolete Fairey Swordfish torpedo-bombers, which managed to disable her steering. After further attacks, *Bismarck*'s captain ordered her to be scuttled. It was 27 May 1941.

Prinz Eugen escaped, heading south. But she encountered engine problems and was ordered to head east to France for repairs, arriving at the port of Brest on 1 June. The RAF immediately attacked the port, dropping a total of 1,200 tons of bombs on its ship-building and repair facilities. She was again severely damaged on 1 July, when a direct hit from an armour-piercing bomb destroyed the control centre and killed sixty sailors. This was a serious setback for the Germans. On 23 February 1942 the Royal Navy submarine *Trident* attacked *Prinz Eugen* off Trondheim and a torpedo killed fifty crew and destroyed her ability to manoeuvre. Once more she was in desperate need

Under repair in Lofjord, near Trondheim: the *Prinz Eugen* (centre with repair ship *Huscaran*). Below, under headland, the cruiser *Admiral Scheer*. Aerial reconnaissance photograph, March 1942. (*Imperial War Museum*)

of repairs. After limping towards Trondheim she was towed into Lofjord, a branch of Trondheimsfjord, well away from prowling British submarines, where she was joined by the *Admiral Scheer* and the repair ship *Huscaran.*

The engineers of the *Huscaran* did a remarkable job of cutting away the damaged stern of the *Prinz Eugen* and replacing it by an improvised aft end with two rudders that could be operated from capstans on the deck.

On 10 May 1942 *Admiral Scheer* left Lofjord and resumed her journey north to Narvik. *Prinz Eugen* left six days later, making a course south for the Baltic. Concerned that rough seas offshore might result in damage to her jury-rigged stern, she was hugging the coast when she arrived in Frøysjøen and became framed in the binoculars of Ole Snefjellå and Eivind Viken. What a prize! A notorious heavy cruiser, clearly damaged, limping south and ever closer to Allied air bases in Britain. They lost no time in tuning their radio to an emergency frequency for a signal outside Operation PI II's regular 'sked' (transmission schedule).

Prinz Eugen was unfinished business, and RAF Coastal Command's 42 Squadron was tasked with putting an end to her streak of good fortune. On 17 May 1942 the squadron spearheaded a force of forty-eight Bristol Blenheims, Beauforts, Hudsons and Beaufighters which took off from RAF Leuchars on the east coast of Scotland. The lead aircraft was piloted by Wing Commander Mervyn Williams. The attack was to take place using torpedoes under cover of darkness. Just locating the *Prinz Eugen* at night was quite an achievement, but her flotilla was found at the south-western tip of Norway off the Cape Lista lighthouse.

The attack itself, skimming the wave-tops at night towards a barrage of fire from the cruiser and her four destroyer-escorts, while hounded by Me109 fighters, took remarkable courage. But the *Prinz Eugen* escaped yet again, and Williams' aircraft was downed. The only survivor from his Beaufort, he was taken prisoner by one of the German destroyers.*

* * *

Even before the sighting of *Prinz Eugen*, Ole Snefjellå and Eivind Viken had been receiving alarming reports from Bergen about an incident in the village of Telavåg on the island of Sotra, 130km south of Sunnfjord. In mid-1942 the determination of the Nazis to put an end to clandestine wireless stations and the running of agents and resistance fighters, weapons and equipment to

---

* Williams ended up in Stalag Luft III for the rest of the war. He became intelligence officer for the camp and was a planner of 'The Great Escape'. In August 1942 he was awarded the DSO.

and fro across the North Sea had been stepped up along Norway's western coast; threats of the death penalty were not working. Telavåg had become an important terminal for the Shetland Bus (the regular link between Shetland and Norway), but the Germans only learned about this by chance. In an act of revenge, a local man who had got into a petty dispute with Lauritz Telle over the sale of a boat, reported him for having an illegal radio.

On 26 April senior Gestapo officers Gerhard Berns and Henry Bertram led a force of SS soldiers and Norwegian NS police in a dawn raid on the island of Sotra. When this considerable unit surrounded Lauritz and Martha Telle's house they were unaware that the elderly couple were sheltering two resistance fighters, Arne Værum and Emil Hvaal from *Kompani Linge* (Norwegian Independent Company No. 1). Woken by the raiders, Værum and Hvaal put up a fierce fight and shot and killed the Gestapo officers. In the ensuing close-quarters struggle Værum was killed and Hvaal seriously wounded. Twelve villagers were immediately rounded up and taken to Bergen, where they were brutally interrogated and tortured. Included among them were Lauritz and Martha Telle, both in their sixties.

For the whole period of occupation the governor of Norway was Reichskommissar Josef Terboven; it was a role for which he was singularly unqualified in every respect except one. In the military (during the Great

Josef Terboven (front 2nd right) with Vidkun Quisling, Heinrich Himmler and Generaloberst Nikolaus von Falkenhorst in 31 January 1941 at an oath-taking ceremony for Norwegian volunteers in the Waffen-SS.

War) he had failed to get beyond the rank of lieutenant; he had studied law at Munich University and political science (an oxymoron if there ever was one) at Freiburg, but failed to graduate from either seat of learning. When he got a mundane clerical job in a bank he was sacked in short order. The exception to this disastrous string of failures was that he proved to be a nasty enough thug to qualify for a full-time job with the Nationalsozialistische Deutsche Arbeiterpartei, the Nazi Party. In the 1930s he reached the rank of Obergruppenführer and even married Ilse Stahl, one of Joseph Goebbels' discarded mistresses. Maybe she liked weedy fascists? However, she refused to join him in Oslo despite the fact he was living in the crown prince's official residence at Skaugum.

The people of Telavåg must have been terrified to see Terboven arrive in their village. The despised tyrant had decided the whole community would pay dearly for the death of his two Gestapo officers. While General Nikolaus von Falkenhorst was the commander of the 400,000 Wehrmacht troops stationed in Norway, Terboven exercised civilian power through the Quisling cabinet, but this arrangement was balanced in his favour by a personal force of about 6,000 SS men and 800 Gestapo agents. From the start, von Falkenhorst, a professional soldier, had demanded that his men extend politeness and respect to Norwegian civilians. He hated Terboven. It was hardly surprising, therefore, that it was the Reichskommissar who determined and carried out the punishment against Telavåg.

His revenge was swift; on 30 April 1942 all men aged between sixteen and sixty were arrested and transported to Sachsenhausen concentration camp,

The razing of Telavåg, May 1942. (*Bundesarchiv*)

north of Berlin. Seventy-two of them died in captivity. During May the SS systematically destroyed every single building in Telavåg. All the fishermen's boats were sunk and all the farmers' cows and sheep were slaughtered. The following year, Emil Hvaal, the surviving *Kompani Linge* fighter, and Lauritz and Martha Telle's son, Lars, were both executed.

At the secret Trandum Forest death camp near Oslo, set up by Terboven, eighteen prisoners with no connection to Telavåg were executed in revenge for the death of the two Gestapo officers. The remaining population of the settlement, mostly women and children, were detained until the end of the war.

It was against this background that the MI6 agents of Operation PI II received reports that the SS and Quisling police were continuing their sweep along the peninsula towards their vantage point at Stavenes, searching every farm and every possible location for a radio station. Then Chester Saltskår, the farmer sheltering the agents, learned that other operatives had already been arrested on the islands to the west of Askvoll. Eivind Viken and Ole Snefjellå could see no easy means of escape and they feared for Chester Saltskår and his family. Eric Welsh and John Turner were equally determined to get their agents back to the UK, but there was no time for them to be reached by a Shetland Bus gunboat or torpedo boat.

The Norwegian Catalina flying boat '*Vingtor*' during a winter sortie, 1942.

A call was made to RAF Coastal Command's Norwegian Detachment at Woodhaven on the south coast of the Firth of Tay, opposite Dundee. Formed only three months earlier, the unit had acquired four Consolidated PBY-5 Catalina flying boats.[6]

The Norwegian crews were still in training, but the unit's commander told Welsh he had an aircraft and crew ready to depart immediately on the hazardous mission. The Norwegian flyers had received the plane, 'Vingtor', from the Royal Canadian Air Force in February, and it had carried out its first special operations mission for the SIS overnight on 1/2 May, when it successfully inserted two W/T agents at Leka, 220km north of Trondheim.

When, on the afternoon of 22 May 1942, pilot Finn Lambrechts pushed the Catalina's throttles forward to take off from the Firth of Tay, Welsh's second-in-command, John Turner, was a passenger. It is not known if he had plans to make a surprise visit to his family in the area. Lambrechts and his navigator, Per Wåge Lea, did a brilliant job of landing at Stavenes in the dark. Waiting for them with Viken and Snefjellå were farmers Chester and Petrine Saltskår and their two-year-old son Harald – the family who had sheltered the agents in the previous weeks. After the events at Telavåg it was far too dangerous for them to be left behind.

Chester had acted as a courier for Viken and Snefjellå. On one occasion he took his fishing boat to Askvoll harbour and told the German harbourmaster he wanted to catch some mackerel. Please could he mark on his sea chart the boundaries of the minefields? The harbourmaster fell for it and obligingly outlined the danger areas for him. Chester took the chart back to the agents, who radioed this valuable intelligence to the SIS.[7]

As they climbed on board *Vingtor* and the crew got ready to take off for Scotland, a Kriegsmarine patrol boat appeared around the headland. Fortunately, it kept going, presumably thinking the aircraft must be German. As the evacuees scrambled on board they left the radio equipment in the rowing boat. It was later found by Norwegians who had the sense to dump it before it was discovered by the Germans. After their successful return, every member of *Vingtor*'s crew were awarded the War Cross with Swords, Norway's highest military medal for bravery.

2.3 Operation ERICA: if he couldn't write, he couldn't code

Atle Svardal arrived off the island of Batalden near Florø on 15 January 1943 aboard a fishing vessel called the *Kvalsund*. For this operation his fellow radio operator was Eivind Viken, another interesting and resourceful character who, with Ole Snefjellå, had been rescued from Stavenes by the crew of *Vingtor* eight months earlier.

When barely more than a teenager, Viken had gone to fight in the 1939–40 Winter War against the Red Army occupying Finland's eastern border region. When he got back to Norway in April 1940, spring had arrived and so had the German military. He enlisted and fought for a while, before escaping across the border into Sweden.

From there he travelled to Finland again, then – somewhat audaciously – to the Soviet Union and through Turkey to Iran. At a Gulf port he signed up as a deckhand on a cargo ship headed for the UK via South Africa. Such determination must have impressed his MI5 interrogator; less so his inability to read and write, an affliction blamed on an interrupted

SIS W/T Operator Eivind Viken. Photo probably taken in 1945.

schooling. He was recommended to MI6 so long as he first filled the gaping holes in his education; if he couldn't write, he couldn't code.

Svardal and Viken's new mission was Operation ERICA, and it was to be based at Husefest on the mainland to the east of Gåsøy Island but overlooking the same stretch of water, the northern access to Florø. However, the plan to put them ashore at Breivik near Husefest was stymied by a warning to be on the lookout for the German patrols in the area. Instead, they stepped ashore on Batalden, an outer island of the Florø group. A crew member of their boat put them in touch with Sigurd Langøy, his wife, mother, and two sons. In his post-operation report, Svardal recorded that 'All of these were excellent people, with the exception of Sigurd Langøy himself, who was nervous [scared] and an extremely scatter brained type.' Word must have got out that they'd arrived, because more assistance was offered by less nervous locals:

All our equipment and stores were taken over in [Langøy's] dinghy. During this work, Saron Karstensen and his son Oddsund came and offered help, which we gladly accepted … They live on Little Batalden and look after the telephone exchange there. (Because of their large family of youngsters, it would be inexcusable to think of living with them.) Before daylight all our equipment, with the exception of the wireless sets, was hidden at an out of the way spot on Skorpa [Island].

On the evening of 16th January, we rowed with all our wireless equipment, accumulators [batteries] and weapons to Solberg, the original contact used by Ulriksen and Svardal. There was an east [head-] wind blowing, so this took us six hours. We were well-received. We sent a message to Dagfinn Hjertenes, an old contact in Florø of Ulriksen and Svardal's. He came on the 18th January with his 17ft motor boat (petrol driven, speed 8 knots). He took us over to [the] Bredvik [farm].[8]

The farm of Isak Bredvik was where they would stay. Svardal's post-operation report includes an interesting section headed 'The Setting Up of the Wireless Station'. It began:

In Brevik there are two farms separated about 50 yards from each other. We had therefore to restrict as much as possible our use of the motor [generator]. We set up our battery-driven set. Bredvik had a 12-volt windmill apparatus of which we made use for accumulator charging. Apart from being a splendid observation point, this was the most important reason for our decision to set up station here …

In the farm the old aerial, in spite of confiscation of wireless sets, was still erected, in a South-North direction. So that the neighbours should not notice any change, we took this down and set up our own aerial in the same direction. The electric light lead from the windmill ran at a distance of 3 metres. We could not make W/T contact, and therefore put up the aerial in an East-West direction. (We had the whole time appreciated that this was the best direction.) All this work could be done only at night.[9]

The post-operation report continues with an account of some important improvisations:

On the 25th January, wireless contact was in order. In case of any trouble, we placed the motor straightaway in the cellar. After various trials, we filled a barrel with wool, cellulose shavings, and asbestos, and passed the exhaust pipe into the barrel. From the barrel there was an exhaust pipe to the chimney. We also built a house [hut?] for the motor. In order to achieve cooling off, the motor house was built comparatively big with air ventilators.

The report includes a hand-drawn sketch of this arrangement.

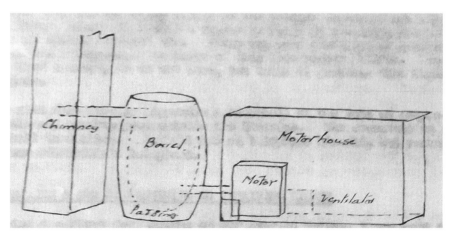

Operation ERICA: concealment of generator exhaust.

At first, the danger of the generator betraying them became something of a preoccupation. It was a few weeks before they could settle into their job:

> We noted that if the motor was used each day it was necessary to moisten the barrel every morning with water, otherwise fire could break out. During entirely calm weather, we could hear the noise of the motor about 20 metres from the house. If there was a wind, the distance was only about 3 metres. It was at any rate impossible to tell where the noise came from. We had a certain amount of trouble with the motor, which had been used before. The voltage was never constant, but varied between 5 and 10 volts.
>
> We tried out the motor-driven wireless set at the beginning of February, and apart from motor stoppages, it was O.K. both on day and night frequencies. We kept watch throughout the 24 hours more or less for the whole of this period. We fetched the rest of our equipment with Bredvik's boat. Everything was carried up to the living house and put in a large clothes closet – in all about 2 tons.
>
> From the 1st February, we kept a record of all shipping that passed both North and South. At the end of every month we sent a review of how much had passed, and how much we had reported.

There was some light relief when, on 15 March 1943, Ingrid Kjørlang, a niece of Isak Bredvik, arrived to work on the farm. Obviously they had to tell her what they were up to, and she must have taken an interest:

> We intended to train Miss Kjørlang as [a] telegraphist. We got her up to speed 30 [words per minute], but then had to move up into the

mountains, which made further training impossible. Miss Kjørlang was indeed very intelligent.[10]

Svardal and Viken must have shown Ingrid the basics of operating the radio to have moved on to Morse. She missed out on the rigours of encryption, but her transmission speed was excellent. Twenty words per minute was the minimum expected of a specialist W/T operator, and most could achieve 25 wpm.

The report moves on to comment on some of their sightings:

> It seems certain that in February there passed a battle cruiser and a cruiser. They went out from Frøysjøen [south of Florø] and into Hellefjord [between Hoveden and Batalden islands] without air escort (in contrast to the cruiser "Nürenburg" [*sic*] on 1st May which followed the usual lead and was escorted by six aircraft).

Most shipping entering or leaving Florø on the north side of the archipelago was clearly visible from the agents' observation post. But they started to worry about warships moving beyond the islands of Hovden, Batalden and Skorpa, which blocked their view. They needed to recruit coast-watchers who had a clear view west from those islands. But how could they share the information with Svardal and Viken so they could radio it back to home base? They decided that the telephone was the only option — so long as they could come up with a smart way of fooling the Germans and the Norwegian police listening in to the conversations:

> To make certain we developed a code for use on the telephone and went out to talk it over with Saron Karstensen who had a telephone. [He also ran the telephone exchange on the island of Little Batalden.] He was to report to us any warships which passed outside the Skerries. We give full details (Appendix A attached) of the code we proposed to use should any warship pass outside the Skerries. The conversation is of course held in dialect.[11]

Sadly, Appendix A is now missing from the report – but we can guess what it might have been like. The use of codebooks is a centuries-old method employed to conceal from the enemy the real meaning of sensitive messages. Essentially it's a look-up table containing innocuous words (or random numbers) to substitute for incriminating ones. For example, 'mackerel' might be used to mean 'destroyer', and 'heavy cruiser' be replaced with 'shark'. (For more on this, see 8.4, the Briefing on Cryptology.)

But the nice twist is in the last sentence. Norway is a country that seems unable to agree what its national language should be. The situation at the time of writing is that there are two *official* written languages, Bokmål and Nynorsk – plus Sami, the language of the indigenous Sami population in the north. Bokmål has its origins in Danish (Norway used to be part of Denmark). Nynorsk is more rooted in the dialects of Old Norse, the language of the Vikings, if you will. Both languages are taught in school, but the majority (87 per cent) of Norwegians prefer to write in Bokmål.

A lot of countries have more than one official language: Canada (English and French); Belgium (French and Flemish); Switzerland (German, French, Italian and Romansh), and so on. Then there are dialects; not just regional accents but variations in which vocabulary, grammar and pronunciation are different enough to make a dialect unintelligible to someone raised in the next valley. The brilliantly funny French writer Lorelou Desjardins explains in her blog[12] that her adopted country has four families of dialects: Østnorsk (Eastern Norwegian, spoken in Oslo and the surrounding area), *Nordnorsk* (Northern Norwegian), *Trøndersk* (Central Norwegian) and *Vestlandsk* (Western Norwegian). Within these dialect families are marked variations – although the differences have faded over time.

Florø lies in Sogn og Fjordane, the only county in Norway where 100 per cent of the town and village councils have chosen Nynorsk over Bokmål as the official written form of Norwegian. But many dialects are spoken – one every 20 km, according to Lorelou, who does her field research by asking a test question: 'How do you say "woollen socks"?' So far her count has reached one hundred variations. In the unlikely event that any of Operation ERICA's messages included the words 'woollen socks', no Germans – or Norwegians who didn't speak the Florø dialect at the kitchen table – would have made any sense of Svardal's conversations. Even if they could, the puzzle of a 'destroyer' wrapped inside the enigma of a 'mackerel' would have had them baffled.

*   *   *

Despite the remoteness of their location, the radio agents of Operation ERICA were under unrelenting threat from the Germans:

> During the first four months of our stay in Norway, there were constantly razzias* in the district. The Germans seemed to favour Sundays especially for this pastime, which seemed to us a pity, as we considered Sunday a day of rest.

---

* Raids. The word originates from the Italian via French and is based on an Arabic word referring to mid-nineteenth century kidnapping raids by Moorish pirates along the Barbary Coast of North Africa. It has now disappeared entirely from everyday use in English.

According to our contacts there were at this time razzias on all the Islands ... Every single house in Florø was searched ...

When an M.T.B. [motor torpedo boat] was lost in Florø, the Germans assumed that the crew had escaped to some place or other on the mainland. More or less the whole district round about was searched. The father of Dagfinn Hjertenes was skipper on board the Germans' launch in Florø, and he often had to act as pilot during night razzias ... Skipper Hjertenes was ordered to pilot the Gestapo to Hovden. He thereupon was ordered to go to Berle [a village on the south coast of Bremanger] where people had been landed in rubber boats. The Germans this time searched only around the houses, and the local inhabitants saw nothing of them. We heard about this, but understood it had happened at Botnane. [Botnane was only 5km north of the Operation ERICA observation post.] Because of the nature of the razzia, and because Skipper Hjertenes believed that further searches were likely, we decided that London should be informed.

As if the attention of the Germans wasn't enough, the locals were starting to make Svardal and Viken nervous: 'There flourished a rumour in Florø of a certain SVARDAL who was "in the Secret Service" etc. There was even a message of greetings sent to one of his relations. Who had spread these rumours, we do not know, but think it was probable that Sigurd Langøy is to blame.' Then, at Easter 1943, a 13-year-old girl, a relative of the farmer, arrived for a visit and 'nosed around in every corner'. The agents decided it was time to relocate. They spent two days on a reconnaissance mission and found a suitable cave in the mountains two hours walk above Bredvik farm. The move was made by moonlight and took three trips, each lasting three hours, to avoid houses near the route. Remarkably, they achieved this without interrupting the flow of radio messages to MI6. During the day they maintained watch themselves; after dark a local farm worker kept a lookout and signalled them with a light if he saw anything.

We were taking no chances a warship could pass unobserved. Before our move, we tested the radio set in the mountains. There was the possibility that some metal content in the mountain might cause disturbance. For this reason, London was asked to listen for us on two frequencies at one period. One frequency being used from the farm, the other from the mountains. In this way, warships could not pass without being reported immediately. It took rather a long time to arrange all this; rainy weather was to blame. A single drop in the wireless apparatus could have resulted in a short circuit.

By the 17th May, we had moved with our wireless apparatus to the mountains, with the most essential part of the provisions and clothes. Wireless contact was better than ever before. The remainder of our stores, over one ton, remained at the first stage well hidden in the woods. We carried by night, and worked by day.[13]

In a letter, the Deputy Director of Naval Intelligence, Captain Charles A. G. Nichols, conveyed his thanks: 'I would like to express my appreciation of the invaluable reports received from this station. The reliability of the reports and the speed of transmission make them of great value.'

* * *

Lines were drawn for anyone who knew what the agents were doing and the consequences for overstepping them were dire:

Relations between the servant Martin and the womenfolk on the farm were very bad. The boy was badly treated, and since he was pretty cheeky, there was always a lot of back chat. The result was that the boy went away on the 1st July. Martin is about 16 years old, and of undeveloped intellect … He came several times to us with the threat of betraying us, but we managed to cure him of such talk. When we left Norway, he had gone to live at his home in Tradsøy. Dagfinn Hjertenes and Ragnar Svardal were asked to watch the boy, and if necessary to dispose of him.[14]

Svardal's report includes an assessment (partially post-mortem) of the radio equipment they used:

The wireless sets were excellent, and worked without trouble the whole time. We used the accumulator-driven set up to our last week in Norway, when the set refused to work. We know now from the experts in London that the fault was due to salt in the clips. If the set had gradually become worse, we should possibly have discovered the fault, but there came an abrupt stop. At the beginning, the vibrator worked, but otherwise there was no sound from the set. We examined all the leads and coils, and changed all the valves, but in vain. In the end we changed the vibrator valve, with the result that the vibrator ceased to function.

The [exhaust system] for the motor had been burnt out two months earlier. Fire broke out in the barrel which acted as silencer. Twenty timber logs and fifteen boxes of moss caught fire. It was a long way to any water and everything was absolutely dry, and that we were not discovered was pure luck for which my lucky hat was probably responsible.

> The motor [generator] was carried away and hidden (at the end of August). Within 24 hours we had fixed up a temporary hole in which the motor was placed. Wireless contact was established immediately. The motor had apparently already been used when we got it. We had trouble with it the whole time. It worked after a fashion, but noise from the motor came through on the radio set so that it was nearly impossible to hear signals.

What finally determined they should be evacuated was the onset of winter, and thus the likelihood of leaving tracks in the snow as they travelled up and down the mountain. They decided to leave all their radios behind for when they returned in the spring of 1944. Word came on 3 September telling them to get ready, and they set to wrapping the equipment in tarred paper and placing it in tin boxes. A layer of oilskins provided further protection, before they concealed everything 'in a large rocky slope 300 metres from [our] working place'. They then searched the whole area, making certain they had expunged all evidence of their presence.

> Isak Bredvik took us over in his rowing boat to Botnene where we arrived at 2230 GMT. At 0100 GMT the MTB arrived … We were well received. Mines were laid at Botnene, and we returned to Lerwick, where we were met by Lt. Cdr. [Eric] Welsh on the 7th September after an eight months' absence.

The presence of Lieutenant Commander Welsh waiting to greet them on the Lerwick pierside demonstrated how much importance MI6 attached to these missions. Hopefully he will have extended the Royal Navy's renowned hospitality by buying them large whiskies at the nearest officers' mess. That wouldn't have taken much encouragement; Welsh was a notorious boozer.[15] He would certainly have warmly greeted Atle Svardal and Eivind Viken in fluent Norwegian, for in the twenty years between the wars he had lived and worked in Bergen for the British company International Paints Ltd, and his wife was

A rare photograph of Eric Welsh, head of MI6's Norway Branch. c.1945.

Norwegian. Arguably his greatest legacy lies in his determination to end the production of heavy water at Norsk Hydro's Vemork plant. Before the war he had provided waterproof paint for the plant's floors.

2.4 Operation CYGNUS: 'persistence and initiative'

That day, waiting on the dock at Lerwick, Eric Welsh already knew Svardal and Viken were not going back to Norway as soon as April 1944. He had a new team poised to take over the observation of German shipping around Florø – in the area called Sunnfjord. Dagfinn Ulriksen and Ivar Møller would be known as Operation CYGNUS. Ulriksen was, of course a veteran of coast-watching in the region, having shared a Morse key and a freezing hut with Atle Svardal in Operation CRUSOE (née ERIC) on the bleak island of Gåsøy during the winter of 1941/2.

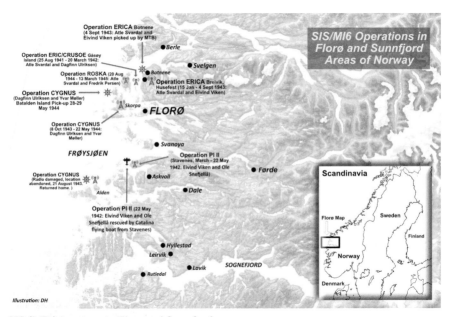

SIS (MI6) locations in Florø and Sunnfjord.

The first of the SIS documents in the Norwegian archives is a letter dated 24 August 1943 from Eric Welsh to Major Knut Ås, his opposite number in the 'E' office of Norwegian intelligence. The note informed Ås that on 21 August an MTB had successfully delivered agents Møller and Ulriksen to Alden (a hump-backed, crab-shaped island 33km south of Florø), where they would set up a W/T station to report shipping movements in the area.

Welsh's claim was somewhat over-optimistic, however, and on 3 September he had to write to Knut Ås again telling him that the radio equipment had been damaged during the landing and the agents were already back in the UK securing a new set. It was not until 10 October that Ås learned the agents had now been delivered to a different island, Skorpa, much closer to Florø and probably easier to support.

Oddly, the first report from CYGNUS is a 12 November 1943 signal about the sighting of two escorted cargo vessels on 11 October – but 'November' looks suspiciously like an error. The next two messages are dated 21 October and report that the 'lead' (passage) between Roten and Botnavaagen has been 'closed with wire obstacles fastened to buoys'. But Møller and Ulriksen soon fell into a routine, most detailed signals being sent on the same day as the observation.

Radio signal
from Operation
CYGNUS, 24
October 1943.
(*Norwegian archives*)

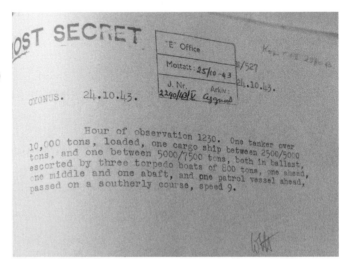

Sometimes, however, the radio station was acting as a relay for critical intelligence gathered by both resistance fighters and civilians determined to support the fight against the occupying forces.

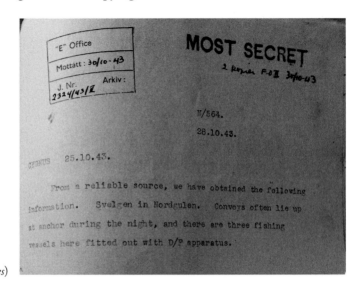

Radio signal
from Operation
CYGNUS, 28
October 1943.
(*Norwegian archives*)

Clearly, the information that German convoys lay up overnight at Svelgen, north-east of Florø, identifies potential targets for RAF Coastal Command bombers and Royal Navy motor torpedo boats. But more alarming for MI6's radio operators is the presence of the three fishing boats fitted with 'D/F' – direction-finding equipment – which could be used to triangulate the location of their wireless set. (See 8.2 Briefing on Countermeasures.) Eight days later, there was more intelligence about enemy defences: 'On Ytteroy there are now 25 Germans and no Norwegians. There is a gun position, an A.A. [anti-aircraft] gun and barbed wire entanglements around the whole island.' And on 24 November: 'A sub-source reports that about 11,000 Germans are to be moved from North Norway to Trondheim by express coastal steamer: about 200 at a time. At present there are three R boats in Florø.' R boats were smaller vessels (40m, 160 tons) used for mine-sweeping, escort duties and the rescue of downed airmen.

But after four weeks of excellent signals, Ulriksen and Møller started to hit technical problems. In a letter of 30 November (N/873), Eric Welsh briefed Knut Ås, quoting from the agents' urgent message:

Tiny Tim [small generator] will not work, and has been bad from the beginning. We have repaired it twice. If possible can we have another? At the same time we would like 50 gallons of paraffin, 10 of petrol, a paraffin stove, 2 reserve burners for a primus, round flashlight batteries and bulbs, white sugar and syrup, one barrel of Solar oil 50 kilo of lubricating oil, and extra lead for Tiny Tim.

If possible, a frequency between 7 and 7.5 for home station and Cygnus as contact is difficult. We cannot hear the home station on the night frequency. We have tried the aerial at different lengths.

Welsh wrote 'We are attending' below his signature. The suggestion of a night-time frequency of 7 – 7.5 MHz would be a routine request for a change to the transmission schedule ('sked') based on their experience operating from their present observation post.

But this wasn't their only problem. Later the same day, Major Ås received letter N/874 from Welsh quoting another message from the Cygnus agents:

We have lately had considerable interference from another station. In the last few days, it has been using the same call sign as Central. Thus it is difficult to say who is who, when one hears two stations with the same call sign.[16]

By late 1943 the allocation and management of call-signs had become more burdensome because of the sheer number of radio operators in the field – not all of them working for MI6, of course. What made the problem even more acute was the fact that call-signs had to be transmitted in clear-text (not enciphered), and this helped German radio intelligence keep track of who was on the air. Therefore good practice dictated that call-signs be changed as frequently as practicable. Welsh had scrawled a PS on the letter: 'This is OK. EW.' Clearly it wasn't OK, so presumably he meant the problem had been fixed.

Tales of woe resumed within 24 hours when Ulriksen and Møller complained it had become almost impossible to establish contact with the UK. They blamed this on weather conditions and asked for a more powerful 'Mark V' set and a new generator. During the first week of December they were given a date and place of delivery for the new equipment. On 6 December they replied, 'We will be on the spot when it arrives. The Germans often make searches around here so we have got to get the stuff away at once.' A few days later, they seemed to be back in business again.

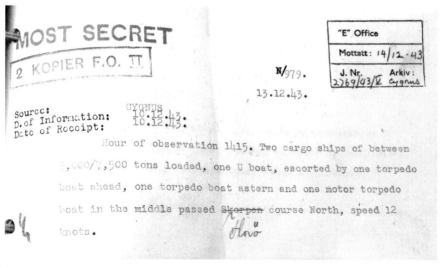

Radio signal from Operation CYGNUS, 13 December 1943. (*Norwegian archives*)

However, searches by the Kriegsmarine and the Luftwaffe were clearly making them nervous:

> Recently the Germans have been extremely active in searches both with gunboats and patrol boats. There has also been lively air activity around the Islands and in the Lead here. We need the motor badly.[17]

The next day Welsh wrote to Ås informing him the equipment had been delivered and the MTB had returned safely. On 16 December they confirmed safe receipt:

We received our stores and everything O.K. The motor is working fine. When does Cygnus II start? Is Cygnus I plan now cancelled? Will the broadcast at 1330 G.M.T. continue? There was one Christmas tree sent for King Haakon and one for Welsh.[18]

No genuine Norwegian Christmas tree for Major Knut Ås? What is not mentioned in the radio traffic is that the two agents took great risks (somewhat reluctantly) to add eleven civilian refugees to the two conifers loaded on the MTB.[19] It didn't help that Ulriksen had been ill for most of the month.

Operation CYGNUS's messages continued through Yuletide and the New Year, but the Germans' determination to track them down did not let up.

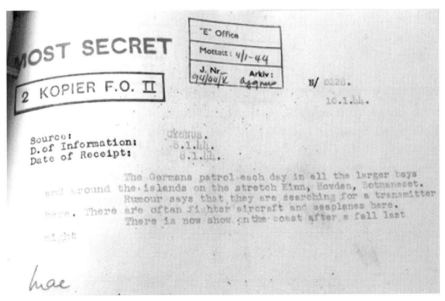

Radio message from Operation CYGNUS, N/0228, 10 January 1944.

A few days later, the weather became so bad that they could no longer operate from the hills of Skorpa and had to relocate the station to the house of a friendly family. Unable to get a good view of the sea passages around the islands, they warned home base that future signals might not be so good but promised to do their best. At the end of February 1944 Operation CYGNUS was re-designated CYGNUS II.

On 1 March 1944 they signalled that a 10,000-ton cargo ship carrying coal had gone aground in a snowstorm near the Årebrot lighthouse and implored the RAF to 'Smash her up!' The same snow caught out 'a small destroyer', which went aground close to Stavang Light in Florø waters: this time they begged Coastal Command to 'Blow her up!' According to a 4 April letter from Welsh to Knut Ås, CYGNUS II was now CYGNUS III and a fresh stock of supplies had been delivered to the station on 27 March. The confirmatory signal reported that the shipment included a prized item: 'Thanks for the fine broadcast receiver.' But a signal dated 11 April confirmed that the Germans were still looking for them: 'A D/F fishing boat has come here, and is lying about 400 metres away. We shall close the station for a while.' Three days later, they reported that the D/F boat had moved off to Skorpevågen, south of Florø, but added, 'There are eight such fishing vessels stationed between Stadt and Haugesund, three of them are between Stadt and Florø.' Every time Dagfinn Ulriksen and Ivar Møller switched their radio to 'transmit', their hearts must have beat faster, all too aware that direction-finding antennae were being turned to find the strongest point of reception.

Another signal dated 11 May reported that the D/F cutter was back and anchored 500m off their position. An error in decryption (at Bletchley Park) delayed delivery of the message by a week. By this time the news was added that 'The Germans are building an RDF station on Liset outside Kalvåg.'[20]

In April 1944 it was Møller's turn to fall ill with 'a great pain in the ear and head'. In fact, he was so unwell that Ulriksen requested his urgent evacuation. However, a local doctor was found for him and he was soon back at the Morse key. But their days were numbered:

> In May 1944, extensive razzias took place in the area and owing to the arrests of some of their contacts, the 'CYGNUS' station was in great danger. We decided to close down the station and an M.T.B. successfully evacuated the two Agents with their main helpers, in all eleven persons.[21]

According to Ulriksen's own account of Operation CYGNUS, the MTB arrived at 0110 GMT on Monday, 29 May 1944, and they rendezvoused in Lerwick at noon the same day. By Wednesday he and Møller were in London. Lieutenant Commander Eric Welsh was clearly determined the courage of his agents in Norway should be recognized:

> They sent in regular and valuable shipping reports, totally nearly 300 ... Great credit is due to Ulriksen's persistence and initiative, which enabled this valuable Coast Watching Station to continue for so long a period.

Sometime in the second half of 1944 Dagfinn Ulriksen and Ivar Møller again deployed to Sunnfjord. Two years on from the crisis that had forced the evacuation of Eivind Viken, Ole Snefjellå and Chester Saltskår's family on the Catalina *Vingtor*, it was deemed safe enough to re-establish the observation and radio post at Stavenes. The Saltskår farm had been taken

Hans Hollevik, Oddny Saltskår and Anton Hollevik after their release in 1945.

over by Chester's sister, Oddny, and her boyfriend, Anton Hollevik. Chester had persuaded them to play host to the new agents.

Unfortunately, rumours soon spread in the area that the station had reopened. A plan to exfiltrate Møller and Ulriksen was quickly put into effect. Oddny and Anton were given the opportunity to leave with them, but they decided to stay because they were worried the Germans would exact retribution on Anton's family. A short time later, they were informed on by one of their neighbours. At this stage of the war, when the defeat of Germany appeared inevitable, it is difficult to understand why anyone would believe they could profit by turning informer. But they did. On 17 March 1945 Oddny Saltskår and Anton Hollevik were arrested by the Gestapo. They were beaten and tortured before being sent to a concentration camp at Espeland near Bergen. There they were kept in solitary confinement for the few remaining weeks of the war.[22]

2.5 Operation DEHLIA: 'the Soviet spy and the submarine'

DEHLIA* was an odd operation about which there is little documentation in the archives. A two-page report[23] on the assignment states the bare facts but provides no background information.

The team comprised three radio agents. Eivind Viken and Atle Svardal were of course veterans of Operations ERIC/CRUSOE, PI II and (together) ERICA. This time 25-year-old Norwegian army officer Alfred Henningsen was added to the group. The agents flew from London on 11 November

---

* Eric Welsh spelled the name 'Delia', the Norwegians spelt it as 'Dehlia'. I have no idea which is correct.

1943, reaching Lerwick the following day. Bad weather in the North Sea delayed the departure of their MTB until 1000 on 16 November. Their boat arrived at 2300 at Hovden Island, west of Gåsøy.

They were amazed to find snow on the ground: 'The temperature was below freezing, and it turned out that the snow had come. On the islands, there was very little, and only on the east side. The mainland, on the other hand, was covered with snow right down to the beach.' It may seem surprising that Norwegians should be caught unawares by snow. However, on the west coast, November temperatures usually range between 3° and 7° Celsius, and precipitation arrives in the form of rain (an average of 260mm over twenty-two days of the month). The snow doesn't usually start until January. At 0030 on 17 November, now carrying three resistance fighters and five civilian refugees, they set a course back to Lerwick, arriving at 1200. Remarkably, they had been in Norway for only 90 minutes; they had concluded that they could not transport their equipment while travelling on skis, and any movement on foot would have left clear traces.

Instead of flying back to London, the agents were told to stay in Lerwick while discussions took place about a second attempt. During the post mortem it was pointed out that it had been 'clearly stated in the plan' that, should there be snow on the ground, the operation was undoable. 'We were now asked,' the report continues, 'if we could make the trip to [location] "Arne" and only act as observation and message station, i.e. without any dealings with the submarine crew.' What submarine crew? What submarine? A double check of the translation confirms that 'ubåtmannskap' does indeed mean 'submarine crew'.

On 14 December 1943 Eric Welsh wrote to Knut Ås informing him that the DEHLIA agents had been evacuated but not mentioning any plans to send them out again. So what were the objectives of Operation DEHLIA? A flaw in the way the system had been operating until late 1943 had been the inherent delay between the sighting of a potential target and the launch of an attack. The sequence went something like this:

1. A destroyer is seen heading south at a speed of 12 knots with an escort of two R-boats. A note to that effect is written and carefully encrypted.
2. At the next scheduled transmission (or on an emergency frequency) the coded message is sent in Morse as five-letter groups and received at Whaddon Hall.
3. From Whaddon the message is forwarded, unaltered, via a secure telegraph line to Hut 10 at Bletchley Park.
4. At Bletchley the message is decrypted, the call-sign indicating which key words to use. It is now in clear-text.

5. Next, the message needs to be translated from (in this case) Norwegian into English. Mostly, this will be done by the same team doing the decryption.
6. A dedicated telegraph line is again used to get the message to London, where a decision has to be made about the armed response to put into effect. Does the Royal Navy have a warship within striking distance? Or is it a job for RAF Coastal Command?
7. Once the decision is made, the response has to be activated, with ship or aircraft being dispatched to the most likely location of the destroyer so an attack can be launched.

There were few ways in which this process could be accelerated; army motorcycle dispatch riders had already been replaced by telegraph lines. So why not cut out the middle men and women entirely and deploy a submarine to the Florø/Sunnfjord region? Fjords are plenty deep enough. Sognefjord itself, for example, is over 1,000m deep for 100km of its length, between Rutledal and Leikanger. If coded radio contact can be established between the observing station and the submarine, the checklist can be shortened to this:

1. A destroyer is seen heading south at a speed of, say, 12 knots with an escort of two R-boats. A note to that effect is written and carefully encrypted.
2. The signal is sent to the *submarine*, not the UK.
3. The submarine attacks the destroyer.

The Royal Navy T class submarine carried sixteen 21-inch torpedoes but would need to be rotated to replenish these and allow for refuelling and provisioning. The idea must have occurred to someone at the time.

* * *

Alfred Henningsen was a man of the north. The son of a fisherman, he was born in 1918 in Kirkenes in Finnmark, the northernmost county of Norway, well within the Arctic Circle. In the south Finnmark borders Finland, and the frontier with Russia is only 35km to the east of Kirkenes. Politically, the Henningsen family was on the left, and Alf was a member of the Labour Party's Workers' Youth League as a teenager.

In May 1940, after the royal family and government had been evacuated from the northern port of Narvik to the UK, Alf Henningsen and his friend Torstein Råby became agents of Soviet intelligence (probably the GRU) in Murmansk, with the job of reporting on German troop movements. They were soon in the sights of German counter-intelligence – probably as a result of a lack of training – and sensibly decided it was time to make themselves scarce. They took to the mountains, heading south into Sweden. From there, probably with the help of recruiters at the British legation, they were flown to the UK. Their former allegiance to the Russians would have been an issue, but it was trumped by their proven willingness to fight the forces occupying their homeland. After a visit to the salubrious Royal Victoria Patriotic School (see Chapter 1) they were recommended to the Secret Intelligence Service, which trained them both as wireless telegraphy operators.

At the end of 1943 MI6 sent Torstein Råby back to his home territory of Finnmark with fellow-agent, Karl Rasmussen; this was Operation IDA. They settled into the coastal village of Alta, successfully staying hidden while they kept a close eye on the *Tirpitz* which, at the time, was anchored in Kåfjord and poised to strike out north into the Barents Sea to wreak havoc among the supply convoys sailing between Britain and Murmansk in Russia. Råby cheekily hid his wireless in a location that enabled him to connect to an antenna set up by a German officer for his own radio. Resistance fighters made numerous attempts to sink the feared battleship but only damaged her, and she had to be moved to Tromsø for repairs. It was there that she was sunk by the RAF on 12 November that year. In May 1944 Karl Rasmussen was captured and tortured, before committing suicide. The SS burned the village of Alta to the ground, while Råby was successfully exfiltrated. In recognition of the important role his messages played in tracking the location of *Tirpitz* and her ultimate sinking, he was awarded the highest Norwegian decoration for military gallantry, the War Cross with Sword; the British awarded him the DSO and the French the Croix de Guerre.

Alf Henningsen carried out four operations in the remaining years of the war. The last year of the war found him back in Finnmark, where the Red Army had crossed the border to help the Norwegian Army drive out the remaining Germans. One day he was relocating his radio station, alone in a rowing boat on the 123km-long Porsanger Fjord, when he was spotted by a Kriegsmarine patrol. As they stopped him at gunpoint, he dumped the wireless set overboard and dived after it into the freezing water. The Germans opened fire and wounded him, but he managed to swim to shore, where he was caught and taken prisoner. The approach of the war's end was probably the only thing that stopped the Germans shooting him out of hand. Instead, he was flown south to Oslo and interned in Akershus Fortress; he and the other prisoners were liberated in a matter of days.

After the war, Henningsen was approached by an academic from the University of Oslo who was looking for a radio operator. Alf had met the man before, a member of the Free Norwegian Forces who had fought in Finnmark from 1944 to the end of the occupation. Would Alf be interested in going on a sailing voyage across the Pacific Ocean? At the time Henningsen was settling into a career in the regular army (he rose to the rank of lieutenant colonel before moving into politics) so he declined, but he vouched for another experienced W/T operator – Torstein Råby.

And so it was that Råby took part in Thor Heyerdahl's Kon-Tiki expedition, an 8,000km voyage on a raft to determine whether the Polynesians

Torstein Råby, SIS and Kon-Tiki radio operator. Probably from the end of the war.

could have originated from South America rather than South-East Asia. During the voyage he made contact with radio hams around the world. After Kon-Tiki he worked as a radio operator on Bear Island and Jan Mayen Island in the Arctic. All this time, Råby had been nursing a heart condition and, sadly, he died in 1964 (aged forty-five) while on an attempt to reach the North Pole on skis.

2.6 Operation ROSKA: 'magnificent work'

After the failed Operation DEHLIA it was eight months before Atle Svardal got back to Norway, this time partnered with Fredrick Persen. On 20 August 1944 they arrived at the island of Hovden on board the Shetland Bus MGB *Hessa* (skippered by Petter Salen) to set up Operation ROSKA. They got ashore with a radio, personal gear and two weeks of provisions, using a rowing boat they had brought with them, but needed the help of the *Hessa*'s power boat to land an additional 120 packages. They concealed everything in a nearby forest, a task that took them several hours. Good fortune was on their side. Just as they completed the offloading, two German patrol boats were spotted, and the MGB had to take off fast, back to Scotland.

While it was still dark they got in their little rowing boat with a radio and some provisions, set off again – concerned the patrol boats might return – and headed east past Gåsøy to Breivik on the mainland. There was a strong northerly blow for the whole crossing. The boat was leaking, and with the spray coming over the side they had to bail; but their equipment still got

Motor Gun Boat *Hessa* leaving Scalloway in Shetland in 1943. With two similar 'sub-chasers' it made 116 crossings to Norway. One of these, the *Vigra*, was later restored and is still operated by the Royal Norwegian Navy for promotional and training purposes.

drenched, and a range-finder never worked again. It was dawn by the time they reached their destination. From Operation ERICA, Svardal knew exactly who to make contact with: first Isak Bredvik at the farm and then his trusty supporters, Dagfinn Hjertenes, Magne Sørbotten, Magnus Uren, Sigrun Solberg, Torbjørn and Arne Øvrebotten. All of them volunteered to risk their lives and help once more.

A quick inspection showed that the cave Svardal and Viken had used during Operation ERICA had been compromised. With Bredvik's help, the agents found another location for the observation post. A ledge 200m (about 600ft) up a rocky cliff a few hundred metres from the coastal trail gave them a great view and would be almost impossible to spot from land. And, no doubt, being close to the farm would help with the supply of provisions. After a trip in Bredvik's boat to retrieve the rest of their boxes from Hovden, they set to building a *hytte* (wooden hut) and carefully camouflaged it so it would also be difficult to spot from the sea. (The agents themselves avoided going out during daylight hours.) Getting all their equipment to the ledge required the rigging of lines to enable them to hoist each box up from below. Aerials pre-set to different lengths ran up the cliff from the hut.

*   *   *

Over the next six months Svardal and Persen sent more than 300 messages to England. The priority sightings – warships, fuel tankers and troop-carriers – were often the subject of attack when they emerged from the shelter of Norway's coastal islands. They would be targeted by the Royal Navy if it

Consequences: RAF Mosquitoes attack a convoy evacuating troops from Norway on 5 April 1945.

had patrols in the right area. Otherwise, the job would fall to RAF Coastal Command's bombers.

After D-Day the Germans were desperate to relocate troops from Norway to mainland Europe to bolster the defence of their homeland; preventing ship movements being targeted by MI6's coast watchers had therefore become an urgent undertaking. From early 1944 agents had noted a steady increase in the number of vessels in the Florø and Sunnfjord areas that were fitted with radio direction-finding antennas – the maximum recorded was eight, and only three were needed to get a decent fix on a covert transmitter.

There is a key archive document which tells us how the previously successful Operation ROSKA came to a tragic end. Shortly after the war, Fredrick Persen wrote a detailed six-page account of the mission. In 2017 his daughters, Anne Kristi Persen and Kari Persen, posted this report on a local history website.[24] According to them, Persen made it clear he and Svardal were cautious about prowling 'D/F' boats:

We were soon aware that the Germans knew about our transmitter. Throughout December [1944] they answered our own call sign when we called [home base in England]. They only did this in cases where [Whaddon Hall] did not hear us. Immediately before Christmas, they started raiding on Hovden and Kallvåg [to the north of Hovden], and we learned they were looking for people who had come from outside. When they later started jamming on the central station's frequency, we realized how eager they were to stop us.

All this made us, if possible, more careful. All boats were suspected of being a D/F boat, and we were never on the air when a boat passed by.[25]

Then they received another alert to the Germans' attempts to track them down:

One time before we were captured, we were notified that the Germans had gone farther north with patrols of two men. The week before, we also received a message that they had mounted bearing [antennae] on board two small boats and were working in the district. On Saturday evening (March 10) Dagfinn Hjertenes arrived with the news that the harbour boat in Florø had been equipped with some D/F equipment and was located at Hovden just west of us. Hjertenes's father, who worked aboard [the boat], had said that some of the crew had access to the cabin and could see this equipment.

What made the agents even edgier was the fact they had received a number of messages from Whaddon Hall earlier that day. They assumed these had all been intercepted.

Then at noon on Sunday we saw a German boat go from Hovdevågen to Husefest and later got a message that soldiers had been put ashore, supposedly to look at a mine. Furthermore, we were notified that they had gone ashore at Urene. This day we stayed away from the air, but on Monday we were on the air for fifty minutes.

The last sentence is alarming. Persen probably means they were on air for a *total* of 50 minutes rather than one message took that long (at the time the recommended maximum was five minutes). Even so, it is a long time to be transmitting when you know you are being D/F-ed. There was a certain inevitability about what happened the following day:

On Tuesday March 13th we were captured. It happened like this. We were to send a signal at 9:35 am and I went outside the cabin to look for boats. Then I was shouted at by a German squatting about 20–30 m away. I turned and ran into the cabin for weapons. I told Svardal there was a German right next to the hut. Svardal immediately fired a shot to make a hole in the wall, and the Germans began shooting back with several sub-machine guns. The incoming fire was so overwhelming that we immediately realized that we had no hope. We wondered about escaping through the window in the north wall, but discovered that that side was covered by a soldier who was posted right above the hut. Svardal was hit almost immediately in the left side, and the bullet must have passed through both lungs. We then cried out that we surrendered and were told that if we didn't come out, they'd throw hand grenades. We then went out, and after we were body-searched, Svardal was given first aid. He was laid on the ground on his sleeping bag. My feet were tied and I had to lie down with a Gestapo officer as guard.[26]

Persen was taken down from the cliff while the soldiers started to recover all the equipment; they forced thirty men from the village of Botnane to do the heavy lifting. These included Torbjørn Øvrebotten's brothers Odd, Halvdan and Abraham, as well as his father, Nils.

After Persen had been beaten with shovels, the Gestapo officer – believed to be notorious torturer Willie August Kesting – started to interrogate him about his contacts. In particular, he wanted to know the whereabouts of Dagfinn Ulriksen and Yvar Möller. When the last of the soldiers came down they told him Atle Svardal was dead. They had dumped his body in the hut before burning the observation post down.

Fredrick Persen pictured in 1949 at the location of Operation ROSKA's observation hut. The words 'ATLE SVARDAL 13-3-1945' were carved into the rock by Svardal's brothers, Ragnar and Per.

Isak Bredvik, Magnus Uren and Dagfinn Hjertenes were also arrested and, with Fredrick Persen, taken to the regional Gestapo headquarters in Bergen. They were interrogated there by Kesting until 4 May 1945, when all the prisoners were released. After a few days in a civilian prison they were freed to make their own way home. Willie August Kesting was sentenced to death for war crimes (ill-treatment and murder) in the Gulating Court of Appeal on 18 March 1946. After the judgment was confirmed in the Supreme Court, he was executed at Sverresborg, Bergen on 8 August 1946.

According to Fredrick Persen's daughters, he remained, until his death in 1990, saddened by the callous way his friend Atle Svardal's body had been treated by the Germans.

The report recommending Svardal for a British medal, a few days after his return from Operation ERICA, was summarized as follows:

> From the point of view of the Intelligence Service [MI6], we are particularly pleased with the magnificent work of this agent, in that on both his expeditions owing to his cool courage and administrative abilities, he has been able to cover up his traces in such a manner that the field has been left open for future operations of a similar nature in the same most important area.[27]

Atle Svardal, Dagfinn Ulriksen and Eivind Viken were all awarded Distinguished Service Crosses by the British. (See Chapter 8.2 Briefing: Countermeasures for a description of how the Germans probably found the Operation ROSKA station.)

According to various sources, there were about 100 SIS radio stations in Norway during the Second World War, involving about 190 agents in total. The most present at any one time (the start of 1945) was over 40. Some 127 of these agents received awards from the Norwegian, British and French governments.

Chapter 3

The Solomon Islands

Without a Teleradio, a Coast Watcher was doomed and useless. So, knowing their lives depended on it, they learnt how to code and de-code, how to operate a Teleradio and effect simple repairs to it.

Eric Feldt, *The Coastwatchers*

3.1 Operation FERDINAND: just smell the flowers

Preliminary sketch for a memorial statue 'Pride of our Nation' by Frank Haikiu, Solomon Islands. (*©2009 Frank Haikius. Solomon Scouts and Coastwatchers Trust*)

With respect to irregular operations in the early years of the Second World War, there was a significant difference between Europe and the region of Australia, New Zealand, the Indonesian archipelago and the South-West Pacific. The deployment of behind-the-lines intelligence and sabotage agents in Europe was very much a reaction

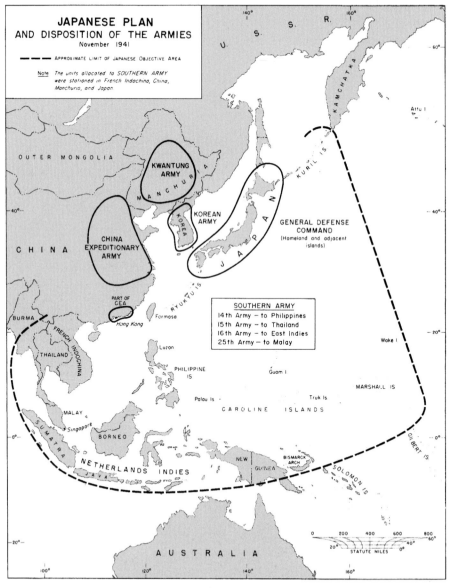

The threat to Australia from Japan in November 1941 is starkly illustrated in this map. (*Louis Morton*, United States Army in World War II: The War in the Pacific, *Center of Military History, United States Army, Washington DC, 1953*)

to the onslaught of German forces. When it came to the threat from Japan, however, Australia was well ahead of the game.

In 1940 the population of Australia was 7 million (less than the Netherlands' 8.8m) and 80 per cent of those lived in the south-eastern states of Victoria and New South Wales. This left most of the country's 36,000km (22,400 miles) of coastline unprotected. The idea of a 'coast-watching' organization was first proposed in 1919 by a senior Royal Australian Navy (RAN) officer, Captain J. G. Clare. Government officials, initially on a voluntary basis, were given the responsibility of monitoring any dubious ship movements along the north coast – essentially the 'top end' of Western Australia, the Northern Territories and Queensland. Even then, the objective was to keep the Japanese out. However, in line with Australia's longstanding policy of 'selective immigration', other peoples of Asian origin were soon included in this ban. Clare's proposal was accepted, and the scheme was extended to New Guinea, Papua and the Solomon Islands.

Consequently, when war broke out in Europe in 1939, Australia already had a defensive intelligence network in place. For a number of reasons, however, it had to be beefed up: the Solomons alone comprised some 1,000 mostly unoccupied islands, and many more watchers needed to be recruited and trained: teachers, district commissioners, fishermen.

The 'Teleradios' the Coastwatchers used were very bulky, and the full kit including batteries and generators required '12 to 16 porters'[1] to relocate it. It is estimated they had to carry 168kg (370lbs), plus the weight of the jerry cans of petrol at about 20kg each, including the can. (See 8.1 Briefing: The Radio Sets.) Also, procedures needed to be introduced to ensure messages were relayed, island-hopping to cover the long distances involved in reaching operational headquarters on the Australian mainland. The range for voice was about 650km (400 miles), and 960km (600 miles) for Morse.

Eric Feldt, a former Royal Australian Navy officer, was brought out of retirement to tackle these problems. Feldt had worked for many years as a civil servant in New Guinea; he knew the other islanders, government officials, planters and missionaries, and they trusted him. The name 'Coastwatchers' was a bit too obvious, so Feldt opted for 'Ferdinand', from an American children's book,[2] as a code name:

> I chose Ferdinand … who did not fight but sat under a tree and just smelled the flowers. It was meant as a reminder to Coastwatchers that it was not their duty to fight and so draw attention to themselves, but to sit circumspectly and unobtrusively, gathering information. Of course, like their titular prototype, they could fight if they were stung.

A Coastwatcher Teleradio being relocated. Fourth in line is the generator.

So the doctrine was that of SIS rather than SOE. Feldt then set off on an extraordinary expedition to get Operation FERDINAND ready for the Japanese:

> On 21 September 1939, with the war sixteen days old, I set out with a sheaf of printed coastwatcher instructions to visit every man in the islands who had a Teleradio. My travels took me by ship, motor boat, canoes, bicycle, airplane and boot throughout the Solomons, the New Hebrides, Papua, New Guinea, New Britain, New Ireland, and their satellite specks of land. I saw nearly everybody and nearly everybody saw me. I already knew more than half of those I met and all were very helpful.*
>
> By December 1939 I had enrolled all existing Teleradio operators, taught them how to code, what to report, and that speed in reporting was the prime essential. With an eye to the future, I also instructed about a hundred others in reporting, although most of these had no means by which a message could be passed to us except by runner to the nearest Teleradio – often a matter of days.[3]

When Feldt started, there were about 600 coastwatchers, but most of those were on the Australian mainland. By 1943 there were over 100 radio stations on the islands, all communicating on a network that employed a special,

---

* The British had passed administrative control of its territories in the Pacific to Australia in 1905.

rarely-used frequency (the 'X-frequency', 6.675 MHz). By that stage, in June 1942, Feldt's organization had become Section C of the Allied Intelligence Bureau (AIB), a co-ordinating centre for United States, Australian, British and Dutch intelligence and special operations agencies. (Section A was Special Operations Australia, a distant outpost of the British SOE.)

3.2 Solomon Islands: the mythical coastwatchers

Wars are won only by fighting, a truth too often forgotten. No claim is made by the Coastwatchers to have done more than to put the fighting man in a position of advantage.

Eric Feldt

On Malaita Island in the Solomons Feldt met with the 24-year-old trainee commissioner, Martin Clemens. Born in Aberdeen, Clemens had won a scholarship to Bedford School in England and later graduated from Christ's College, Cambridge with a degree in agriculture and natural sciences. In 1938 he joined the Colonial Service (long since absorbed into the UK Foreign and Commonwealth Office) and was sent to serve a three-year cadetship on Malaita. He was promoted to district officer of San Cristobal, in the south, in November 1941. After the Japanese attack on Pearl Harbor Clemens volunteered for the military but was refused on the grounds that he was in a reserved occupation.

On 28 February 1942 he became the District Officer and Coastwatcher assuming responsibility for some 15,000 native islanders and the handful of Europeans who had decided to remain. He was also a captain in the British Solomon Islands Protectorate Defence Force but had no uniform or military accreditation. In addition to his duties on behalf of the British government, he was soon sending radio reports on Japanese activities to Australian naval intelligence.

Clemens was on leave in Australia when the RAN sent a commercial passenger ship, the *Morinda*, to rescue the Europeans and Chinese on Guadalcanal and Tulagi. Clemens hitched a ride and, on reaching the island as the only passenger, stayed there. (He nearly didn't make it; as the *Morinda* approached its destination harbour it was bombed – unsuccessfully – by a Japanese flying boat.)

It was 8 February 1942. Clemens' first call was to pay his respects to the Resident Commissioner, 'a bewildered elderly Englishman named William Marchant'.[4] Marchant dispatched him to take over the district office on the island of Gizo, but Clemens wanted to go to the more strategic Guadalcanal, where he thought his presence as a W/T operator could make a difference.

Coastwatcher W.F.M. Clemens and six scouts on Guadalcanal, 1942. Right of Martin Clemens is Daniel Pule (his clerk), left is Corporal (later Sergeant) Andrew Langabaea.

And that's where he went, arriving on 11 February 1942. District Officer Dick Horton and assistant Henry Josselyn in the village of Aola east along the north coast were delighted to see him – both wanted to get back to Australia and join the military. (They were probably unaware that they too would be considered to be in reserved occupations.) The two colleagues briefed him, showed him the radio and promptly disappeared, leaving him in charge.

Meanwhile, Marchant – probably still bewildered – was moved east 100 miles to Malaita, and Feldt ordered his navy liaison officer, Lieutenant D. S. MacFarland, to relocate to a radio station midway along the northern coast of Guadalcanal. Feldt's next move was to order Coastwatcher F. Ashton Rhoades to cover the western reaches of the island from his present position managing a copra plantation at Lavoro.

Eric Feldt had recruited Rhoades twelve months earlier but had been unable to supply him with a Teleradio. Now supplies were coming through from AWA (makers of radios), Don MacFarland, Martin Clemens and a resolute old stay-behind planter called Kenneth Houston Dalrymple Hay teamed up on 24 March 1942 for a trip across the island; together, they assembled 'Snowy' Rhoades' shiny new wireless and rigged the aerial. After he was taught the rather useless Playfair code and how to send in Morse, Rhoades was nearly a fully fledged Coastwatcher.

For the time being at least, these three men – Clemens, MacFarland and 'Snowy' – had Guadalcanal covered.

* * *

Martin Clemens first alerted Eric Feldt to a Japanese presence on Tulagi early in May 1942. April had been a tense month; the enemy had taken Buka, Bougainville and the Shortland Islands. Clemens was still trying to perform his duties as district commissioner for the island while he watched from afar as Japanese bombs rained down on the RAAF base at Tulagi; the defending Australian Imperial Force (AIF) platoon had no anti-aircraft weapons. The arrival of the Imperial Navy and its force of marines seemed imminent – so, on 21 April 1942, he organized a cricket match. This was still, after all, a British protectorate.

In June he radioed another urgent message to Townsville saying the enemy had now arrived on Guadalcanal itself and were already busy constructing an airfield. They had landed unopposed. This was a heads-up the Allies could not afford to ignore; Japanese fighters and bombers based in the southern Solomons would create havoc among the defensive forces and the supply routes between America, Australia and New Zealand. Allied generals immediately planned what would become the first major assault of the war against Imperial forces.

Meanwhile, Clemens disassembled his bulky Teleradio and, on 19 May 1942, with his team of scouts and porters, headed for a new vantage point at Paripao high in the mountains, well away from enemy patrols. It was a huge procession, twelve men carrying the Teleradio and another twenty burdened with the bullion-laden office safe. The arduous trek would sometimes be along well-worn paths, but at higher altitudes they had to labour through dense jungle – the 'long bush'. They were reassured, however, by the knowledge that the Japanese would have to do the same to locate them.

Don MacFarland was also on the move. With the help of Ken Hay and a dozen native porters he loaded his Teleradio and other essentials into a truck and headed inland to Bamboo Creek, then travelled on foot up to a prepared location at Gold Ridge. Hay returned to the coast, planning to join them later.

The go-ahead for Operation CACTUS came from Washington DC. The assault would be led by the 1st Marine Division under the command of Major General Alexander A. Vandegrift, but Operation FERDINAND would provide the intelligence. While responding to the pressure to maintain a steady flow of reports from his lofty hideout on the whereabouts of Japanese forces, Martin Clemens and his team were running out of life-sustaining essentials: food, medical supplies and, most importantly, fuel for his generator, were in desperately short supply; without the generator his Teleradio would soon be no more than dead weight. But his intelligence system was working. Unarmed scouts around the island were keeping an eye on the enemy. Whenever they were repositioned or reinforced, the scouts would tell the armed island policemen; the police would then relay the information up the mountain to Clemens, who would encode and transmit a signal to Coastwatcher home base in Townsville on the Queensland coast. Consequently, when the landings came, the Marines pretty much knew where all the Japanese were.

Clemens' morale must have been boosted by the arrival in June 1942 of Sergeant Major Jacob Vouza, who had just returned from a visit to Malaita. Vouza, his senior police officer, was a stalwart character.

Early in August, the Japanese got a hint that their building of an airstrip at Henderson Field was about to be interrupted:

> Beginning on 5 August 1942, Japanese signal intelligence units began to pick up transmissions between Noumea on New Caledonia and Melbourne, Australia. Enemy analysts concluded that Vice Admiral Richard L. Ghormley, commanding the South Pacific Area (ComSoPac), was signalling a British or Australian force in preparation for an offensive in the Solomons or at New Guinea. The warnings were passed to Japanese headquarters at Rabaul and Truk, but were ignored.[5]

The Marine Raiders' landing craft touched the beaches on 7 August 1942, and they headed inland unopposed. On 8 August 1942, Coastwatcher Jack Read on Bougainville – 550km (342 miles) to the north-west of Guadalcanal – alerted American forces to an upcoming raid by forty Japanese 'Betty' bombers, and thirty-six of these enemy planes were destroyed by fighters waiting to pounce on them.

It was 15 August before Martin Clemens and his team of Coastwatchers came down from their mountain hideaway and walked into the beachhead at Henderson Field. Clemens was barefoot; his boots had long since disintegrated. There they were able to get their malaria, dysentery and tropical abscesses treated, and rebuild their strength. But Jacob Vouza was missing. He had been caught by a Japanese patrol in possession of a US flag given to him by the Marines. They beat him brutally with rifle butts and bayoneted

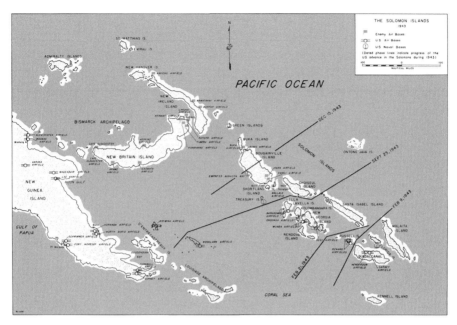

US Marine Corps map showing progress of advance against the Japanese through the Solomon Islands.

Jacob Vouza with US Marine sergeant on Guadalcanal,15 September 1943.

Down from the hills, Coastwatcher Martin Clemens (left) briefs Lt. Col. Buckley (2nd left), Commanding Officer Division 2 (Intelligence), US 1ˢᵗ Marine Division, Lt. F. Kidd (3rd left), Division 2, United States 1st Marine Division, Flight Lt. Charles Widdy (right), RAAF, a guide with the 1ˢᵗ Marine Division. Photograph taken on 18 August 1942, Guadalcanal. (*Australian War Memorial archive PO2803.00*)

W/T operator Sergeant William Bennett MM, British Solomon Islands Protectorate Defence Force, operating an AWA 3BZ Teleradio at Coastwatchers' station ZFJ5.

him seven times, before leaving him for dead; he obviously wasn't going to talk. But he wasn't ready to die, either, and he crawled in agony to Henderson Field. Clemens said Vouza was in such bad shape that he could hardly stand to look at him.

After treatment in the US Navy field hospital, the islander declared himself fit for duty and volunteered to deploy again as a guide for the Marine Raiders. Clemens and his intelligence network also went back to work reporting the movements of the enemy.

Later that year, Clemens was awarded the Military Cross by the British and, in 1944, the Legion of Merit by the US. The Americans gave Jacob Vouza the Silver Star for refusing to reveal information under torture and the Legion of Merit for his outstanding service with the Marines. The British gave him the George Medal for gallantry, the MBE for public service in the Solomon Islands and, on the recommendation of Clemens, a knighthood. Both men lived into their nineties.

Other Coastwatchers who served on Guadalcanal were Ken Hay, Leif Schroeder (a Norwegian trader), William Bennett, Donald MacFarland and Ashton 'Snowy' Rhoades. With the help of native islanders, they helped locate and rescue an increasing number of downed Allied pilots.

So frequent were Japanese bombing raids on Lunga – now renamed Henderson Field – that the Coastwatchers had to bury their home radio station.

Coastwatcher Donald S. MacFarland at Lunga Point, Guadalcanal. (*Australian War Memorial archive*)

The Coastwatcher dugout radio station KEN at Henderson Field airstrip (Lunga). The operator has a 3B Teleradio on the right and a US military set on the left. From 16 August 1943 all Operation FERDINAND traffic in the Solomons was routed through here. The fact that the operator is not wearing a shirt suggests conditions in the dugout were horribly sweaty. (*Australian War Memorial archive*)

3.3 Buka Island: Coastwatchers open for business

Bougainville is at the northern end of the Solomons group of islands; mountainous and enveloped in dense jungle, two live volcanoes add to its drama. English, French and German place names document its colonial history. It was originally discovered by the Spanish in 1567, but they did not stay long enough to establish settlements. The presence of a golf course and – as on Guadalcanal – a cricket pitch confirmed the British had been its most recent rulers (since 1893).

William John 'Jack' Read and Paul Edward Allen Mason were deployed there in December 1941. Both men had been recruited as Coastwatchers by Lieutenant Commander Eric Feldt. Aged forty-one, Mason was a short, quiet man who wore spectacles and was a little deaf. What made him a key recruit for Feldt was the fact he had spent most of his working life managing a plantation on Bougainville and was familiar with every nook and cranny of the island. He knew the native islanders and spoke the local Pidgin fluently; the 250km (160 miles) long island boasts twenty-six languages. An added bonus for Feldt was Mason's invaluable skill as a radio technician.

Jack Read was born in Sydney in 1905. He joined the Australian Administration as a Cadet Patrol Officer and was twenty-three years old when posted to New Guinea. For most of 1931 he had been back in Sydney for additional training, including instruction in tropical medicine. This proved useful, for on his return to New Guinea he contracted amoebic dysentery.

Once fully qualified as a patrol officer, Jack Read progressed through the ranks and, when Japan attacked Pearl Harbor, he had been an Assistant District Officer for five years and was currently serving as the top man on Buka Island, off Bougainville's northern cape.

Coastwatcher Sub-Lt. Paul Mason RANVR (*Australian War Memorial archive*)

Separating Buka and Bougainville was the 350m-wide Buka Passage; Eric Feldt described it eloquently:

> Read's headquarters was set in the Passage itself, on Sohano, a small island [at the western entrance to the passage] containing two bungalows, an office, quarters for native police and labourers, a jail, a native hospital,

Lt. Jack Read, RANVR, Coastwatcher. (*Australian War Memorial archive*)

and a storehouse. To the north lay Buka, 30 miles long and 10 miles wide, a flat island with low hills near its western shore. To the south was the flat, mangrove-fringed shore of Bougainville, stretching away to high mountains in the blue distance.

The demographic make-up of Bougainville and Buka Island was typical of the south-west Pacific – the 'North-East Islands' if you are Australian – at that time. Europeans owned the plantations, with the local population providing the labour. Chinese families ran import-export businesses and operated the local utility stores. More Europeans and North Americans were there to bring their preferred god into the lives of the people, while running schools and clinics. Feldt continued:

> To the west of the village, a small huddle of Chinese stores and dwellings was dignified by the title of Chinatown. Here Cantonese and their descendants sold cloth, knives, peroxide, lamps, and such items to the natives, and in return bought copra and ivory nuts. By day there was little movement in the drowsy Passage. Sometimes a motor schooner passed through with a muffled throb of engines and a white moustache of wave beneath its bow.

However these idyllic days in the tropical sun were numbered:

> But now the inhabitants of Buka Passage tensely watched war approach. Twenty-five soldiers of the Australian Imperial Forces, under the command of Lieutenant J. H. Mackie, had been stationed at the Passage to guard a partly completed airfield and its fuel and bomb stores. At Soraken, a plantation ten miles to the west, two of our Catalinas were temporarily based for carrying out daily searches to the north. Mackie's men were members of the 1st Independent Company, trained as Commandos, hard-bitten men, most of them older than their officer, which made his command no easier.

Australian Imperial Forces (more correctly, the Second AIF) were volunteer soldiers in the Second World War. By law, only volunteers could serve outside Australia. With the bulk of the Second AIF deployed in the Middle East, several companies were trained as 'commandos' to fight in Bougainville, New Guinea and elsewhere in the South West Pacific as the main force returned to Australia.. The Second AIF was disbanded after the war, and today's regular army was formed in 1948.

Tough though they were, Mackie's AIF platoon was a token force compared with what the approaching Japanese could throw into the fray. He decided

Lt. J. H. Mackie (back row, 3rd left) with members of his platoon of AIF soldiers and armed scouts, Bougainville, early 1944. (*RAN Historical Collection*)

they needed to abandon the unfinished airfield and go into hiding for the time being. Feldt described what happened:

> The first sign of the Japanese was their reconnaissance aircraft, lazily circling over the two islands from time to time. On 21 January 1942, the crews of our two Catalinas took off suddenly, carrying with them the bits of personal gear normally left ashore. This was an ominous sign, not lost on Read and Mackie. Read, determining that he would not be tamely caught when the enemy arrived, took advice from those who knew the local geography and selected a place called Aravia as a retreat. To reach it, it was necessary to travel twenty miles eastward along the Bougainville coast and then to walk inland for two hours, climbing a thousand feet.

Read urged all the Europeans he could contact to make themselves scarce but, strangely, most resisted his advice and decided to stay put. The Cantonese families did not: 'The Chinese, well aware that a corpse has no dignity, followed the advice,' wrote Eric Feldt, and continued:

> The night after word reached Read and Mackie of the fall of Rabaul [a port at the easternmost tip of New Britain Island, only 300km, 185 miles,

to the north-west], they set their natives to work. In the darkness, surefootedly picking their way along the familiar paths to the beach, the workers carried rice, tinned meat, clothing, benzine, cooking utensils, and trade goods, and loaded them into boats that made trip after trip to the Bougainville shore of the Passage. There other natives unloaded the boats, and began transporting the supplies to Baniu, farther along the coast. Read set off for Baniu by launch, taking with him a native crew, two police-boys, cash, office records, and the Teleradio.

He had made his preparations only in the nick of time. It was daylight when he started for Baniu in the launch, and he had gone about a mile when he sighted a plane at great height. As he headed for shore, the plane turned and pointed low toward the defenceless launch. Machine guns stuttered and a crop of white splashes jumped on the water. Then the plane banked, disappeared for a moment over Buka Passage, and reappeared leading a formation of five. Bombs dropped over Read's headquarters, Chinatown, and the airfield, and machine guns strafed the native houses.

At the airfield, Mackie's men turned their machine guns on the planes and apparently brought one down in the sea. Then the guards blew up the fuel and bombs and left for the Bougainville shore.

Meanwhile, Read and two government employees managed to reach a quiet place on the coast and, with help of local islanders, carried the Teleradio and supplies up the steep slope to Aravia. There they built a camp using local materials. Some islanders brought them wild fruit; their own supplies mainly comprised tinned meat and rice.

While their wood and kunai grass huts were being built, Read got the Teleradio working. As he listened to the depressing broadcasts about Japanese advances, two scouts arrived with more bad news – this time about events at the port of Kieta, further down the east coast. Planters and missionaries in the area had panicked and left aboard a sailing schooner with the intention of reaching Australia. They had brazenly stolen the Teleradio of aging Coastwatcher Tom Ebery, who was based south of Kieta. Once they had departed, the town had been looted. Regardless of his own safety, Read got back into his motor launch and headed to Kieta under cover of darkness.

At the dock he was greeted by Dr Bruno Kröning, who had been a district commissioner during the German administration of Bougainville, a post that naturally ended at the conclusion of First World War. Kröning now informed Read he was in charge again. We do not know the Australian's exact reaction at hearing this claim, but it seems the German's self-awarded promotion was

Many volunteer soldiers of the Australian Imperial Force served with the Coastwatchers, performing close protection and reconnaissance duties. Some also trained in the field as radio operators.

both optimistic and short-lived. After taking control, Read found some of the native police he knew and sent them to recover all the goods, mostly food, that had been looted. He had this transported to concealed inland dumps as a contingency. Eventually, most of the planters and missionaries changed their minds and agreed to leave. Read added Dr Kröning and his wife to the passenger list, and they duly set off for Australia and a few years of internment.

Read's and Mackie's next objective was to redeploy their coast-watching assets to reflect the fact the Japanese were not just offshore but on terra firma. Feldt takes up the story again:

> Read and Mackie now decided to set up watching stations, each with a Teleradio: at Kieta; at Numa, which was on the east coast north of Kieta; at Buin, on the southern shore of Bougainville; at the Aravia camp; and at the northern tip of Buka Island. This would cover the two islands except for the undeveloped west coast of Bougainville, which was unlikely to be visited by the enemy first.
>
> Four of Mackie's men were sent to man the station at Buin, and another four were sent to Numa. Read himself manned Aravia.

Paul Mason was assigned to the observation post covering Kieta on the east coast of Bougainville. Like Percy Good, he was skilled with a soldering iron:

> Radio had been one of his hobbies, and he had taught himself all that was to be known of frequencies, condensers, inductions, and circuits. He could wind his own coils, make his own repairs, send and receive in Morse. He had maintained communication with Port Moresby [on the south coast of New Guinea] and Tulagi when others in his vicinity were unable to do so, and while Read was in Kieta he had sent and received all signals for Bougainville. It was he who gave Tulagi warning of its first bombing.

However, there was a radio station to the far north where Read faced a tough decision:

> Percy Good, a coastwatcher planter, was already at Kessa near the northern tip of Buka. He was a man of fifty or more who, before he became a plantation owner, had been a radio mechanic for Amalgamated Wireless. Because of his age, it had been expected that he would evacuate, and we had instructed him from coastwatcher headquarters to cease reporting.
>
> He felt this decision keenly and, remaining in spite of it, offered his services to Read. Read arranged that his Teleradio should be moved to high land near Cape Henpan, at the very tip of the island, above Good's

low, exposed plantation, and he sent four of Mackie's soldiers to man it. Good was hurt by this decision but acquiesced and remained at his plantation, leaving his offer of service still open.

Percy Good had done an excellent job as a civilian Coastwatcher since he joined the group in 1939, but Read was clearly concerned about his safety once the Japanese arrived and began hunting radio operators. Read was unable to force him to leave his copra plantation but would have been pleased about his 'offer of service' – clearly a reference to the fact he would be available to fix any broken 3B radios; Good even had a workshop and spare parts, so he could do just that. This would have dire consequences for him:

> On the morning of 8 March [1942], six Japanese cruisers and two destroyers anchored in Carola Haven, near Kessa, and a Japanese landing party debarked at Good's plantation. For the time being, they put Good on parole. News of this reached Read by native runner, and he immediately signalled it to Port Moresby [the capital of what was then Papua]. He was mystified about why he had not received a radio message from the party of soldiers stationed at Cape Henpan, and when he could not make contact with them through his Teleradio, he set off to find out what had happened. When he reached Buka Passage, he met the soldiers, who were on their way to the Aravia camp. For some reason they had been unable to work the radio properly and, upon being warned by natives that some Japanese were approaching, had dismantled and hidden it and then left the post. Natives were sent to retrieve the radio and the party was reinstalled near its original place, with hopes that it would do better next time.

Without the immediate re-establishment of the Cape Henpan observation post the Coastwatchers would have no eyes on the Imperial Japanese Navy's activities around Buka Island. But something unexpected – and disastrous – now happened:

> Our [radio] news broadcasts now took a hand, and announced that Japanese warships had been seen off Cape Henpan. The Japanese, listening in, rubbed their eyes. They knew none of our aircraft had seen the ships. Their presence, they reasoned, must have been reported by Good, the man who apparently had no workable radio but did have a room full of radio bits and pieces. Two days after the broadcast, the Japanese ships returned to Kessa. A party landed, killed Good, then marched up the coast, took a missionary prisoner, and carried him off on

board ship. Once again, someone in ignorance had effectively betrayed a coastwatcher.

The Japanese shore party tortured Percy Good before murdering him, presumably in an attempt to get him to reveal the location of the radio. There are no reports of any attempts to search the Cape Henpan area, so we can assume he did not tell them. Good was honoured posthumously, and his wife received a full military widow's pension for the rest of her life.

*   *   *

Paul Mason, as the Coastwatcher in charge of the important Kieta area with its harbour, was also having a difficult time. Not only was he under threat from the Japanese, he was also having trouble with unfriendly islanders and hostile missionaries. On 26 March 1943 he wrote a letter to Lieutenant Commander Feldt in Townsville about his experiences over the previous twelve months:

> I was just out of Kieta when the first raid was made there. Four large destroyers and a cargo vessel attacked at 3 a.m. 31st March or 1st April [1942. Three weeks after the Japanese Navy arrived off Buka Island.] One force was landed on the N. W. side of the Peninsula whilst another went into Kieta Harbour and landed there attempting to cut off all on the Peninsula. There had been four A.I.F. there, but two were out on patrol, and the other two were saved by a warning, circular message received from Macfarlan which I received and sent to them. They climbed the wireless hill at 3 a.m. to see if their native watchers were on the job and ran into a party of Nips. They raced down the hill to get their packs and finding another party in possession of the town, promptly got into the bush.[6]

The Japanese soldiers exploring the town probably headed to the Catholic Mission, because it was the biggest building in Kieta:

> At the Mission were an old French Father and a young German one, together with three brothers. I had visited the Mission a few days previously and heard that Bishop Wade's orders were that they were all to leave their stations in the event of a raid; but all excepting one brother, a Luxembourger, remained although I sent warning the night before of the impending raid. As soon as the ships left I went into Kieta to see that the A.I.F. were safe, and the missionaries admitted that they had told the Nips where I was, and what I was doing, also when questioned

about the A.I.F. Buin party, disclosed there were four men there. I immediately let the boys there know that their position was known, but they failed to move out until a landing was made at Buin [near the southern capes of Bougainville], and they lost their equipment ...

Then the four A.I.F. from Buin and I asked permission from Mackie to take Wigley and Otter to Buin. Our trip there was delayed by unfriendly natives and we arrived there as the enemy ships were leaving for Tulagi and the Coral Sea Battle. I myself went to Kaiserina Augusta Bay [Empress Augusta Bay] to try and find the first stores dropped, and whilst I was away the Nip fleet came back from the Coral Sea Battle (I presume that is where they came from), the set broke down and no one knew how to get it going again until my return. From this time on, except for a food shortage we had an easy time as Read sent police boys and cash and the natives in this district remained friendly. The Mission was also friendly and helpful here, until the Nips grabbed them.

Buin, high in the south of the island, provided the Coastwatchers with a good sight of the many Japanese warships passing around the cape or anchoring in Tonolei Harbour. In the north, on 28 August 1942, Jack Read heard a sound indicating that the nearby airstrip was finally operational and signalled KEN:

FIGHTERS NOW TAKING OFF, CIRCLING, LANDING BUKA DROME. SAW FOURTEEN UP SAME TIME THIS MORNING.[7]

It was an ominous signal. Japanese pilots could now operate from a base 300km (190 miles) nearer to Guadalcanal than their previous airfields at

Australian Coastwatchers (probably AIF) on Bougainville. Date uncertain.

Rabaul on New Britain Island. They would be a similar amount closer again when the airfield at the south cape of Bougainville was completed.

On 9 October Read radioed in an alert to warn of the Imperial Navy's third (and penultimate) attempt to recapture Henderson Field and Guadalcanal. Mason and his team had eyes on a large fleet poised to head south-east down the Slot:

> SHIPS VISIBLE BUIN AREA: 3 NATI, 1 KAKO, 1 SENDAI, 1 TATUA CLASS CRUISER, 17 DESTROYERS, 13 CARGO SHIPS, 1 TANKER, 3 MYSTERY SHIPS—COULD BE LARGE SEAPLANE CARRIERS. AT 11 A.M. 1 TATUTA CLASS CRUISER AND 5 DESTROYERS WENT SOUTHEAST.[8]

On the night of 13/14 October the Japanese remorselessly shelled Lunga, damaging 85 of 90 aircraft at Henderson Field and blowing up the fuel dumps. The KEN radio dugout was also destroyed and had to be re-excavated further from the runway. The build-up to a further (and final) naval assault took place early in November 1942. On the 10th of that month, when KEN decoded Mason's priority signal, it read as follows.

> AT LEAST 61 SHIPS THIS AREA, VIZ 2 NATI, 1 AOBAI, 1 MOGAMI, 1 KISO, 1 TATUA, 2 SLOOPS, 33 DESTROYERS, 17 CARGOES, 2 TANKERS, AND 1 PASSENGER LINER OF 8,000 TONS.

Meanwhile, Mason reported that the population in the south of Bougainville was proving friendlier than those at Kieta on the east coast:

> To give you an idea of the natives' attitude here, they were ordered to go to work on [an aerodrome, probably the airstrip at Kahili], which they did from all around where we were, as well as from elsewhere. Our cook-boy went with them to work on the 'drome and get information. After this we had more trust in the natives as they told the Nips repeatedly we were not anywhere in the district. We got them to search for dropped supplies. So they worked for the Nips by day and for us by night.

After the torture and killing of Percy Good, Paul Mason was acutely aware of the risk of exposure. The situation on the island was now dire, and there was no mercy for any captured Coastwatchers.

> I suspect the Kieta natives told Tashira that I was still in Buin. [Tashira was a Japanese expatriate who had lived in Kieta before the war. He was with the raiding force when it landed.] They sent many patrols and enquiries were made about me; but out of thousands of natives none

betrayed us. We had given the stick to some beach natives who told the Nips about us previously, before the Nips actually occupied Buin. These same natives told us to move, as the Japs meant business this time 'as they were bringing their beds ashore' just before they occupied Kihili.

When we moved out of Buin about 21st December, some natives from the Korimina district heard where we were from others at a Christmas gathering, and all the Kieta natives with Japs came after us. The Kieta natives called themselves black dogs, raping, killing and looting as they came. Tom Ebery was caught, taken to Kieta and made to accompany the 'black dogs'. It was thought he knew where we were, but he didn't, he had just recovered from twelve months illness and was forced over gorges and mountains. Beaten with sticks and rifles most of the time, he died near the headwaters of the Mailal River in Buin. The local natives found the body and buried him on the banks of the river, marking the spot so that they could show us when we came back, but we did not return that way.

The reign of terror has spread across the island and along the coast as far as Numa and South to Taimonapu.

Giving cash to the islanders was a reliable way of securing some form of loyalty. Paul Mason had funds available for such purposes – but there was never enough. Feldt recalled:

Fortunately, money still held its value, as the natives used it among themselves even when there were no trade articles to buy. Read had not only saved the Government's cash at Buka Passage but on his second visit to Kieta had called a miner to his aid to dynamite the office safe there and had added those funds to his money for carriers and food.

Coastwatchers in a high observation post. Such nests were often reinforced with additional leaves and branches. (*Australian War Memorial archive*)

Meanwhile, far to the north on Baku Island, local AIF officer commanding, Lieutenant Mackie, and some of his men were also in a perilous situation. Eric Feldt described the crisis they faced and how a friendly priest came to their rescue:

> Before taking any measures to escape, Mackie signalled the arrival of more Japanese warships off Cape Henpan. He and his four men were in a very serious position. Their retreat through the island was blocked at Buka Passage, and the coastal waters were patrolled by enemy picket boats. In this extremity, a Fijian missionary, the Reverend Usaia Sotutu, came to their aid. He provided them with canoes and guides and slipped them through the patrolled waters by night, until they reached Bougainville.

But Feldt knew there would be no more intelligence on Japanese naval movements around Buka for the time being.

The situation was no better to the south, as Feldt reported:

> Read, accompanied by Sali, in the meantime walked across Bougainville to the east coast. Crouched in the mangroves by the shore, the two men watched hundreds of Japanese troops being disembarked by launches and landing barges from a transport and destroyers. As they watched two cruisers head in from the east, they knew that this was no mere raid, but a permanent occupation. To the south, below Bougainville, the Japanese meantime occupied Faisi in the Shortland Islands [15km (9 miles) off the southern tip of Bougainville]. The Buin party of soldiers reported the landing but, in spite of warnings from headquarters, remained in their house near the beach.
>
> Within a week, the Japanese landed at Buin. The soldiers escaped with only their lives, losing their supplies and Teleradio.

When Paul Mason moved away from Kieta to the safety of a supply dump further south he fell victim to tropical disease. Feldt again:

> On his arrival there, he was laid up for several days by a severe attack of malaria. The soldiers who had been with him at Kieta had moved on to the Aravia camp, and he was alone except for two native houseboys. After a few days, however, he was joined by the four hungry and bedraggled soldiers who had fled Buin. Fortunately, his fever abated until, as he said, he 'could eat nearly as much as the soldiers', this being, in his experience, the ultra in superlatives.

Realizing that Buin should be covered, he applied to coastwatcher headquarters for permission to move his station there. Air reconnaissance had shown us that the Japanese landing in the Shortland Islands was a permanent occupation, so his request was quickly approved. Two of Mackie's soldiers and two native police were added to his own natives to make up the party.

On the night of their arrival in Buin, Mason and his party heard the welcome sound of bombs being dropped by our aircraft on enemy ships at anchor …

For his observation post, Mason selected Malabita Hill [half-way between Buin and Kangu on the coast], from which he could see the whole area enclosed by the Shortland Islands, Fauro Island, and Bougainville—an area which was to become a principal anchorage for a large part of the Navy of Japan. A few miles inland from his observation post, in very rough country, he set up his camp.

As the Japanese tightened their grip on the island, with more warships at anchor, airstrips under construction and Marine and army troops seizing much of the coast, the Coastwatchers – with their AIF soldiers, island police and native helpers – settled into observation posts and radio bases, from which they could keep a watch on the enemy and report his every movement:

[Jack] Read, meanwhile, was searching for an observation post from which to keep watch on Buka Passage. He first tentatively selected a mountain from which he could see the whole of Buka Island and the sea to east and west in fine weather, but from which nothing was visible when the clouds descended in a damp, grey mist. Further search disclosed a better site, named Porapora, not so high and closer to the Passage. Knowing that his location could not long be kept secret from the natives, Read, with foresight that was part of his nature, did not use this second location but reserved it for the future. His principal nightmare at this time was the thought of a Teleradio breakdown. Mason, the only technician, was more than a hundred miles to the south. So Read developed a mild phobia about the care of his set.

After the sad loss of Percy Good and Tom Ebery, the situation on Bougainville had shifted a little, from dangerous chaos to something closer to settled:

The pieces were now set on the board; the Japanese at their bases with their ships visiting the coast; Read and Mason at their observation posts; Mackie and most of his men in their camp near Aravia; the planters and missionaries at their homes; the natives in their villages.

During this period, eyes constantly on their personal safety, the Coastwatchers continued to do their invaluable jobs: signal updates on enemy activities and rescue downed pilots:

> All this time, Mason and Read had been reporting the arrivals and departures of ships, the position of Japanese supplies and troop barracks, and the building of installations. This information was passed on to the Air Force to guide its bombers. Sometimes, after one of our air raids on Buka Passage, Read would signal back to us [at Coastwatchers HQ in Townsville] the results of our strikes, information which had been passed on to him by [the missionary] Usaia's scouts.

But Feldt also raised a legitimate question: why weren't the Japanese more successful at hunting down these active radio stations?

> The Japanese, of course, were not ignoring the presence of the coastwatchers during this period. The enemy knew they were in the jungle, but not exactly where. The presence of Mackie's soldiers, even though they had made many blunders and had not yet adapted themselves to conditions, also gave our watchers a distinct advantage. Simply because of the numbers on the coastwatchers' side, the Japanese commander knew that if he sent out a patrol to kill or capture our men, it would need to be a strong one. The larger the patrol, the more slowly it would move, and the less likelihood it would have of catching our men. In the meantime, the commander had his bases to build up and defend, and he could not spare a large patrol for any length of time.
>
> That Japanese commander must later have realized that his toleration of Read and Mason was the most serious blunder he could have made. At coastwatcher headquarters, we already knew that before the summer was out Read and Mason would be filling a vital niche in the Allies' plans. We could not even hint of this to our two men, of course, but we knew that up to now they had filled in the blanks themselves and that they had allowed no consideration to divert them from their intelligence role. So, without any portentous insinuations of what was to come, we simply continued to depend on them.

During January, February and March of 1943 the Coastwatchers settled into a well-ordered routine of keeping KEN and the Allied commanders on Bougainville supplied with intelligence on the enemy's activities at the northern end of the Slot. In the middle of March, they were delighted to get a morale-boosting visit from Lieutenant Commander Eric Feldt. Sadly, though, he fell ill on the 20th, suffering a stroke. He could no longer continue in his important job and was replaced by RAN Lieutenant Commander J. C. McManus, an intelligence officer with long experience in the Islands.

It would be a long and hard battle to gain total control of Guadalcanal, but Allied commanders had already decided that the next objective in the campaign to drive the Japanese back north towards their home islands would be Bougainville.

3.4 Bougainville: climbing through the 'long bush'

So secret was this organization of Coastwatchers, operating behind enemy lines, that its existence was never admitted during the war.

Eric Feldt

The messages which saved so many American lives were coming from Coastwatchers on Bougainville. Japanese planes were operating from airstrips at Kavieng on New Ireland and Rabaul on New Britain, and the contemporary map shown below illustrates how their routes took them over the enemy-occupied island of Bougainville, where they were spotted by Australian Coastwatchers Jack Read and Paul Mason (see 3.3 above). From their concealed radio positions they would then use their 3B Teleradios to alert the Marines on Guadalcanal.

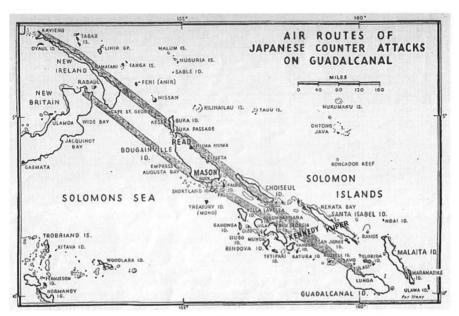

Coastwatcher map showing air routes of Japanese bombers attacking US Marine Corps positions on Guadalcanal. (*Australian War Memorial archive*)

These invaluable warnings of imminent aerial onslaught were often picked up first by other W/T operators closer to Guadalcanal and relayed. Coastwatchers Donald Kennedy on New Georgia (300km, 190 miles distant), and Geoffrey Kuper on Santa Isabel (190km, 120 miles distant) were able to relay the signals ahead to KEN. If one didn't pick up the transmission, another would see the incoming squadron and send his own alert to Henderson Field, giving the US fighters time to take off and climb to an attacking altitude.

As the Allies slowly but surely gained control of Guadalcanal – it would take a year – planners at combined operations were considering the next target. A key decision was made to avoid getting tied up in too many deadly skirmishes on the beaches of the smaller islands in the archipelago and leapfrog these to take the next big island, Bougainville, which would position them well for attacks on occupied New Britain and New Ireland.

Lieutenant Commander Hugh Mackenzie, now Supervising Intelligence Officer (SIO) for the Solomon Islands, ordered Jack Read to make recommendations for the deployment of additional Coastwatchers on Bougainville; no Japanese soldier was to visit the heads without the fact being signalled back to HQ. Read filed his report to Lieutenant Commander Pryce-Jones, who had taken over as Deputy SIO from Mackenzie. The document, dated 26 April 1943, was copied all the way up to the Director of Naval Intelligence in Melbourne. At the bottom of the cover sheet is a handwritten note: 'After you have finished with this may I have it for historical records?'

Gratitude should be extended to whoever wrote that note; Jack Read's report is a case study in how to plan a comprehensive surveillance operation incorporating the use of covert radio agents. It includes a sketch map of the islands (see opposite).

Read's report starts like this:

Sub-Lt. Keenan, with 2 AIF personnel, will cover Buka Passage area. He will have a 3B Teleradio based somewhere near Lumsis Village; and a 208 Field W.T. Set will report back to him from the observation post formerly occupied by BTU, and which commands an uninterrupted view from Soraken on the west to Baniu on the east. It takes in the whole of Buka Passage, Buka Island and the airfield thereon, and all that area north of an imaginary line Soraken to Baniu. This lookout position is 2,400ft. a.s.l. [above sea level]. It is seldom clouded in. Any activity on the airfield [on the north side of the Buka Passage] can always be seen or heard. All shipping entering or leaving Buka Passage can be observed; and any shipping passing 50 miles or more to the east or west can be seen. It covers also the nearer enemy outposts of Porton, Chabai, Tarlena and Chundawan.

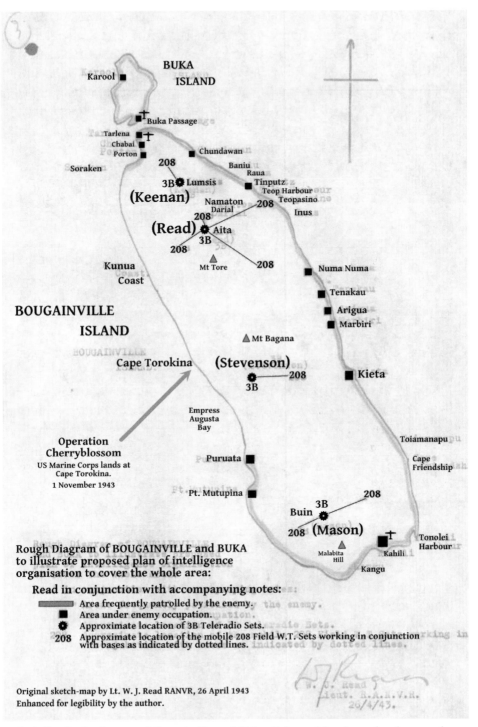

BUKA ISLAND

Karool

Buka Passage

Tarlena
Chabai
Porton
Soraken

Chundawan

208

Baniu
Raua

3B Lumsis
(Keenan)

Tinputz
Teop Harbour
Teopasino
Inus

Namaton
Darial
208

208

(Read) Aita
3B

208

Mt Tore

208

Numa Numa

Kunua
Coast

Tenakau

Arigua

Marbiri

BOUGAINVILLE ISLAND

Mt Bagana

Cape Torokina

(Stevenson)
208
3B

Kieta

Empress
Augusta
Bay

Operation Cherryblossom
US Marine Corps lands at
Cape Torokina.
1 November 1943

Puruata

Toiamanapu

Cape
Friendship

Pt. Mutupina

3B 208
Buin
208 **(Mason)**

Malabita
Hill

Kahili

Tonolei
Harbour

Kangu

**Rough Diagram of BOUGAINVILLE and BUKA
to illustrate proposed plan of intelligence
organisation to cover the whole area:**

Read in conjunction with accompanying notes:

    Area frequently patrolled by the enemy.
    Area under enemy occupation.
    Approximate location of 3B Teleradio Sets.
208 Approximate location of the mobile 208 Field W.T. Sets working in conjunction
      with bases as indicated by dotted lines.

Original sketch-map by Lt. W. J. Read RANVR, 26 April 1943
Enhanced for legibility by the author.

W. J. Read
Lieut. R.A.N.V.R.
26/4/43.

Jack Read's sketch map of Bougainville and Buka. Enhanced by the author because the original in the archives lacks legibility.

The position of the 3B Teleradio itself commands a full view of the East Coast extending from a point just north of Baniu as far south as Teop Harbour. Its height is 1,500ft. a.s.l. affording an horizon as far as the Cartaret Islands [110km, 70 miles]; and its nearness to that section of the East Coast abovementioned enables a close contact with the beach road for quick information of any enemy movements thereon.[9]

An Australian soldier using a Model 208 field radio set. The small box is the battery. Note the aerial lead. (*Australian War Memorial archive*)

The '208 Field W.T. Set' Read refers to is the standard portable radio used by the Australian Army. This was manufactured by AWA, the same company that produced the 3B Teleradio. The 208 was Morse-only and operated between 2.5 and 3.5 MHz. With all its accessories and the battery it weighed 8kg (18lbs) and could be carried in a backpack, but had to be removed for operation.

With a very clear and easy-to-use control panel (see below), it was very popular with both soldiers and Coastwatchers. Read later wrote:

We have four of these mobile sets; and we have asked for four more. So far they have withstood satisfactory tests here; and I am certain they will be of great value to us. The unwieldy 3B Sets can be safely based while these small jobs are used by scouting parties to report the information

The control panel of the Australian WS 208 Mk II short-wave radio set.

back. They have worked well here over a distance of 30 miles which is more than we ask.

Lieutenant Read's report moves on from the northernmost of the four observation posts south to the next – his own mountain retreat:

> Lt. Read together with Capt. Robinson and Lt. Bedkober will be based at Aita. As yet I am not in possession of any first-hand facts re Aita; but I understand that its altitude is about 3,000 feet [900 m] a.s.l., and that it commands an uninterrupted view of the East Coast from Inus Pltn [Plantation] as far south as Kieta. Thus it overlooks the enemy occupied area extending from Numa Numa Pltn south to Marbiri Pltn. I propose to move to Aita immediately following the arrival of the balance of the new AIF Section.
>
> A 3B Teleradio will be established at Aita; and it will have communication with 208 Field W.T. Sets at the following points: [Namatoa; Dariai; the West Coast; and Numa Numa].

Thus, so far as the Aita Base is concerned the proposed plan will leave 4 AIF personnel on hand there for any job arising.

Read's sketch map (above) is a little misleading; the Buka Passage is only 360m wide at its narrowest. Buka Town and the airfield are on its north bank, with what looks like a suburb on the south bank (reachable only by boat). But this shortcut was frequently used by Japanese warships. An undated signal by Lieutenant Read reported:

> A ship, which may be a cruiser, and probably another, entered Kessa 1 p.m. believe from north. Heavy destroyer and light cruiser, derrick on stern, just entered Buka Passage. Unusual air activity today; nine fighters landed at drome. Believe about twenty fighters and bombers now here. First mentioned ship now leaving Kessa believe may come this way.

In fact, it could be argued that by funnelling its ships through the Buka Passage the Japanese Navy made it easy for the Coastwatchers to keep eyes on them, count them and report their movements.

Read's 26 April 1943 report went on to describe the deployment of two further observation posts in the south of Bougainville:

> Sub-Lt. Mason and Lt. Stevenson accompanied by 8 AIF personnel will cover the Kieta-Buin area. That party will leave Aita equipped with two 3B Teleradios and three 208 Field W.T. Sets and move south through the centre of the island … The subsequent disposition of the party personnel is dependent on what progress is achieved as it penetrates towards the two objectives of Kieta and Buin. However, it is very probable that Stevenson will base a 3B Teleradio somewhere as indicated on the sketch map, using the 208 Field W.T. Set to cover at closer range whatever enemy activity is current around Kieta, Marbiri, Arigua, etc; and that Mason will be able to get back again to the Buin area, basing his 3B Teleradio and using two 208 Field W.T. Sets to the best advantage. Such is the plan in general for this party – future developments depend entirely on its progress.

Read's suggestions are sensible, practical and well thought out:

> Subject to any instructions to the contrary, as soon as the evacuation of the old AIF Section has been accomplished, and the incoming personnel are to hand, the plan as outlined above will be put into effect. By the end of May [1943] it should be in full working order; and it will mean that the whole of Bougainville will then be covered to the maximum advantage. We will then be in a position to give maximum compliance to any order from Headquarters as to any specific information required.

AIF commandos on Bougainville taking a meal break. Model 208 radio front right.

After setting out his plan for the pre-invasion phase of Coastwatcher activities, Read added a few more pages of comments and a number of special requests.

The first of these was a bid for ten additional soldiers – 'preferably signalmen' – to boost his available manpower. He also revealed that regular air-drops had been taking place into Bougainville: 'We now know by experience that the stores drop on the present basis will feed another ten men.'

> We are very appreciative of the organization which has enabled regular drops those past months; and, often under unfavourable conditions, the pilots have made our ground work easy by their skilful and accurate placing of the parachutes. Occasionally 'chutes have failed to open; but our loss in that respect has been only slight.
>
> At present we have two approved drop sites available to us, viz, Aita and Dariai. While present circumstances hold it is intended to prepare still more drop sites for use should same ever be necessary. Thus, by maximum conservation of stores we should eventually have emergency food dumps dispersed without the difficulty of ground transport.
>
> There will never be any difficulty for us to forward stores, as required, to Keenan and party covering the northern end of the island, from the

drops at Aita, Dariai, or such other central site as may be used, but the Mason-Stevenson party comprising 10 units all told cannot be so served – it would not be practical to carry stores for so large a party over the arduous and sparsely populated mountain route intervening. The alternative is for that party to arrange its own drop site for direct supply as required. If not practical to give them a monthly drop, then one every two months should suffice.

The selection of stores comprising each drop is most satisfactory. Flour is about the only item which usually runs out before the end of the period. Our enforced move to the interior has meant the curtailment of our fresh meat supply hitherto provided by plantation cattle on the coast. That means so will need more tinned stuff than in the past. I have heard mention of Dehydrated Meats – such as, that 1lb of dehydrated mutton is equal to 7lbs of fresh mutton, etc. What are the possibilities of more dehydrated foods being included in each drop, please – and, presumably, there should be a considerable saving of space in the plane?

Quinine Tablets – we need 1,000 five-grain tablets each month, please. In the past the drop has included only a couple of hundred or so – not enough for the existing personnel. The original supplies of quinine which we were able to retrieve from Buka Passage and Kieta prior to enemy occupation have enabled us to carry on to date; but these supplies are now just about exhausted.

Regarding Teleradio requirements: Each drop should include 2 gallons S.A.E.20 Engine Oil, and two 5-gallon drums of Benzine.

The Coastwatchers did not seem to have an equivalent to the well-regarded portable sets of SIS and SOE.

Eric Feldt's respect for Jack Read's attention to detail was not misplaced. Read wanted extra writing paper for the AIF soldiers who would be using the 208 radios, since single sheets are easy to destroy, but a lost notebook would provide Japanese radio intelligence with an unwelcome insight into Operation FERDINAND's activities.

* * *

Like Paul Mason, Jack Read was appalled by the treatment meted out to Europeans and Chinese by Japanese soldiers. However, he placed much of the blame on the enemy's local native allies and used the opportunity of his report to HQ to put some of the worst incidents on record:

There is the more recent case of Roche. Native betrayers led the Japs to his place in the Kieta hinterland. He was brutally handled by the natives before the Japs took charge of him. They forced him to walk for a whole day, having first tied his head forward and down between his legs. When Roche was at the stage of exhaustion they beheaded him. Fr. Muller is said to have located the body the next day and performed the burial rite.

The same natives first introduced the Japs to the Numa Numa area where a number of Chinese were in hiding. One, Jack Lee, was caught and murdered after being subjected to such torture as having fire-sticks poked in his eyes and mouth.

There are other numerous incidents which could be quoted concerning the misuse of Chinese women by both Japs and natives – however, they are but victims to the Jap method of instigating them to acts of self-incrimination as the best means of divorcing them from the European …

Our contra-propaganda, to the effect that drastic action will be taken against any natives collaborating with the Japs against us, is having good results hereabouts. The same attitude will be adopted by the Mason-Stevenson party when moving to the other end; and I have no doubt that results will be commensurate. In our circumstances, the Japs by themselves are no real menace to us; but with the help of natives they become a serious danger.

However, it wasn't all bad news. Some of the native islanders may have been torn between acknowledging the British and Australians or the Japanese as their masters, but most remained loyal to the regime they knew:

Practically the whole of the peace-time native police force is with us. In accordance with early instructions they were duly attested [sworn in]; and I presume their position is alright officially.

In addition, we also have many natives with us who were indentured to the Administration in peace-time. Two of these lads are very good W.T. operators and will prove very valuable with these small 208 Field W.T. Sets we now have. They are Tomaira and Tamti. I would like to see whatever is needed to be done to place them on an official footing please.[10]

Read goes on to add a brief update on the situation regarding enemy forces in the north of the island:

Jap. Situation: There is little of any value that can be stated in furtherance to our signals. I would say that there is anything from two to three thousand troops, ground staff, etc, at Buka Passage – which includes the outposts of Karoola, Tarlena, Chabai, Porton, Chundawan; and also the hundred or so at Tinputz [see sketch-map above]. We know that there has not been a ship of any size at the Passage for at least two months past. We know also that they are having difficulty in getting enough native foods. A system is in vogue whereby certain villages provide food on certain days; but due to the strain on their own supplies, and also because the payment, if any, is poor, the natives are tending to dodge the issue. Every indication is that the Japs are hard pressed for food ...

Unfortunately I am not able to include much concerning the Kieta-Buin area [central and south Bougainville] – we've been cut off from that part ever since Mason was forced to get out some four months ago. I am certain that in the near future we can furnish some information about that area when Mason and Stevenson get on the job.[11]

Read took a particular interest in the airfields north and south of the Buka Passage. Before the Japanese arrived he had a comfortable base for his radio station on Sohano Island in the western entrance to the passage. At that time

Buka Passage seen from the north-east, early November 1943. This photograph was taken as Grumman F6F Hellcats from the USS *Saratoga* bombed the airstrips at Buka (right) and Bonis (left). The triangular island at the far entrance to the passage is Sohano, where Coastwatcher Jack Read had his HQ before the Japanese arrived on 31 March 1942.

the Royal Australian Air Force was building the airstrip on the north side, the workers, fuel and munitions being guarded by twenty-five AIF soldiers commanded by Lieutenant John H. Mackie. This platoon had time to blow up much of the equipment, fuel and bombs before heading for the hills with Read, but the Japanese completed the airfield and made it operational. Read continues:

> Regarding Buka Passage airfield it is reliably reported that the 98 planes which raided the Solomons about three weeks ago all took off from there. Intelligent natives counted them as they took off, and they made the number 98 – which was the figure subsequently stated over the air. I believe it to be correct – in which case the ground activity at Buka is more than I thought …
>
> We know that the Japs are well aware of our existence in the bush. They even know that we are operating a Teleradio and that its callsign is BIO – and yet to date no serious attempt has been made to contact us. We prefer the opinion that the frequent coastal patrols although out to get information are reticent about venturing into the hills. They know of our stores drops. In my opinion we need not expect much danger of them coming after us. It would be a big operation for them to keep up a supply line, etc; and they could not hope for any success without native guides. The latter were eager to lead the Japs to unarmed individual civilians; but I am certain they will never exhibit the same eagerness against our number and arms.

Jack Read concludes his report by making some practical suggestions about how the anticipated increase in radio traffic from Bougainville should be organized:

> Three, and probably four, 3B Teleradios will shortly be in operation throughout the island; and my object is to do the work necessary with as little traffic as possible.
>
> Present instructions are that in addition to sending all coast-watch reports to KEN [Coastwatcher HQ at Lungi, Henderson Field] it is also necessary to keep VIG informed. That has been easy in the past few months, and has not entailed any material increase in traffic, because BTU [near Lumsis village in the north of the island] has been more or less the only station on the air here. But when these other stations get going a continuation of the same order must mean somewhat of a cluttering up of the air in so small an area. I would suggest that all stations continue to report direct to KEN in the matter of coast-watch reports; but that whatever is necessary to be passed on to VIG be decided

and done by KEN. KEN has better facilities to do that than we have here. Approval of that suggestion would make things much easier here; and would leave BTU only to keep the usual daily skeds with VIG for any emergency purpose arising in the island.

It is interesting to compare Operation FERDINAND with the behind-the-lines operations of the SIS and SOE in Europe. Eric Feldt laid down strict rules from the start that the Coastwatchers should just do what their name implies – monitor and report the activities of the enemy, but try hard to do that without letting them know you exist. Ferdinand the bull is only allowed to fight to defend himself if in danger of being stung. However, the isolation of the radio agents in the South Pacific probably made it harder for them to stick to the rules.

New Zealander Donald Kennedy and his Coastwatcher team on the island of New Georgia, north-west of Guadalcanal, was responsible for keeping eyes on the heavy Japanese marine traffic travelling up and down the 'Slot' or 'Cut' through the Solomon Islands. Warships were unable to move along this crucial waterway without being seen and reported by Read and Mason on Bougainville, Waddell on Choiseul, Keenen on Vella Lavella and Kennedy

US troops inspect Japanese Navy supply barge beached on Guadalcanal in 1942. (*Australian War Memorial archive*)

on New Georgia. Japan had, as usual, overstretched its logistics in this theatre and was forced to use barges to transport munitions and supplies.

The barges comprised little more than a sturdy hull, an inboard diesel engine in the stern and, at the bow, a ramp for loading and unloading on beaches. But they were vulnerable to air attack and assault by PT boats during daylight. As the sun rose, Coastwatchers would see them heading for the nearest island to conceal themselves close to shore or even right in the mouth of a creek. One day, when watching this happen, the temptation grew too much for Kennedy. Eric Feldt describes what happened:

> One day, a Japanese barge, straggling from its course, headed for Segi [New Georgia]. Kennedy, reasoning that the secret of Segi could be kept inviolate only by wiping out the Japanese, waylaid the barge at an anchorage with his native force, and killed every Japanese in the party. From the barge, he obtained Japanese arms and ammunition, which he issued to his expanded force. Later, two more barges were reported approaching and again Kennedy ambushed them and wiped out all except two men, whom he captured.

Kennedy was ticked off by Feldt and reminded of the FERDINAND rules: agents were supposed to operate like SIS, not SOE. It is not known what the former civil servant's reaction was, but not long afterwards, this happened:

> Then his scouts at Viru [on New Georgia] reported a patrol of twenty-five enemy soldiers moving overland in the direction of Segi. Kennedy attacked them in their camp at night, but they escaped in the darkness. Their equipment and diaries were captured, the latter showing that the coastwatcher [Kennedy] was the object of the patrol. In this last action, Kennedy was wounded by a bullet in the thigh, and two of his scouts were also wounded. But in all the affrays there were no other casualties in Kennedy's forces, while fifty-four Japanese were killed. Kennedy treated his own wound and continued on duty.

There was no reprimand after this incident; the radio station had been under serious threat, and Kennedy had responded appropriately.

One thing is clear: the level of cooperation between the radio agents in the field and the Australian and US forces they were there to support was much higher than in Europe. There was little or no bickering between agencies as there was between the Free French and SOE F-Section, between the RAF and SOE (over bombing versus sabotage) and of course between SOE and the SIS. Today's documentary film-makers prefer to depict the conflict in the Solomon Islands as an all-American affair, but the commanders of US forces

Dinner for VIP guests at Captain Donald Kennedy's Segi Coastwatcher station (ZGJ5). Left to right: Lt. Carson, United States Navy Reserve; Capt. Boyd, United States Marine Corps; Capt. D. G. Kennedy, British Solomon Islands Protectorate Defence Force; unknown US Marine; Lt. William Ferrell Coultas, USNR. New Georgia, Solomon Islands, March 1943. (*Australian War Memorial archive*)

at the time knew the truth – Operation FERDINAND was indispensable to them. Many of the downed pilots rescued by the Coastwatchers expressed amazement that there were Allied units active on enemy-occupied islands. They were even able to entertain them to dinner – see the photograph below.

The liberation of Bougainville was dependent on the Allies' ability to break the Japanese grip on Guadalcanal. Operation WATCHTOWER began on 7 August 1942, when the US Marine Corps landed a considerable force on Guadalcanal, Tulagi and the Florida islands. But it would be 184 days before the Japanese withdrew the last of their forces, on 9 February 1943.

During that time the US Navy's Construction Battalions, the 'Seabees', threw everything at completing the airfield, even using captured enemy plant. But the Japanese were determined to recapture this valuable asset, and there followed four failed invasion attempts, three land battles, seven naval engagements (including two between carrier battle-groups), and regular daily bombing raids from the north. Fighters based at the newly-completed Henderson Field wrought havoc on the Japanese air force, and it never really recovered from the losses.

Once Allied commanders considered Guadalcanal secure, it was time to drive north; after securing the Solomons they would be poised to pounce on the significant Japanese airbase and naval station at Rabaul in New Britain. By 25 September 1943 the Coastwatchers on the key islands of Tulagi, the nearby Russel Group, New Georgia, Santa Isabel, Kolombangara, Rendova and Vella Lavella had all seen US Marine Corps landing craft drop bow ramps on their beaches. Any pockets of resistance had been left for Australian forces to mop up.

Jack Read and Paul Mason on Bougainville had only another five weeks to wait. The amphibious assault came on 1 November 1943 at Cape Torokina, north of Empress Augusta Bay on the western coast of the island.

Landing craft circle, waiting for the signal to head for the beach at Cape Torokina (still being shelled), 1 November 1943. The high mountain in the distance is the volcanic Mt Bagana, Bougainville. (*US Navy archive*)

A US Navy historical account of that day's events sums up its significance:

The beachhead on Bougainville, established on 1 November 1943, represented not so much an advance of the South Pacific frontier against the Japanese as it did a leap beyond the frontier into enemy territory. The landings at Cape Torokina were made some 80 miles behind the heaviest concentrations of enemy land forces in the area – those in the Shortland Island area and Southern Bougainville. To the rear of the beachhead also lay enemy airfields, seaplane bases, and fighter strips at

Ballale, Porporang, Kieta, and Kara. About 70 miles beyond and to the northwest of our newly established holdings at Empress Augusta Bay were located the two active airfields of Buka and Bonis, lying parallel to each other on opposite sides of Buka passage at the northern end of Bougainville Island. Farther to the northwest, but still within easy bombing range was the great Japanese sea and air base of Rabaul, which the enemy had elected to make the main bastion of his position in the New Britain-New Ireland-Solomons area.[12]

Once the beachhead had been established, there were a number of key objectives if the Allies were to progress across the island. The first of these was the establishment of effective and reliable radio communications between the newly-arrived Marines and the Coastwatchers with eyes on the Japanese airfields, and naval bases and ground forces (primarily the US Marine Corps 6th Division at Buin).

US Marine signallers reinforce their radio base near the Cape Torokina beachhead c.1–9 November 1943. See long aerials reaching up into the trees. (*USN NHHC*)

The days following the initial landing at Cape Torokina were the most critical period for the new operation. While the enemy forces were strongly emplaced to the southeast, with several well-developed airfields, the position of the Marines at Torokina was precarious and undeveloped. Allied airfields

USMC Cpl. Henry Bake Jr. and PFC George H. Kirk, Native-American Navajo code-talkers, on Bougainville, December 1943. (*USN NHHC*)

Australian Coastwatchers arrive on Bougainville by PT boat from New Ireland, 30 November 1943. (*USN NHHC*)

were yet to be cut out of the jungle and built up from mangrove swamp, and American forces were crowded into a narrow strip of beach between swamp and sea. Reinforcements and supplies for the beachhead had to be convoyed over a route that was patrolled from enemy airfields and invited attack from enemy bombers. The threat of superior surface forces descending from Rabaul had to be guarded against constantly.[13]

Jack Read did not immediately get the ten additional signallers he had requested in his letter of 26 April 1943, but he did get a delivery on 30 November of five Coastwatcher radio operators with no fewer than nine armed scouts. They had been relocated from New Ireland in the north, transported by PT boat. They were to be kept busy; fighting continued on Bougainville, with pockets of resistance staying dug in, until Japan surrendered on 2 September 1945.

Once again, the Americans moved on when the situation was stable and left Australian forces to ensure the remaining Japanese soldiers were unable to hinder the Allied attack on Rabaul and its five airfields. Many Pacific Islanders fought courageously with them to free their homes from the Japanese.

Chapter 4

The Red Orchestra: Nazis versus Soviets

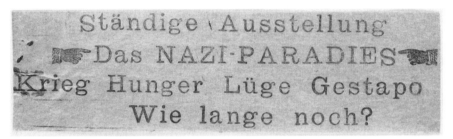

German resistance sticker reading:

'Permanent Exhibition
The NAZI PARADISE
War Hunger Lies Gestapo
How much longer?'

4.1 Moscow's Players: the sound of music

Of course, the British and the Americans were not the only Allies operating agents behind enemy lines. The Soviet Union had a network of spies across the whole of occupied Europe – or rather a network of networks, which functioned together when they shouldn't have and shunned each other when they should have been in a close embrace. The CIA's history of this remarkable undertaking includes chapters on the following countries: Belgium, Holland, France, Germany and Switzerland; also subsections on Austria, Bulgaria, Canada, Czechoslovakia, Italy, Poland, Portugal, Romania, Scandinavia and Yugoslavia.[1]

This remarkable network of spies, couriers and radio operators was known to the Germans as *Die Rote Kapelle* – usually translated as 'The Red Orchestra'. The introduction to the CIA history explains the origin of the name:

The term 'Rote Kapelle' ('Red Orchestra', 'Red Band', 'Red Choir', or 'Red Chapel') was a cryptonym coined by the German central security office, the Reichssicherheits-hauptamt (RSHA), to designate the Soviet networks of espionage and subversion discovered in Western Europe after the outbreak of the Russo-German war in 1941. *The espionage reports were transmitted primarily by radio.* [Author's italics.] The 'music' on the air had its pianists (radio operators), a maestro in the field (the Grand Chef), and its conductor in Moscow (the Director). This analogy was not new to German counterintelligence. 'Kapelle' was, in fact, an accepted Abwehr term for secret wireless transmitters and the counterespionage operations against them.[2]

The expression *Rote Kapelle* first came into play in August 1941, when a Soviet intelligence radio station was detected in Brussels by the Funkabwehr, the W/T intercept and cryptanalysis unit of German military counter-intelligence. Their investigation, however, soon extended into Holland, France, Switzerland, Italy and Germany, and the designation *Rote Kapelle* was also adopted for these expanded operations. In November 1942 the Gestapo set up a counter-espionage unit called Sonderkommando Rote Kapelle (Task Force *Rote Kapelle*), headquartered in Paris. It seems that Gestapo officers referred to this unit, confusingly, as '*die Rote Kapelle*'. Everyone else just called it the 'Sonderkommando'.

There were three phases in the life of the *Rote Kapelle*: the 'COMINTERN' pre-war era, when Moscow was trying to spread the message of communism and recruit adherents abroad;* the period of the ill-fated Molotov-Ribbentrop Pact (the Treaty of Non-Aggression), which ran from 23 August 1939; and

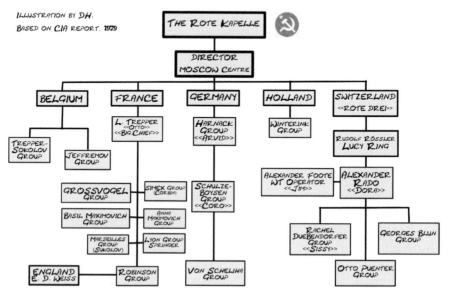

The *Rote Kapelle* (based on CIA report, 1979).

---

* Perhaps its greatest success was the recruitment of the 'Cambridge Five', including Kim Philby, who became a senior MI6 officer during the war while working as an agent for the Soviets. He later defected to Moscow.

finally, from the end of the Pact on 22 June 1941 when the Germans launched Operation BARBAROSSA (the invasion of the Soviet Union) to the end of the war in the summer of 1945.

The *Rote Kapelle*'s most active area of operation pre-war was in Spain during the 1936–39 Civil War, when the Soviets supported the left-leaning Republican Government against General Francisco Franco's nationalist insurgents. On their return home, many of the French volunteers – socialists, anarchists and communists – who had supported the defeated Republicans joined the Maquis* resistance units and took to the hills to fight the Nazi occupiers. Their longstanding affinity with the Soviets did not dissuade SOE from supplying weapons and training to the Maquis, and in 1944 the American OSS worked jointly with these resistance units during Operation JEDBURGH. (See Chapter 6.3 on Western Europe.) The success of Europe's communist parties in the first post-war elections had a lot to do with the contribution they had made to the Resistance, particularly in France and Italy, where voters repaid their endeavours. The author of the CIA's history of the *Rote Kapelle* even pays this unexpected tribute to the network's agents:

> The leading Soviet Rote Kapelle officers independently gave corroborating testimony to the effect that Moscow began to set up the first Rote Kapelle nets in Europe as early as 1935 and 1936. For this purpose, specially trained and first-rate Red Army intelligence officers were employed. Some matriculated as students in European universities, whereas others applied for positions as technicians and as merchants in need of practice and experience abroad.[3]

However, there is ample evidence of disruptive infighting behind embassy walls and of weeks off sick – all stories with a vodka-fuelled theme in a Russian context. And the network was far from being tight-knit; the French, Dutch and Belgian groups were rarely, if ever, in contact with each other.

* * *

With Stalin as its primary client, the *Rote Kapelle* was controlled from 'Moscow Centre'. If the Centre had a leg-man in the field it was Leopold Trepper. Code-named 'Otto', he was born in 1904 into a Jewish family living in Nowy Targ, Poland (then part of the Austro-Hungarian Empire).

---

* The name adopted by the Resistance, referring to the dense and tough scrub vegetation characteristic of Mediterranean coastal regions.

As a teenager he closely followed the revolutionary events in Russia, and after leaving school he went to Kraków to study history and literature. This background is reflected in the quality of writing in his book[4] but, sadly, his parents could not afford the fees and he ended up working in a Silesian coal mine, where he joined the Polish Communist Party. The strike he organized in 1923 earned him an eight-month jail term. On his release, Trepper went to Palestine and transferred his allegiance to the Palestine Communist Party and the Zionist socialist movement *Hashomer Hatzair*. The occupying British objected to his presence and expelled him in 1929. He then travelled to France and joined a subversive political organization (*Rabcors*), which was dismantled by French security in 1932.

Trepper then left for Moscow, where he was recruited and trained by the GRU. Under a new identity he spent the next six years travelling between Moscow and Paris. This work bore fruit and, when war started, he had already set up the *Rote Kapelle*; underground operations were well under way in Germany, France, Switzerland and the Netherlands. Former MI5 officer Peter Wright described Trepper as one of the 'great illegals', a group that included Richard Sorge (working as a German diplomat in Tokyo) and Alexander Radó (in Switzerland, see Chapter 4.2):

Leopold Trepper, the *Rote Kapelle*. Code name 'Otto'.

> They were often not Russians at all, although they held Russian citizenship. They were Trotskyist Communists who believed in international Communism and the COMINTERN. They worked undercover, often at great personal risk, and travelled throughout the world in search of potential recruits. They were the best recruiters and controllers the Russian Intelligence Service ever had.[5]

But the *Rote Kapelle* was more than a loose collective of GRU* and NKVD†

---

* GRU (*Glavnoje Razvedyvatel'noje Upravlenije*): the Main Directorate of the General Staff of the Armed Forces of the USSR (now the Russian Federation). In other words, 'Military Intelligence'.

† NKVD (*Naródny komissariát vnútryennikh dyél*): the People's Commissariat for Internal Affairs. The name is misleading, because before the Second World War it had been responsible for COMINTERN operations and was Moscow Central for the Rote Kapelle. It was the predecessor of the KGB, now the FSB.

officers stationed overseas. Although much of its activity involved espionage targeting the highest levels of the Nazi regime (the resulting intelligence being routed to Moscow via radios located *outside* Germany), it also included sabotage, aid to persecuted minorities, the printing and distribution of anti-Nazi pamphlets and assassination attempts against Hitler.

A lot of the high-quality intelligence traffic went through Belgium, but the German underground was fairly dependent on the Swiss branch of this Europe-wide network. (See Chapter 4.2 *Die Rote Drei*)

The Soviet 'Tensor' (or 'Tenzor') portable radio was introduced in 1942. The designers opted for a modular approach, with each component packaged in almost identical containers. The round-cornered boxes and clever use of colour components make this device look remarkably modern. It even came with a leather shoulder-bag. Of course, none of this says anything about its functionality or reliability. For a brilliant explanation of how it worked, go to www.cryptomuseum.com/spy/tensor/index.htm. (*Photograph by permisssion of Crypto Museum*)

4.2 Die Rote Drei: oder vier… oder fünf …

> *I must pay the Russians a compliment: in this war Russia was the only country whose cryptographic systems remained practically unbreakable throughout, although first-rate experts in other countries were attempting their solution.*[6]
>
> Wilhelm F. Flicke, German cryptanalyst

Rudolf Rössler was born in the Black Forest town of Kaufbeuren, 75km west of Munich, in 1897. He was thus old enough to be conscripted into the German Army in the First World War. That conflict over, he went to college in Augsburg and on graduation became a journalist on a local paper in the city. He did not long endure the brain-numbing grind of reporting weddings and funerals and soon relocated to Berlin, where he got a job as a literary critic.

Weimar Berlin was an exciting place for all the right and wrong reasons. Film, literature, music, architecture, the visual and performing arts all flourished.[7] This liberal – if not a little raunchy – culture existed alongside (but did not survive) the growth of the Nazi party. Rössler's work as a journalist inevitably brought him into contact with the denizens of the scene; some were Jewish, many were left-inclined, all hated Hitler. As the twenties

Rudolf Rössler, founder of the Lucy Network.

drew on, his friends and acquaintances realized their days were numbered and many fled the country. Hitler's manipulated rise to Chancellor on 30 January 1933 was the last straw for Rössler. The following year, he and his wife departed south and set up a business publishing anti-fascist books in Lucerne, Switzerland; the city gave him his cover name, 'Lucy' or 'Lucie'.

The company performed well enough financially for him to be able to afford regular and – considering the propaganda he was turning out – somewhat hazardous trips back to Germany. He had kept his contacts alive and was able to secure discreet meetings with senior people in the arts, politics and even the military who felt the same way he did about the direction in which their country was heading. Some agreed to supply him with information that would help the Allied cause. Rössler would later claim he had sight of German military plans within 24 hours of their being drafted.

The intelligence he obtained was of the highest strategic significance and included detailed plans for the invasion of Poland and, later, France, Belgium and the Netherlands. But at this stage Rössler had no means of conveying the information to Moscow by radio. He was forced instead to make use of the services of Dr Xavier Schneiper, a Marxist who was already working for Swiss Federation Intelligence Service (FIS). The cut-out between Schneiper and the FIS was a front company called 'Bureau Ha', which posed as a press-cuttings agency. So Rössler's valuable intelligence was only reaching the Swiss, who may or may not have been sharing it with MI6.

Rössler's risky networking in Berlin really paid off when he was contacted by two senior Wehrmacht staff officers, Rudolph von Gersdorff and Fritz Thiele. Along with Thiele's commanding officer, Erich Fellgiebel, they were part of a conspiracy to assassinate Hitler. Neither was a minor player: Thiele, a Great War veteran, was chief of staff of OKW communications;* Von Gersdorff's regiment had recently been involved in the invasion of Poland and would later be engaged in the Blitzkrieg against France and the Low Countries; at the time of the approach to Rössler he had been posted as an intelligence liaison officer to the Abwehr Army Group Centre, where Thiele worked. The group resented being under the command of a supreme leader who had ordered war crimes and mass murders in Poland and would later do the same in Ukraine.

General Fritz Thiele, a leader of the anti-Nazi resistance. He was hanged on 4 September 1944 at Berlin's Plötzensee prison.

These veteran commanders approached Rudolf Rössler because they wanted him to channel the detailed military intelligence that crossed their desks every day to any Allied power engaged in the fight against the Nazis. Rössler was more than willing to help, but they faced the usual problem: how were they to get the intelligence from Berlin to Lucerne?

As a senior officer in OKW communications, the solution was in the hands of General Fritz Thiele. Brazenly, he supplied Rössler with a standard issue army radio set *and* an Enigma machine. He had him listed as a military signals station with the call-sign 'RAHS'. This was 'hiding in plain sight' with a vengeance; he was even able to get an Army W/T signaller to work for them, because the operator would be ignorant of the incriminating contents of the messages.

All this plotting and intrigue took place in the massive Bendlerblock† building just south of Berlin's Tiergarten (Zoo) on Stauffenbergstraße. Originally constructed at the start of the First World War, and expanded by the Nazis, it was occupied by the OKW, the Abwehr and the Defence Ministry's communications centre. So as well as being clever, Thiele's means of communicating with Rössler in Switzerland was also highly convenient.

* * *

---

* *Oberkommando der Wehrmacht* (*OKW*), 'High Command of the Armed Forces', oversaw the Heer (Army), the Kriegsmarine (Navy) and the Luftwaffe (Air Force).

† In the aftermath of the 20 July 1944 attempt on Hitler's life, many of the leaders of the conspiracy were summarily shot in the courtyard of the Bendlerblock. They included Claus Count Schenk von Stauffenberg, Werner von Häften, Ludwig Beck, Albrecht Ritter Mertz von Quirnheim and Friedrich Olbricht. The Bendlerblock is now the site of a memorial to the German Resistance.

The veritable flood of intelligence traffic coming into the Lucy Ring from the Bendlerblock put pressure on Rudolf Rössler to ensure that his own lack of wireless resources did not delay its onward transmission to Allied command headquarters. This was where the *Rote Drei* (Red Three) branch of the *Rote Kapelle* joined the chorus.

The leader of the Red Three was Hungarian-born Alexander (Sándor) Radó. Born in 1899 to Jewish parents, he became a socialist while a student at the Budapest Gymnasium (high school) and later joined the Communist Party during the Russian Revolution of 1917. In 1919, when the short-lived communist government in Hungary was overthrown, Radó fled his homeland for Austria and then Germany. He was brilliant enough (and his family was wealthy enough) for him to secure a place at the University of Jena. He originally enrolled to study law but switched to a geography and cartography course. Before he had drawn more than a few contour lines he was whisked off to Moscow to join the Secretariat of the COMINTERN. After receiving his first training in espionage he was posted to Soviet organizations in Sweden and Austria. After three years away from his studies he was allowed to return to Jena, and graduated in 1925. Next, he was dispatched to Berlin, where he harvested political and military intelligence while working as a cartographer for Lufthansa. He then undertook further assignments in France and Italy, before he and his family relocated to Switzerland.*

It was 1936 when Radó, his wife Helene, his two sons and his mother-in-law settled in Geneva. He had been on Moscow's payroll since 1919, but now, with no Russian legation in Bern (the capital) and no way of transferring his stipend into his account each month, the family was in dire financial straits. His only sources of income were intermittent consultancy work with the International Labour Office† and whatever cash the Soviets could get to him by hand. He urgently needed

Alexander Radó, Soviet agent and head of the Swiss resistance group, the Red Three. (*Chronos*)

---

* For a more detailed account of Radó's inter-war exploits see: Louis Thomas, *Alexander Radó*, Central Intelligence Agency, Center for the Study of Intelligence.

† A League of Nations body.

money, and while in Paris he had run a news agency called 'Inpress', which specialized in 'maps and geographic data related to current events'.[8] Inpress had not been particularly successful, but Moscow agreed to let him try again and provided the funds to establish a new business called 'Geopress'. Now Radó was a Fellow of the Royal Geographical Society, this business worked out better for him. The CIA recorded:

> Geopress was more successful than Inpress because of better organization and the increased demand for news maps in the advancing shadows of World War II. As cover for an intelligence operation it proved ideal. Its normal activity – news collection and dissemination – provided justification for contacts with businessmen, officials, diplomats, journalists, and military leaders, some of whom became intelligence sources. It also justified a large volume of telephone and telegraph traffic, extensive postal business, and the maintenance of a courier system.

As he expanded his network of contacts and his options for getting intelligence to Moscow, Radó also worked on strengthening his own cover. This included preparing (with Marthe Rajchman) an *Atlas of Today and Tomorrow*.[9] At this time he added Rudolf Rössler as a major source, thus giving him access to the valuable intelligence flowing from the Operation VALKYRIE conspirators in the Bendlerblock HQ of the Wehrmacht. Distrustful of a conduit not of its own making, Moscow Centre expressed its displeasure with this arrangement, but Radó ignored them and paid Rössler for whatever intelligence he passed over. Initially, he got this material to Moscow by sending it via courier to Paris, from where it could complete the rest of the journey in the diplomatic bag (a method used extensively by the *Rote Kapelle* before short-wave radios became more readily available), but that route closed with the fall of France.

Another early member of the Red Three was German communist Ursula Hamburger (née Kuczynski).[10] Born in Poland to a Jewish family, her code names were 'Sonja' or 'Sonja Schultz'. She had been trained in Moscow by the GRU and was the Lucy Ring's radio operator from autumn 1938 to December 1940. During that time she divorced her first husband, Rudolf Hamburger, and married a British GRU

Allan Alexander Foote (1905–57), British radio operator of the Red Three spy network.

agent called Leo Charles Beurton (or Len Burton), enabling her to become a British citizen and move to the UK.

Sonja had met Beurton through another Englishman, Allan Alexander Foote.[11] Foote was born in Kirkdale, Liverpool in 1905 to a Scottish father and English mother but was raised across the county border in Yorkshire. In the 1930s he was one of some 2,000 British volunteers who fought in the International Brigades supporting the Republican cause in Spain; 500 of them were killed. Late in 1938, he returned to the UK, where he was recruited to work for Soviet military intelligence (the GRU) by his former 'political commissar' in Spain, Douglas Springhall. His role was not that of agent – he had no intelligence to give them – but as a full-time officer on a monthly wage of US$150.

In his briefing at an apartment in St John's Wood, North London, Foote was ordered to travel to Lausanne in Switzerland, thus avoiding conscription ('the call-up'). In Lausanne he was to make contact with a woman at 12 noon outside the central post office. He was to carry a belt in his hand and be ready to answer a question about where he had bought it. His contact would be carrying a bag containing a green parcel and holding an orange in her free hand. Foote arrived in good time, but at first he could not see anyone who fitted the bill.

> Then I noticed her. Punctuality may be the politeness of princes but it is certainly a perquisite of Soviet spies. Slim, with a good figure and even better legs, her black hair demurely dressed, she stood out from the Swiss crowd. In her early thirties, she might have been the wife of a minor French consular official. Her bag contained a green parcel and she held an orange. 'Excuse me, but where did you buy that belt?'[12]

Contact had been established. It was Sonja Schultz.

When he joined the Lucy Ring, Foote expected to be sent to Moscow for training. However, he was told the political situation was escalating too rapidly and he was going to have to learn on the job. Sonja taught him and Beurton W/T operation and encryption, so they could take over those roles after she had departed for England.

In his book he describes his cover as that of 'a gentleman of leisure' and an

Career Soviet spy Ursula Maria Kuczynski. Code name Sonja Schultz.

'*embusqué*'* Englishman. On a practical level, Foote did not get off to a good start because he had difficulty concealing his radio's long antenna. To resolve this, he approached a sympathetic electrical engineer in Geneva, Edmond Hamel, and trained *him* to operate the transmitter. Hamel's wife performed the encoding. Happy with this cosy arrangement, Radó paid them 1,000 Swiss francs a month. Radó even roped in his mistress, Marguerite Bolli, to provide a further channel. Her radio was concealed in a portable gramophone, and she transmitted pre-encrypted messages three times a week between midnight and 1.00 am. The 800 francs he paid her was probably a nice supplement to the pay she got serving tables at a Geneva restaurant.

After training the Hamels and Marguerite, Alexander Foote eventually got his own station operational. It must have been a fairly new radio set – maybe the Tensor shown above – because he was able to conceal it in a typewriter. Radó paid him too – 1,300 francs a month. Foote was officially a captain in the Red Army, but his pay probably reached him infrequently, if at all.

It was now the summer of 1941 and the *Rote Drei* had three 'pianists' and plenty of traffic to keep the frequencies humming with valuable intelligence for Moscow Central. However, the fact they were transmitting from Switzerland did not mean they were avoiding the attentions of German radio intelligence officers, especially Wilhelm Flicke, a cryptanalyst, who recalled:

One such agent center had been organized in the summer of 1941 in Switzerland. This network, which spread from Switzerland to Germany, had three radio stations, all located in Swiss territory. The traffic was soon spotted and monitored currently by the German intercept service but for a long time it was not possible to decipher the radiograms. This radio net was called the 'Rote Drei' …

The first messages were intercepted in September 1941 and they had [sequence] numbers running from 200 up; i.e., the first 200 radiograms escaped the German intercept service. Probably this organization began to function immediately after 22 June 1941.

While the German troops were storming forward in the east and special reports of their victories were being broadcast, in Switzerland (and in other countries) an intensive Russian espionage activity began. Day by day radiograms went to Moscow and supplied the intelligence section of the Russian General Staff with the basis for conducting its operations. It was an invisible struggle that was developing here.

---

* The French term for a draft-dodger, someone seeking to avoid military service or, more generally, a work-shy individual.

Flicke's 1953 account of the *Rote Kapelle* for the NSA includes some statistics for the network's call signs. The level of traffic going east out of Switzerland was unquestionably high. He estimated it at 5,500 messages in total, an average of five per day over a period of three years. A lower estimate – made in the Trepper Report – put it at 2,000 over two years. The matter was resolved in 1993, when the CIA Library analysed the Red Three's signals in their files and came up with a figure of 5,000, suggesting Flicke was right all along.

Arguably, quality is more important than quantity, so what did the messages contain? Flicke again:

> Through confidential agents in Switzerland and the German counterintelligence office in Dijon, France, an attempt was made to get at this organization, above all to get some clue to the cryptographic system, so as to be able to read the tremendous volume of traffic over this net. Not until the summer of 1944 was Germany able to read those messages. The contents were enough to take a person's breath away.

Flicke included a useful sample in his report for the NSA. These mostly come from post-summer 1944:

- 'According to a High German Officer in Brittany, 30 divisions are being transferred from the West to the East Front.'
- '400,000 Germans are holding strategic points in Italy as guarantee against a separate peace by Italy. Feeling in Italy increasingly anti-German.'
- 'Swiss Military Attaché in Italy reports increasing tension between Italian Army and Fascist Party.'
- 'All information of Swiss General Staff comes from a German Officer located at OKW.'
- 'Due to losses most German divisions on the eastern front have lost homogeneity. Along with people completely trained they have men with four to six months training and less.' [Another signal reports that military training camps across Germany were deserted. They were running out of men.]
- 'Stock of German Aircraft now 22,000 machines of first and second line, also 6,000 – 6,500 Ju 52 transport planes.' [By 1941 Britain and America had already far outdone Germany in aircraft production.]
- 'Number of planes lost on east front averaged 45 daily from 22 June till end of September.'
- 'New Messerschmitt ground attack plane has two cannon and two machine guns. All four mounted laterally on wings. Speed 600 km per hour.' [This may refer to the Focke-Wulf Fw 190, introduced in August 1941.]

- 'High officers of German occupation in Paris estimate duration of war at two more years and expect defeat of Germany … Masses still believe in final victory but intellectuals and high military circles skeptical regarding outcome in east.'
- 'Victories on east front cost elite of German army. Russian tanks often superior. Lithuanians and Estonians convinced Soviets are coming back.' [They did indeed come back. On 22 September 1944 Red Army troops entered the Estonian capital of Tallinn.][13]

Breathtaking indeed; this is intelligence of the highest order. But how were the *Rote Kapelle*'s codes broken? Before we consider that, you might need to read the Chapter 8.4 Briefing on Codes and Cryptology. This section is important, because only when the codes were broken could the Funkabwehr slowly but surely arrest the members of the network and hang them.

4.3 The Brussels Suburbs: a basket of rabbits

Leopold Trepper's job as trouble-shooter was to keep the agents safe and ensure the intelligence kept flowing. In reality, he spent at least as much time mopping up after the mistakes made by the Centre. If the high command in Moscow had trusted him, he would have been more successful and the *Rote Kapelle* would have lasted longer. His very readable book[14] – written in 1977 while he was in retirement in Israel – is critical of Red Army intelligence and its refusal to take seriously his reports from the field. So confident was the Centre of the group's safety that they sent 'Otto' to Brussels to make sure that network kept sending.

Johann Wentzel, Soviet radio specialist.

For many years the head of the Belgian branch of the network had been Johann Wenzel. Born in 1902 in Niedau (or Nidowo), 40km south-east of the port of Gdańsk in Poland, he took an active interest in left-wing politics throughout his youth. On leaving school he moved to the Ruhr in Germany, where he started an apprenticeship with a coal-mining company, before securing a job with the industrial giant Krupp. After joining the KPD (*Kommunistische Partei Deutschlands*, Communist Party of Germany), he was sent to the USSR for training. He worked in the field for several years under the cover names of 'Horst' and 'Hermann' before, in 1935, being recalled to Moscow for an intensive course as a specialist W/T operator. He would act as an instructor, radio repairman and adviser to other agents when he returned the following year to set up the networks in Belgium and the Netherlands. For two years he was an invaluable member of the team, who knew him as 'The Professor', and he regularly shared the workload on the Morse key.

The disbandment of the circuit began in Belgium, in the summer of 1941. Trepper had been concerned for some time by the number of arrests being made and argued with the Centre that the three stations in Brussels urgently needed to be closed down. The Centre refused, thus giving German radio intelligence more time to locate the primary station. Wilhelm Flicke was an eyewitness to some of what happened:

> The radio traffic itself was soon intercepted by German stations, for the first time on 26 June [1941]. However, it was not possible to solve the cryptographic system and read the contents. Furthermore, it was a long time before the German D/F service was able to fix the station [geographically].
>
> Not until November 1941 was it ascertained that the station was certainly in Brussels. Now the close-range search began. On 12 December the transmitter was fixed definitely so that steps could be taken for picking it up. On 13 December it was captured by representatives of German counterintelligence in Brussels. This was the first transmitter of its type that had been spotted in Western Europe.
>
> The villa* in which it had been set up and from which it operated had been rented during the summer of 1941 by the Russian espionage service and was cared for by a Belgian housekeeper. The building served not only as the location of the radio station but also as shelter for members of the agent group and as calling point for agents and informers.

What happened in Brussels on that day was even more dramatic than suggested by Flicke's account. Sharing Otto's concerns about security, Wenzel had already shut down transmissions from 101 Rue des Atrébates. Trepper arrived in the city from Paris on 11 December and assessed the situation as dangerous. At midday on the 12th he went to the house, where Polish cipher clerk Sofie Poznanska described how bad security was. An agent (Mikhail Makarov) who operated with a Uruguayan passport in the name 'Carlos Alamo' had been bringing to the house men and women who were unknown to the group. Otto made a quick decision to send Sofie – whom he had

---

* The use of the word 'villa' in this translation is misleading. The location (which still exists) is a five-storey terraced town house on a narrow street.

known in Palestine – and another agent called 'Kamy' to Paris as soon as possible. Wenzel would have to find replacements. He arranged for them all to meet at 101 Rue des Atrébates at noon the following day, 13 December.

When the raid came, it was led by Abwehr Hauptmann (Captain) Harry Piepe. Greeting him inside on the ground floor was housekeeper Rita Arnould, a Dutch sympathizer who had rented the group the building but knew nothing about their activities. On the first floor, Sofie Poznanska was busy deciphering traffic when she heard the commotion below. Realizing she was about to be caught red-handed, she scooped up all the papers and threw them on the fire. A German soldier managed to retrieve half of one page. Next to be arrested was Kamy. He was caught listening to a radio, monitoring the outgoing traffic of another station. Somehow he managed to duck past the Germans and reach the street, but was caught after what Trepper called 'a wild chase'.[15]

At 11.30 the following morning (the 14th) the eccentric Carlos Alamo turned up in good time for the meeting called by Otto. He must have looked quite a sight to the Germans who opened the door to him; he was scruffy, unshaven and carrying 'a basket of rabbits for dinner'. He told the men behind the rifles he was a black marketeer selling rabbits door-to-door, but his Uruguayan passport failed to convince them, and he was detained.

An equally unsuspecting Leopold Trepper rang the doorbell dead on 12 noon. It was easy for him to show genuine surprise when a uniformed German opened the door. He said he hadn't expected the house to be used by the Wehrmacht and that he must have come to the wrong address, but he was unceremoniously dragged inside. The Abwehr had caught its arch enemy, the head of the *Rote Kapelle* spy network.

What happened next was quite remarkable. Wilhelm Flicke describes the arrest of R/T operator Carlos Alamo (he of the rabbits) on 14 December but makes no mention of the far more important Trepper. The Germans had already trashed 101 Rue des Atrébates in their search for incriminating materials, and Otto could see Alamo detained in another room. Before the soldiers could demand his papers, he calmly produced them and handed them over. They were stunned. The papers, complete with official German stamps and signatures, stated that 'Monsieur Gilbert' had been commissioned by the head of Organisation Todt* in Paris to secure vital material and supplies for the Wehrmacht. The documents requested that all German military give Monsieur Gilbert every necessary support in the completion of his task.

---

* The Organisation Todt, named after its founder Fritz Todt, was a massive industrial and military engineering group which operated between 1933 and 1945. It started with construction of the autobahn and 'graduated' to building the concentration camps that housed the 1.4 million slave labourers it had grown to depend on as the war progressed.

Trepper spun a tale that he had come to check the availability of scrap metal at a garage across the road, but the place was closed and so he was enquiring at Number 101 about when it usually opened. With Monsieur Gilbert's convincing credentials in his hand, the soldier reassured him but said he would have to wait until Hauptmann Piepe arrived. Otto protested, saying he had to catch a train back to Paris and couldn't wait. The soldier did not like the way things were developing and telephoned Piepe, who reprimanded him, called him an idiot and ordered him to release Trepper.

Back on the street – fifteen minutes later – Otto's relief was tempered by the knowledge that the work of the Belgian branch of the *Rote Kapelle* was at an end. He had to assume the Germans had their hands on paperwork that would help them crack the group's codes, and his concerns were well-justified. Wilhelm Flicke later wrote:

> Among the material found were some 500 enciphered radiograms forwarded by this transmitter, hence there was no doubt that the encipherment and decipherment had been done in the house and that the cipher keys must be there somewhere. Until these were found, nothing could be done with the traffic. It was only possible to learn that a grille [grid?] system was involved which was obviously re-enciphered with a so-called book key. As book key, any book may be used by agreement between sender and recipient. From the text an 'additive sequence' is derived and decipherment is not possible without having the book used.

These assumptions were to prove correct, as we shall see later. Trepper rushed off to find 'Kent' (see below) and other agents still at large to get them out of the country. But Wenzel stayed behind, changed his identity, relocated his radio and continued transmitting intelligence to the Centre. It was an act of remarkable courage. Among the warders at Brussels' St Gilles Prison* were a number of resistance supporters who kept Wenzel informed about the interrogations of the captured *Rote Kapelle* members. When they started talking, he might have to move again.

4.4 A Scrap of Paper: how the code was cracked

Although the Funkabwehr's D/F people deserved credit for pinning down the location of the radio station at Rue des Atrébates, the Brussels office of counter-intelligence refused to let them anywhere near the place after the transmitter had been seized. Of those arrested only the housekeeper,

---

* This notorious jail was a military prison under German control during the war. It has been estimated that 30,000 Belgian men, women and children were interned there between 1940 and 1944.

Rita Arnould, talked under interrogation, and it was soon concluded that she knew nothing about the spy ring she was making coffee for. Counter-intelligence said their actions were 'for security reasons'; Flicke said they were about 'egotism' and a desire to take all the credit. The 'villa' was even released back to its original owners in a matter of days.

However, six weeks later, counter-intelligence sent a report to the radio security team. It boldly declared that an attempt by the cipher section of OKW to decrypt the radiograms had proved successful. This was a bit rich considering that the cryptanalysts had not been given access to the cipher text of the messages. But tucked into the back of the report were photographs of all the material found. The code-breakers could now get to work. Flicke explained what happened:

> These photographs were subjected to a careful check at the central office of 'Radio Defense' and it was discovered that one of the scraps of paper which had been photographed contained a so-called 'Caesar' key,* such as is employed by the Russians for enciphering plain text. [This doesn't make sense; the Caesar code is trivial.] This scrap of paper showed several rows of the encipherment of the radiogram and this proved that encipherment had been carried on within the house. Hence the books used must also be there.

Flicke also recalled that 'Some notes in secret ink and certain letters contained hints that the organization had branches in France and Holland.' This implies that some of the original documents must have been included with the report; text written with secret ink cannot be revealed from a photograph. Some of the analysts worked with other scraps of cipher text and discovered (probably statistically) that the book being used must have been in French. This was a small breakthrough, but they would still need to identify the title and secure the same edition.

Another Russian agent, Alexander Foote, although he did not work in Belgium, describes in detail in Appendix A of his book the way in which he prepared his messages for transmission:

> The process of enciphering messages for the Centre was divided into two parts. The first stage is comparatively simple and can easily be carried in the head, and ... I frequently made notes in this First Stage Cipher for ease and convenience. The second stage involves the 'closing' of the first simple encipherment against the text of a code book. (In this case, a 'code book' is any ordinary published book that may be selected.)

---

* See briefing: Chapter 8.4 Codes and Crypto.

Foote says that the book he used was a Swiss volume of trade statistics.

At first it looks as though the initial stage of the encryption is going to be some kind of transposition based on the Playfair method. (See briefing: Chapter 8.4 Codes and Crypto.) The keys have six letters and are changed periodically by Moscow Centre. Foote's example uses the word 'PLAYER' (equivalent to Sørli's key, 'TRØNDELAG'). This is how a 6 x 5 table is created; the key is followed by the remaining letters of the alphabet in sequence.

P	L	A	Y	E	R
B	C	D	F	G	H
I	J	K	M	N	O
Q	S	T	U	V	W
X	Z	@	.		

The Rote Kapelle code. Stage 1 (Left to right, top to bottom)

Now forget about Playfair. The next stage is to convert the letters to numbers. Some are converted to 1 to 9 (excluding 4), others to 00 to 09, then 40 to 49. This is a fairly clever way of introducing an additional key (also changed frequently by the Centre). In his example, Foote has to designate A, S, I, N, T, O, E and R as the letters to be replaced – the sequence doesn't matter. He calls 'ASINTOER' the 'mnemonic', and it can be changed at any time by Moscow. After the 1 to 9 (without 4) substitution the table looks like this.

		3		6	8
P	L	A	Y	E	R
B	C	D	F	G	H
1				7	9
I	J	K	M	N	O
	2	5			
Q	S	T	U	V	W
X	Z	@	.		

The Rote Kapelle code Stage 2. (Top to bottom, left to right)

Starting at the top left corner and going down each column, the letters of the mnemonic have been numbered 1 to 3 and then 5 to 9 as they occur. Next, the agent fills in the blanks in the same order from top left numbering them 00 to 09 and then (from '@') 40 to 49. (Now you know why the first sequence cannot include '4'.)

00	04	3	41	6	8
P	L	A	Y	E	R
01	05	08	42	46	48
B	C	D	F	G	H
1	06	09	43	7	9
I	J	K	M	N	O
02	2	5	44	47	49
Q	S	T	U	V	W
03	07	40	45		
X	Z	@	.		

The Rote Kapelle code. Stage 3. (Top to bottom, left to right)

The result is a substitution table for a 26-letter alphabet plus '@' and '.'. Here is the message Foote uses in his example:

'DIRECTOR.HAVERECEIVEDYOURNRS.@68.69.70@.JIM. NR.@41@.'

This is a simple acknowledgement to the Centre that he has received message numbers 68, 69 and 70. The @-signs are used to left- and right-bracket any numbers. Now the substitution can take place, each character of the plain text being replaced with a number of one, two or three digits. Note that plain text numerals are repeated twice: '2' becomes '222', '8' becomes '888', and so on.

D	I	R	E	C	T	O	R	.	H	A	V	E	R	E
08	1	8	6	05	5	9	8	45	48	3	47	6	8	6
C	E	I	V	E	D	Y	O	U	R	S	N	R	S	@
05	6	1	47	6	08	41	9	44	8	2	7	8	2	40
6	8	.	6	9	.	7	0	@	.	J	I	M	.	N
666	888	45	666	999	45	777	000	40	45	06	1	43	45	7
R	@	4	1	@	.									
8	40	444	111	40	45									

Now forget about the plaintext and write down the cipher text as five-number groups.

08186	05598		45483	47686	05614
76084	19448	78245	40666	88845	66699
94577	70004	04506	14345	78454	04441
	11404	50000			

The third and sixteenth groups have been left blank for the 'designator' groups. SOE and SIS put their designators at the beginning of messages, but this variable method is obviously safer. The final group has been filled out with zeros.

At this point – halfway through the process – the reader is entitled to take the view that the Soviet system used by *Rote Kapelle* is complicated enough for any agent under pressure from Funkabwehr search teams. Two, possibly three variables are involved: the keyword ('PLAYER' in this case); the 'mnemonic' ('A, S, I, N, T, O, E and R'), 00-09 and 40-49 could be changed to something like 10-19 and 70-79. In the last case, the '7' would have to be omitted from the initial 0-9 instead of '4'.

Even at that level of complexity, the Soviet cryptologists obviously did *not* think it was secure enough and added a further level of encoding, which Alexander Foote described as follows:

> At this point the first stage of encipherment is complete. It is now necessary to 'close' the message by re-enciphering it against the selected portion of the 'code book'.[16]

Here comes another variable: the page number, line number and first word of the 'selected portion' of the text (Foote's Swiss book of trade statistics). The second stage consisted of putting that random piece of text through exactly the same encipherment process of the clear-text message and then combining the resulting cipher text with that of the message. The latter was done by adding the five-figure groups without carrying the tens. All that remained to be done then was to calculate and insert the two 'recognition' groups. Foote's final cipher text looked like this:

52911	69255	79920	59637	23984	43290	49168	45878
84069	29006	28621	08031	59434	16340	65236	89482
83516	23491	95112	57784	94110			

This, then, was what a Funkabwehr W/T operator monitoring Foote's transmitter would have written down as the cipher text of his message. Along with the call-signs, frequency, and time of day, it would represent the starting point for German code-breakers. If Wilhelm Flicke was right in claiming that 'Russia was the only country whose cryptographic systems remained practically unbreakable throughout', it is clear that outcome was not achieved without some considerable ingenuity by Soviet cryptologists and hard work by radio agents in the field.

*   *   *

The scraps of paper found at the Rue des Atrébates were going to help the Germans, but they urgently needed the book that was being used in the second stage of the encryption. As Flicke records, they went back to the housekeeper:

> By carefully questioning the Belgian lady [Rita Arnould, the Dutch supporter] who had run the house it was possible to learn little by little the titles of eight or nine books which might have been used by the Russian agents. Now it was a question of getting these nine books. The only way was to purchase them on the open market, since the villa had meanwhile changed hands and the entire library had disappeared. Even though the titles of the books were now known, there was no guarantee that the proper edition would be found in a book store, i.e. the edition which corresponded exactly in pagination and in text to the one used.

Although Alexander Foote boasted he could write notes holding the first stage of the encipherment in his head, that skill was clearly beyond the talents of the Soviet agents working in the Belgian villa. For example, when they needed to add the five-figure groups from the book text to the five-figure groups from the message, they wrote it down. And, fatally, *they failed to destroy the pencil notes that revealed their workings.* Flicke takes up the story:

> A half destroyed sheet used in encipherment was the critical factor. After some six weeks of work the make-up of the additive sequence was learned. On the basis of other agent traffic it was finally possible to turn these digits into letters and the short sentence obtained contained a significant name 'Proctor'. This name was found in one of the novels which had been procured and thus the key book was revealed and the system was broken.

According to Trepper's account there were just five books that sat permanently on the desk of the cryptographer, Sofie Poznanska. The only one containing the word 'Proctor' was a French novel titled *Le Miracle du Professeur Wolmar.*[17]

Diligence and patience had paid off. This meant that it would be considerably easier to break future radio traffic from the *Rote Kapelle* to Moscow Centre, but they could also return to message 201, the point at which they had started recording the transmissions. Flicke wrote about the prospects of this work:

Now some [but NB not all] of the captured radiograms could be deciphered. The addresses of a number of agents were disclosed and an opportunity was opened for penetrating a widely ramified Russian agent network extending over the west and into Germany itself. The deciphered messages proved that 'Radio Defense' [Funkabwehr] was on the trail of a very clever man who must have connections in the very highest command, since he transmitted in November 1941 the intention of the German command to carry out an attack in the Caucasus in the spring of 1942. Furthermore, his reports on gasoline consumption and existing stocks of fuel and planes showed that he must have contact with the Air Ministry or with the High Command of the Air Force. He even transmitted to Moscow the prediction of an impending extremely cold winter which had been made by German astronomers and weather experts. He even gave a clear calculation of the time when German fuel reserves would be exhausted.

But the Germans had not finished tracing the other two transmitters operating out of Brussels. On 30 July 1942, using street-level receivers, the Funkabwehr's D/F team pinpointed a busy signal emanating from 12 Rue de Namur, a small house in an narrow street in the district of Laeken only 200m from the Royal Palace. It was Johann Wenzel's new base, and he was actually sending at the time his door was broken in by an Abwehr entry team commanded, again, by Hauptmann Harry Piepe and supported by local police and Luftwaffe.

As boots thundered up the stairs of the multi-storey building, the Soviet agent jumped out of an attic window and scrambled across the roof to the adjacent

Hauptmann Harry Piepe. He had a background as a public prosecutor.

house, bravely firing back at his pursuers with a hand gun. He entered his neighbour's house and ran down through the building to the basement. But Piepe had the place surrounded, cutting off the agent's escape routes and capturing him.

Meanwhile, Hauptmann Piepe caught his breath after the race upstairs – he was forty-nine years old – and searched the room containing Wenzel's radio. Next to the set he found a stack of cipher texts awaiting transmission and two clear-text messages awaiting encryption. They were in German, and Piepe, a veteran cavalry officer of the Great War who had been seconded to the Abwehr from a tank regiment in France, was shocked by what he saw: the intelligence in the messages could only have come from the highest Nazi sources in Berlin. Piepe was immediately ordered to drive to the German capital and to report the findings personally to Abwehr chief Admiral Wilhelm Canaris. The admiral brought in Field Marshal Wilhelm Keitel, who headed the OKW at the time. It seemed the Germans didn't entirely trust Enigma to protect the intelligence on their telegraph or radio links.

By this time the 'Professor' was in the hands of Karl Giering, director of the Brussels office of the Gestapo; Wenzel was known to them as a wanted Communist agent. Giering also knew he was responsible for getting him to talk about the *Rote Kapelle* and the code systems the network was using. But who was supplying the intelligence?

There was no 'good cop' during the interrogation. The torture was brutal and unrelenting. It is to Wenzel's huge credit that it took more than six weeks of cruel beatings for the goons to break him – long enough for vulnerable members of the network to make themselves scarce. After telling the Gestapo all he knew, he agreed to co-operate in a *funkspiel* ('radio game') operation, using his own radio at a safe house of the *Sonderkommando Rote Kapelle*.

Leopold Trepper was an aggressive and bold commander of

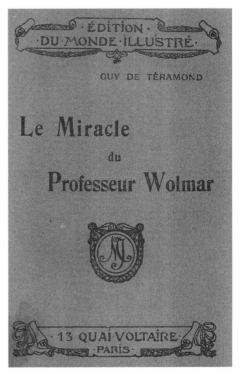

The first edition of *Le Miracle du Professeur Wolmar* by Guy de Téramond, 1910.

espionage field commanders. After moving the agents still at liberty over the border, he took a short trip to Paris himself before returning to the Belgian capital, where he had unfinished business. He had left in place a surveillance team – 'watchers' in the jargon – and they were reporting that the Germans seemed to have lost all interest in 101 Rue des Atrébates. Otto had personally seen the mess created by the entry team's search and did not trust their thoroughness. In another audacious plan he had Gestapo identity papers made for two of his men and sent them into the house to undertake a more painstaking search for Sofie Poznanska's five code books. Nothing was found, and it was only in May 1942 that a copy of *Le Miracle du Professeur Wolmar* was located in a bookshop.[18]

Johann Wenzel had the last of very few laughs emanating from these events. The Gestapo guards at the safe house on Rue de l'Aurore became careless. After all, their prisoner was co-operating, so everyone could – and did – relax. On 17 or 18 November 1942 Wenzel noticed that a Gestapo officer had closed the front door without turning the key in the lock. The instant his minders looked the other way, Wenzel dashed outside, taking the key with him and locking them in. He survived, and died in East Berlin in 1969.

4.5 Following the Links: to a deadly outcome

The head of the cryptanalysis section of the Funkabwehr was a mathematician, Dr Wilhelm Vauck. With a small team of fellow mathematicians he was responsible for breaking the codes used by the W/T operators sending traffic out of Belgium to Moscow. Their starting points were: the cipher traffic recorded by the monitors; the messages and working notes seized during the raids on the stations in Brussels; and the information beaten out of Johann Wenzel by the Gestapo. It was enough to enable Vauck's team to start breaking the intercepted traffic from Brussels to Moscow dating from October 1941. Of 300 such messages about one-third were encrypted using a sentence from *Le Miracle du Professeur Wolmar*.[19]

What they harvested from a high volume of messages was useful, but inevitably somewhat out of date. It was clear that the lead agent in Belgium used the cover name 'Kent', at least during 1940 and 1941. He was a veteran Red Army intelligence agent who moved to Marseilles in 1942 after the Brussels network was broken. His full name was usually given as 'Victor Sokolov' but he also used the aliases Sukoloff, Fritz Kent, Arthur Barcza (his mistress, later his wife, was Margaret Barcza), Victor Gurevich (possibly his real name), Fritz Fritsche, Vincente Sierra and Simon Urwith. Colloquially he was referred to as 'Petit Chef', the 'Grand Chef' in the *Rote Kapelle* being Leopold Trepper, Otto.[20] 'Kent' was the code name used mostly in radio traffic. His travels around Europe underscored the importance of the little boss. The new decrypts detailed his journeys to most parts of Germany and south into Czechoslovakia and Switzerland.

More importantly, it was revealed that Kent's main source was a member of the German resistance referred to in messages as 'Coro'. This was an important breakthrough, because the identification of Coro could lead to the naming of his co-conspirators. A

Passport photograph of Red Army intelligence agent Anatoly Markovich Gurevich, alias 'Victor Sokolov' or 'Fritz Kent'.

serious and unforgivable blunder by Moscow Centre made this task far easier for Wilhelm Vauck's team than it should have been. The 'skeds' used by the British were worked out well in advance, and these dictated which call signs should be used and the exact dates and times of transmissions. If you missed a transmission it didn't matter; the 'sked' told you the time and call sign to use on the next upcoming date. (See Chapter 8.3) The Soviets did it differently, indicating in each message when the next radio exchange should take place; in other words there was no advance 'sked' but a daisy-chain. The problem with this lay in the difficulty of reconnecting the chain if it broke. It was rather like putting bus timetables on the buses instead of the bus stops.

In October 1941 Moscow Centre lost radio contact with the three main agents in Berlin and sent Kent a message ordering him to travel to the German capital to sort the mess out. He was required to speak to each agent and help them re-establish their

Dr Wilhelm Vauck, head of the cryptanalysis section of the Funkabwehr.

regular W/T traffic with the Centre. But Kent didn't know who these agents were or where they lived.

For nine months Vauck's team slogged its way through an in-tray piled with cipher texts sent from Brussels to Moscow. On Tuesday, 14 July 1942, a critical signal was broken, a shocking message that spelled the end of the *Rote Kapelle* group at the heart of the Nazi hierarchy. Dated 18 October 1941, the clear text of the message read:

KL 3 DE RTX 1010-1725 WDS GBT FROM DIRECTOR TO KENT/PERSONAL PROCEED IMMEDIATELY BERLIN THREE ADDRESSES INDICATED AND DETERMINE CAUSES FAILURE RADIO COMMUNICATIONS. IF INTERRUPTIONS RECUR, TAKE OVER BROADCASTS. WORK THREE BERLIN GROUPS AND TRANSMISSION INFORMATIONTOPPRIORITY.ADDRESSES:NEUWESTEND, ALTENBURGER ALLEE 19, THIRD FLOOR RIGHT—CORO; FREDERICIASTRASSE26A, CHARLOTTENBURG, SECOND FLOOR LEFT—WOLF; 18 KAISERALLEE, FRIEDENAU, FOURTH FLOOR LEFT—BAUER. REMIND BAUER OF A BOOK WHICH HE GAVE TO ERDBERG AS A PRESENT NOT LONG BEFORE THE WAR. CALL NAME HERE 'EULENSPIEGEL'. PASSWORD: DIRECTOR. REPORT PROGRESS BY OCTOBER 20. NEW PLAN, REPEAT NEW, IN FORCE FOR THREE STATIONS GBT AR KLS RTX.[21]

Through either arrogance or ignorance, Moscow Centre had assumed that its encryption procedures were rock solid and they could write anything they liked inside their signals. Not only did this idiocy result in the destruction of an invaluable group of sources – Coro, Wolf and Bauer – it cost them their lives. Seeing their exact addresses, right down to the number of the floor if they lived in an apartment building, is quite chilling. Within two days the three locations were under close surveillance by undercover Gestapo officers.

The first address, 19 Altenburger Allee in the residential area of Neu-Westend, was the home of Luftwaffe First

Luftwaffe 1st Lieut. Harro Schulze-Boysen ('Coro').

Lieutenant Harro Schulze-Boysen, who worked in the PR section of the Air Ministry and, later, in the ministry's Attaché Group. He was considered to be highly intelligent, before the war had taught law at the University of Berlin and had played an active part in left-wing politics before Hitler came to power. He had retained an extensive network of friends with like opinions and similar contacts with the USSR. Given his open hostility to the Nazis, it is not unreasonable to ask how he managed to secure a position at the Air Ministry (although not a rank of any significance). His family and social connections might have had something to do with that: he was a member of the family of Grand Admiral Alfred von Tirpitz, Secretary of State of the German Imperial Naval Office until he fell out of favour during the Great War.* Schulze-Boysen was not merely a whistle-blower on German military planning, he was an active organizer of the resistance movement.

The Gestapo was soon able to sketch out Coro's circle of contacts. He was followed by plain-clothes officers to meetings in the nearby Berlin Tiergarten with Councillor Dr Arvid Harnack of the Ministry of Economics and openly exchanged information with him. (Surprisingly, Harnack used his first name, Arvid, as his cover name in radio traffic.) The Gestapo's investigation led them on to an agent Flicke calls 'Z'. A skilled engineer who worked at the Loewe Radio Company, Z was a committed Communist. His usefulness stemmed from the fact he headed research and development into radar and electronic navigation aids for the Luftwaffe. Such was the importance of his role that the ability of the German Air Ministry to exploit this important new technology lay largely in Z's hands. His freedom to hire and fire the engineers on his team enabled him to sabotage the R&D operation. The best radar engineers were transferred to other, supposedly more important, jobs or even sent to the military for service on the Eastern Front. They would be replaced by less experienced, less competent technicians.

Dr Arvid Harnack, Ministry of Economics and member of the *Rote Kapelle*.

---

* Tirpitz was something of an anglophile and spoke English fluently. His two daughters attended the exclusive Cheltenham Ladies' College in Gloucestershire.

And all the while, this technology moved ahead in leaps and bounds in Britain and the USA. [22]

For as long as they could, the Gestapo held off from arresting Harro Schulze-Boysen, Arvid Harnack and the third leader of the Berlin network, journalist Adam Kuckhoff. They wanted to keep watching them closely so they could trace the extent of their network; but that plan came to nought by accident.

Another agent in the Berlin network was Corporal Horst Heilmann. He was a member of Dr Wilhelm Vauck's code-breaking team but had no knowledge of Moscow Centre's compromising signal of 18 October 1941. According to Wilhelm Flicke, Schulze-Boysen had invited Heilmann to go sailing with him one weekend on the Wannsee, a long, narrow lake about 20km south-west of the Brandenburg Gate. At the last moment, Heilmann was detained at his

Corporal Horst Heilmann, a member of Dr Wilhelm Vauck's code-breaking team and a radio operator in the *Rote Kapelle*'s Berlin network. Reputedly he was also one of Libertas Schulze-Boysen's young lovers. On 22 December 1942 Heilmann was hanged at Plötzensee Prison, aged nineteen, alongside eight other members of the group.

office and had to cancel; he found a newly-installed phone and rang Coro's house. A servant answered – Coro had already set off. Heilmann left his apologies and the number of the phone he had used and went back to work.

On his return home the next day, Coro saw the message and dialled the number. As luck would have it, Dr Vauck was walking past the phone when it rang. He heard a voice say it was Schulze-Boysen returning his call. Vauck panicked, thinking the Luftwaffe officer had discovered he was under investigation. They could not afford to delay any longer, and a few hours later Coro was arrested by the Gestapo. It was Sunday, 30 August 1942.

Within one month sixty members of the Berlin network had been detained. Schulze-Boysen was talking – but only to scoff at the allegations and demand he be released without delay. At first, his self-confidence and superior intelligence reassured his supporters that he would soon be freed. However, others were not so resilient, and names were being named. That group may have included Arvid Harnack. By 30 October the total of arrestees had reached 130, many of them completely innocent. One hundred and fifty suspects were in Gestapo cells by the end of the year. In December the first sixty suspects were dragged before the Nazi puppet judges and condemned to death.

The *funkspiel* was soon brought into play, with fake intelligence being sent to Moscow. Some incoming agents were caught on arrival. Outside Germany, more arrests were being made. Kent was captured in Marseilles and Leopold Trepper was arrested on 24 November 1942 in his dentist's chair in Paris. In the hope that he could be 'turned', he was not executed and, in 1943, he managed to escape. He kept his head down until the Liberation, and after the

Libertas Schulze-Boysen, a member of the *Rote Kapelle* executed by the Nazis.

war went to the USSR, where Stalin promptly imprisoned him, on the false charge of betraying other agents. Released in 1955, he went to Poland, but in 1975 he settled in Israel and died there in 1982 at the age of seventy-seven.

4.6 CODA: doubts and diversions

The preceding description of the work of the *Rote Kapelle* during the war is primarily based on the near-contemporaneous accounts of a participant from each side: Leopold Trepper for the Soviets and Wilhelm Flicke for the Germans. But it should not be assumed that such accounts are 100 per cent reliable, and it is not difficult to find the occasional anomaly. For the sake of completeness, it may be worth adding a few short comments about more recent research.

Unsurprisingly, it has been suggested that the Red Three's British radio operator Alexander Foote was in reality an SIS agent and that he was copying to London all the signals traffic that went through his hands. After his network was closed down by the Swiss authorities, Foote was detained for a while. On release he went to live in the Soviet bloc. He trained to undertake a GRU mission in South America to hunt down escaped Nazi leaders, but seemed uninspired by life in East Berlin and defected to Britain with the help of the SIS. It seems that MI6 took no further interest in him – although he is sure to have been thoroughly debriefed on his time as a Russian agent – and he settled into a job at the Ministry of Food and Fisheries. During this period he made friends with former communist and

SIS officer, writer Malcolm Muggeridge. Muggeridge firmly took the view that the intelligence Foote was sending to Moscow Centre 'could only, in fact, have come from Bletchley'.[23] This is a reasonable assumption but does not exclude the possibility that GC&CS might have delivered the intelligence directly to Alexander Radó or Rudolf Rössler. There is no definitive answer to this question, but if SIS did recruit Alexander Foote, Switzerland would have been the perfect place to do it.

In the same year that Muggeridge's book was published it was also alleged that the *Rote Kapelle* was no more than a channel used by the SIS to get Ultra intelligence to Stalin.[24] The Soviet leader was notoriously blind to any material originating from Western sources; it was postulated that he might have been more inclined to believe it if he thought it originated in Germany. However, a number of prominent authors have dismissed these claims. Harry Hinsley, the official historian of the British intelligence services in the Second World War, has stated that there is no truth in the theory. Phillip Knightley makes the practical point that the intelligence was reaching Moscow within 24 hours – far too fast for it to have gone through Bletchley Park en route. In his book, Knightley proposes that a key figure in the conduit between the Bendlerblock and Switzerland was a Czech military intelligence officer called Karel Sedlacek. Sedlacek admitted he had received information from dissidents within German High Command.[25] Maybe, one day, SIS will reveal the truth?

The dispute was not resolved until 2009, when the German Bundestag (Parliament) annulled the Nazi accusations of 'treason' against them and rehabilitated all members of the *Rote Kapelle*. A plaque in their memory now stands in the grounds of the notorious Bendlerblock building in Berlin.

Chapter 5

SOE and OSS in Sweden and Norway

*The Norwegians impressed him the most, for bravery, for readiness to run
risks, and for steadiness in facing the dangers of sabotage.*
George Rheam, Head of SOE Station XVII, Industrial Sabotage[1]

5.1 The Rickman Affair: gelignite, detonators and timers

The Nazi invasion of Norway pushed Britain into an ambivalent
position regarding Sweden's neutrality. Norwegian resistance fighters
and Allied agents had a lightly-policed border over which they could
infiltrate and exfiltrate the occupied territory, and Stockholm provided a more
convenient headquarters than London for irregular operations in Scandinavia.
However, Sweden's interpretation of neutrality gave the Germans freedom to
move troops and materiel wherever they wished.

At the start of the conflict, Britain's intelligence services were in something
of a muddle. Under one wing of the Foreign Office, SIS (MI6) was responsible
for espionage. Under another wing was Section D, a unit responsible for
irregular warfare against the enemy. Across Whitehall at the War Office was
Military Intelligence Research (MIR), a small unit charged with studying
the *means* of guerrilla warfare (but not with actually carrying it out). The
Political Intelligence Department at Electra House in the City of London
specialized in propaganda. On 19 July 1940, Section D, MIR and Electra
House were combined into the Special Operations Executive (SOE) – the
agency created by Winston Churchill to 'set Europe ablaze'. This was much
to MI6's annoyance; its previous dominance of the secret services had been
undermined.

Watching events from the British Legation* in Stockholm was a diplomat
called Peter Tennant. This graduate of Cambridge University was a brilliant
linguist, reputedly able to speak most European languages fluently. Married
to a Swedish woman, he specialized in Scandinavian tongues, could speak

---

* Until the end of the war most diplomatic outposts around the world were called 'legations'; only those
in major capitals were 'embassies'.

Peter Tennant, Alexandra Jartseva (Soviet Union) and Carl Jensen (US): three press attachés sailing in 1944.

Swedish like a native and could give a passable rendition of many of its dialects. These talents had already had him marked out as a candidate for espionage work should war break out. In the meantime, he was Press Attaché, perfect cover for this sociable character to build an extensive network of useful contacts in Sweden's capital.[2]

An office not too far from Tennant's was shared by renowned Arctic explorer and adventurer Andrew Croft[3] and Malcolm Munthe, the son of the Swedish queen's doctor and lover, Axel Munthe. (Supposedly, King Gustaf V preferred male Russian tennis players.) At the outbreak of war Malcolm had gone to London and become a UK citizen so that

Major Malcolm Munthe MC, son of Dr Axel Munthe.

he could join the Gordon Highlanders and fight Germans. In 1940 Tennant knew these two characters were more than just great dinner companions; they were members of Military Intelligence Research and were busy breaching

Swedish neutrality by transporting arms from ports in northern Norway, across Sweden to Finland. So a precedent for many further infractions had been set.

By virtue of their jobs in MIR, Croft and Munthe joined SOE by default; Peter Tennant had to be formally recruited, a simple task undertaken by Charles Hambro. Although of Danish origin, this Old Etonian member of the banking family had been awarded the Military Cross in the First World War as a 19-year-old Coldstream Guards officer. After the war he had resigned his commission, joined the family business and was appointed a director of the Bank of England at the age of just thirty. After the second war broke out he was put in charge of Scandinavian operations, essentially sabotage and smuggling. Tennant would be part of the team he selected.

There were a couple of early setbacks. Before the war, Canadian Bill Stevenson, the head of the British Security Co-ordination Organization in New York, came up with a plan to stymie the German war effort by sabotaging the port of Oxelösund in Northern Sweden and thus interrupting the export of Swedish iron ore. When the security police searched the premises of a British engineer called Freddie Rickman they discovered a hoard of gelignite, limpet mines, detonators and timers. Rickman was sent to prison for eight years. This was an embarrassing matter for Peter Tennant: while busy working with Charles Hambro to set up SOE Scandinavia, he was having to bat off accusations that he was involved in the conspiracy. He wasn't; it was an MIR operation funded locally by the SIS.[4]

While all this was going on – and their agents were being put through the ropes at the Special Training Schools in Britain – Hambro and Tennant were tackling a problem that would seriously hobble any operations undertaken by the SOE. It seems that the radios they had been sent were intended for fixed locations (e.g. in a legation or consulate building) and were far too cumbersome for concealed transport and use behind enemy lines. The solution came when a socialite friend of Tennant's told him she knew someone who could make radios, and this man and his wife were soon turning out the compact and light short-wave radios that were needed.

What was more, this came with a bonus: the man also invented a device for the super-fast transmission of Morse signals. This used a rod on which metal rings could be threaded. The rings had two lengths, short for a dot, long for a dash, and Bakelite insulators kept them apart. Electrical contacts connected to the radio set via the socket for the Morse key could then be stroked quickly and smoothly along the rods. Done in a few seconds, this would shorten transmission times so much that it would make life difficult for the D/F teams of the Swedes and the Funkabwehr.

One assumes the new radios – including the Paraset – being issued to agents across Europe were also sent to Stockholm as diplomatic cargo.

Without them Peter Tennant would have problems with another activity, the planning and establishment of a 'stay-behind' network in case Germany decided to invade Sweden. This involved the installation of hidden radios in pre-determined locations across the country, and the training of local agents in using them. Tennant's book does not reveal how far these plans went.

From the summer of 1940 to the summer of 1941 the SOE in Stockholm settled down to supporting its operatives in the neighbouring occupied countries, especially Norway, from where exhausted agents would often arrive after walking and skiing over the snow-capped, mountainous border region. They also recruited new agents among Norwegian refugees and Swedish volunteers, sometimes sending them westward over the hills to catch a 'Shetland Bus' fishing boat for Scotland. The Swedish Security Police (Säpo) was especially suspicious of Peter Tennant; his telephone was tapped throughout the war, and at one time he was followed 24/7 by a team of watchers. Tennant dealt with the latter annoyance by having a colleague sneak out of the legation on Strandvägan and photograph the watchers hiding in the bushes in the Nobel Park opposite. He then gave the photographs to a newspaper, claiming he was being followed by the Nazis. Embarrassed, the Säpo withdrew its watchers.

5.2 Olga and Lisbeth: the home-brew plan

SOE Sweden's home-brew wireless wasn't the only portable short-wave radio manufactured secretly for use by resistance fighters. Across the border was a Norwegian set nicknamed 'Olga'. Early in 1941, scores of insurgent groups had sprung up around Norway, and it soon became clear they would be more effective if they co-operated; the government-in-exile therefore ordered them to work together as the 'military organization', or 'MILORG'. By operating as a single fighting force they would be more effective in supporting the hoped-for Allied invasion of Norway.

Once this reorganization had taken place, a further problem had to be addressed. It was crucial that MILORG and the SOE did not trip over each other during sabotage operations against the Germans. With the agreement of the Norwegian high command in London, MILORG was brought under SOE control. That left the issue of communications. The various geographically widespread units of this fighting force needed to be able to co-ordinate their operations by radio. But SOE was concerned that the wireless traffic with its agents should not be cluttered with MILORG's traffic on the short-wave frequencies. It also had to get its hands on a lot more radios as quickly as possible.

Stepping into the breach was Salve Staubo, a native of Oslo and the director of a company which manufactured domestic radio receivers, the kind that would sit in your living room in a nice polished wooden box and enable you to receive the broadcast news, documentaries and music. (He had worked in England and the USA between 1924 and 1928.) Staubo recruited friends and employees to make short-wave radios for MILORG. They worked in twos and threes in their cellars and on their kitchen tables. The power transformer and a few other components were made at the factory, using parts which were used in home receivers and therefore would not attract the attention of the Germans. Coils were wound by hand in Staubo's nearby home. Harry Kongshavn built the transmitter and the power supply in his cellar. The receiver units were assembled by Staubo and his cousin, John Gundersen, on his kitchen table. The components were all married together in Kongshavn's basement cellar and then moved to the factory, so that Arne Hannevold could carry out final testing.

Salve Staubo (left) and his cousin John Gundersen assembling radios for the Norwegian resistance. Post-war re-enactment. (*Used by kind permission of the Staubo family*)

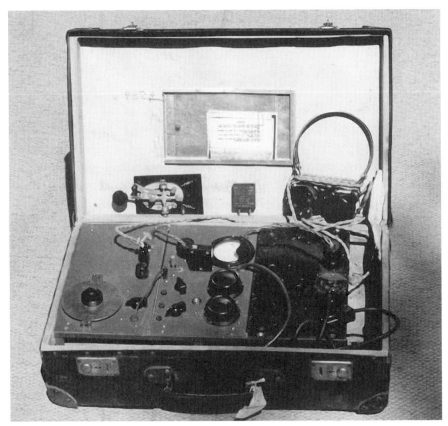

The Norwegian OLGA radio set. It could operate in the frequency ranges 3–7 MHz and 7–16 MHz and weighed 12kg. (*Used by kind permission of the Staubo family*)

Some cover for the factory was afforded by the fact that the Germans gave Staubo's company the job of collecting confiscated radios. This enabled the firm's van to drive around the city unmolested by Abwehr patrols, a fact that after the war caused him to be accused (wrongly) of collaboration.

The OLGA radio set was mostly built from components Salve Staubo already had in stock, but SOE was able to supply him with any parts he was missing. Finn Willoch designed and built a Morse key. The finished product appeared early in 1943, and it wasn't pretty. Indeed, it was deliberately made to look like a radio ham's home-build. Over a hundred of them were built in the last two years of the war – a remarkably brave undertaking for half a dozen men and their families.*

---

* Much of this account is based on a December 2002 report written by Salve Staubo's son, John Peder Staubo. It can be found in full on the website of the *Norsk Radiohistorisk Forening* (Norwegian Radio History Association), http://nrhf.no/radiohistorie/SalveStaubo/forord.php

5.3 Operation LARK: storms along the Norwegian coast

Dina Mohr Ås is a splendid woman, who hates the Germans just as much as she loves her son, and is willing to sacrifice everything for our sake. She naturally got to know where I came from, but not, of course, what my work consisted of. I lived on the fat of the land, and was invited the stay as long as possible.[5]

Olav Krause Sætten

Agents were able to operate into and out of France with relative ease. It is not too far across the English Channel (*La Manche*), and there is plenty of flat countryside on which to land a small aircraft or for a parachutist to arrive without breaking their ankle, an occupational hazard. The Westland Lysander, with a cruising speed of about 300kph (185mph), could get from southern England to northern France in two or three hours and touch down and take off again in 300m (1,000ft). Clearly, such a trip would not be without its discomforts and its heart-stopping moments, but Norway was a different matter; getting there and back was much more of a challenge.

Take the case of SOE Operation LARK and its offspring LARK BLUE and LARK DUMP. The first team included two organizers, Odd Sørli and Herluf Nygaard, with an all-important W/T operator, Ewald Hansen. In addition were three men whose jobs made it clear this was no coast-watching operation – Arthur Henry Pevik, Arne Christiansen and Olav Krause Sætten

Left to right: brothers Kjell, Odd and Øivind Sørli.

were arms instructors. These men were trained in Scotland and England, and their objective was to help local resistance fighters to kill the Germans occupying their home county of Trøndelag and its capital, Trondheim.

Part of the operation was to build up a stockpile of explosives and weapons so that the resistance was well armed enough to support any invasion by the Allies. In addition to a Mark III suitcase radio with two batteries and a rotary converter (weighing 90kg), the March 1942 shipment comprised: a hundred Sten guns, ten Bren guns and fifty 9mm automatic pistols (plus ammunition and maintenance kits for these); ten Mark I compasses; 4,000 hand grenades; six Torpedo limpet mines and six 'Maundy' mines; 250 gallons of petrol and twenty drums of lubricating oil. The 'Maundy' mines were small enough to be laid in rivers from rowing boats and were intended to encourage enemy vessels to take to the open sea, where they would be easier to attack.

This cargo, plus the SOE agents – and quite often SIS agents – would travel on one of the Norwegian fishing boats anchored in Shetland waters across to the many offshore islands guarding the entrance to Trondheimsfjord. (See map below)

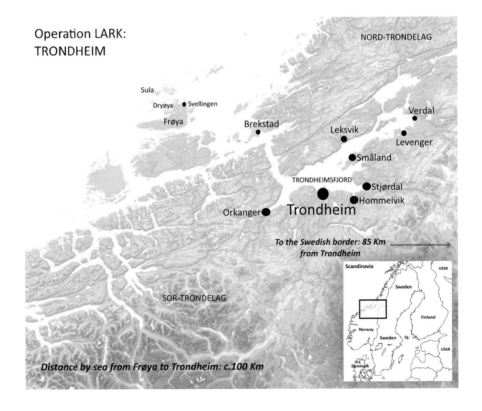

Operation LARK: TRONDHEIM

Distance by sea from Frøya to Trondheim: c.100 Km

In October 1942, Olav Krause Sætten, one of the arms instructors, wrote a report describing how the Operation LARK team concealed their radios and weapons.[6] It is an excellent illustration of the intimacy of Norway's coastal communities and demonstrates why British-born agents would not have survived there more than a few days.

> We left Shetland on the 17th April [1942] and came to Frøya on the afternoon of the 19th. The vessel anchored by a little island belonging to Lars Johansen [Arthur Pevik's uncle], lying about half-an-hour's rowing distance from his home. We lay there and waited for darkness while Arthur Pevik got into contact with his uncle. Pevik came back a few hours later and was able to tell us that Lars was willing [to help], and that he was now looking for a suitable hiding place for the arms. He found an excellent place in a mountain cleft on the above-mentioned island, that is to say, just where we were lying.[7]

Note how quickly family connections came into play. Now they had a nearby hiding place they faced the hard graft of unloading the boat.

> When darkness fell we lay-to and began to discharge the cargo. We had landed about ten cases of explosives, 160 cases of hand grenades, 100 Sten gun and ammunition cases and also 10 Bren guns and 60 rifles, when we discovered that there was no room for any more at that spot. After having well covered the depot with tarpaulins and some blankets and camouflaged the lot with heather and stone, Lars Johansen, Arne Christiansen and myself left the vessel and rowed with the provisions by the shortest way between the islands to Lars' home.

And of course relatives had relatives, some of them in very useful jobs.

> The [fishing] vessel sailed round and into Dyrøysundet, and Pevik went to see his cousin, a nephew of Lars Johansen, who is the postman at Dyrøya ['Animal Island', off the north coast of Frøya]. The latter showed them a place on an island further out to sea suitable for the remainder of the shipment, that is to say, about 130 crates of explosives and the Luger pistols.
> This was Sunday night, the 19/20th April. It turned out that the [coastal] line-steamer, 'Hitra' or 'Frøya', had returned to Trondheim on Sunday morning, so Arne and myself had to wait a whole week out there for the next steamer.

After a quiet week on Frøya they caught the next ferry. When they reached the dock at Trondheim they were welcomed by a familiar face, Øivind Sørli (Odd's brother), who turned out to be an old classmate of Sætten's.

So, everyone had relatives, knew people across the community and had a good idea whether they could be trusted not to betray them. The radios were established in a matter of days, and London was reassured that the agents of Operation LARK were getting the job done.

Operation LARK's first real setback came later in 1942. Having trained a local recruit to operate one of the radios, W/T operator Ewald Hansen left for Sweden with Odd Sørli, Olav Krause Sætten and Arne Christiansen, reaching Stockholm on 12 September 1942. They were no doubt looking forward to getting back to London; they were safe from the Gestapo in Sweden, although the Security Police, the Säpo, could throw them into jail as undesirable aliens. But when Sætten, Christiansen and Sørli got on the UK-bound plane, Ewald Hansen was not with them. Reports had come in saying the new operator he had trained was unable to make his wireless function. On 28 September Hansen set off on the long trek north and across the border back to Trondheim. It didn't take him long to get the troublesome set humming again and, no doubt, he gave the trainee some additional tuition.

Then his luck ran out. On 16 December 1942 Ewald Hansen and Herluf Nygaard were arrested by the Gestapo after the Funkabwehr discovered their location through radio direction-finding.[8] A few days later, Nygaard managed to escape and alert the other LARK agents before heading back over the border into Sweden. He spent Christmas in Stockholm and was flown back

F/V *Arthur* departing Shetland for Norway. Date uncertain.

to the UK in January 1943.[9] The Gestapo tortured Hansen until he died in Falstad concentration camp on 4 April 1943. He was twenty-six years old.

While in Stockholm in August 1943 Odd Sørli wrote a remarkable account of his attempt in February that year to get two urgently-needed radio sets and a further shipments of arms to the Trondheim area. With him was new wireless operator, Erik Gjems-Onstad; they were Operation LARK BLUE.

> Left London February 9th, '43. Arrived at Shetland on the 11th. The intention was for the journey to be made by a fishing vessel [*Harald II* from Scalloway], changing over to a small boat outside Godøy near Ålesund, and then row to a certain address at Godøy.[10]

From Shetland due east to the nearest point of Norway's western coast is about 320km (170 nautical miles). Godøy is 240km south of the entrance to Trondheimsfjord. The weather was not very promising on 9 February 1943, but they cast off with some optimism:

> The weather was not too good, but the crew thought it might improve, and we left on February 14th. When we had reached the most northern part of Shetland the skipper decided that it was no good going on, so we returned to Haroldswick. As the weather improved during the night we made a fresh start the following morning at 8. But the weather got worse and worse and when we were 50 nautical miles off the coast, we were forced to turn and go back to Lerwick, as the weather forecast we

Crossing the North Sea in rough conditions. At the centre is Sgt. Åsmund Wisløf, left is Arthur Pevik. Date uncertain.

received indicated that it was storms along the Norwegian coast. We had been out for 7 days.[11]

The diesel engine in a 1940s fishing boat probably pushed it along at no more than 10 knots (nautical miles per hour), so crew and passengers must have been bounced around all day, and they would not have arrived back until after dark. Sørli continued:

> After a week's rest we started again. This time we got as far as seeing German searchlights on the waters outside Godøy. But there was a considerable storm which made it quite impossible to reach the shore without being caught by the searchlights. It would of course have been impossible to change over to the small boat. The skipper therefore decided that we should return to Shetland. The fact that we got back safely was only due to the crew, they did a marvellous job. Thoroughly wet and practically without sleep they worked continuously for 8 days. When we were approx. 50 miles from Shetland the situation was, however, so hopeless that we had to call for assistance. The boat was leaking and the storm was as fierce as ever.

Shetland has two lifeboat stations, one in Lerwick and another in Aith which covers the Atlantic coast.* There is no question that the Lerwick crew would have gone out to rescue them – regardless of conditions – but there was certain to be doubt about their exact location.

> Towards evening the weather improved and we were able to go on slowly. By midnight we could see a lighthouse off the north coast of Shetland. We proceeded the whole night in a southerly direction. At 7 am the following morning 3 Spitfires flew across looking for us. Three boats had also been sent to our assistance. We managed, however, to get to Lerwick without any help. All our equipment, which was stored in the hold, including two wireless sets was destroyed by water. The small motorboat which was to have been used for getting ashore had been smashed.[12]

They probably saw the Muckle Flugga lighthouse and that would have reassured them a little. Just as comforting would have been the sight of the Spitfires, which could have been photo-reconnaissance aircraft of 602 Squadron from RAF Sumburgh at the southern end of the archipelago. The fact that these planes and three vessels were sent to look for the fishing boat

---

* UK lifeboat services are provided by the volunteer Royal National Lifeboat Institution (RNLI).

underscores the importance placed on their mission. However, the destruction of their equipment and the radio set meant there was going to be a further delay while everything was replaced.

According to the Meteorological Office's Monthly Weather Report for Shetland in February 1943 the wind was averaging 60mph (96km/h) and gusting up to 95mph (150km/h) from 280° for nineteen days.[13] They set off again a week later and arrived at Bjørnør, 60km north of Trondheim, at 11.00 pm on 12 March. It had taken them thirty-one days to travel 320km. Determination and courage had seen them through. Now they were in Norway, but still had to get the radio sets and other equipment from the little fishing village of Bjørnør south to Trondheim.

5.4 Erik Gjems-Onstad: the telegraphist's tale

With Odd Sørli on the February 1943 North Sea odyssey was radio agent Erik Gjems-Onstad, another of the many colourful characters among SOE's Norwegian section. Erik-Ørn Gjems-Onstad (to give him his full name) was born to a lawyer and an architect in Oslo on 22 February 1922. At the age of fifteen he bunked off school and ran away to sea, working as a cabin boy on voyages to ports in Asia and Africa. He returned to complete his education in 1940, winning all the Scout badges for orienteering with map and compass.

When, on 9 April 1940, Norway was invaded, he and a friend headed north to evade the advancing Nazis, but gave up south of Trondheim and returned to Oslo. Back home, he enrolled at university and immediately started making contact with other students eager to begin a resistance movement. After becoming involved in the disruption of a *Nasjonal Samling* (NS) fascist party meeting he was arrested and fined. Undeterred, he got into a fight with some other NS members and was beaten up.

Erik's group of young and bruised resisters included an engineer who had come up with some bright ideas for new weapons, and four of them crossed the border to try these out on the Norwegian military attaché's office on Skeppargatan in Stockholm; but the legation expressed no interest in the inventions.[14]

Someone, probably an official at the Norwegian legation, suggested to Gjems-Onstad he should go down the road to the British legation near the Nobel Park and ask for Major Malcolm Munthe, head of SOE Scandinavia. Munthe was certainly interested in the inventions but was probably even more interested in Gjems-Onstad as a potential recruit. However, before Munthe could get the young man to the UK for training, the Swedish police did the job for him. He was arrested on 25 March, jailed until 23 May 1941 and then transferred to a refugee camp at Öreryd, 100km east of Göteborg (Gothenburg).[15]

Malcolm Munthe must have been annoyed that his promising new recruit had been detained by the Swedish authorities. In October 1941 he got a message to Gjems-Onstad telling him to escape from Öreryd refugee camp and head north the 325km to Oslo. Munthe probably assumed it would be easier to get him to Britain if he started from a different place. The camp was far from being a 'maximum security' facility, and Gjems-Onstad was soon on foot, heading home. He didn't make it. He was surveying his options for getting across the border when the Swedish Home Guard caught him. This time the Swedes had had enough; they formally barred him from ever entering Sweden again and put him on one of their own planes to Britain.

A Norwegian ID card for Erik Gjems-Onstad showing his name as 'Rolf Knutzon' and his age as twenty-three. (He was actually nineteen on the date of issue.) The card is a complete fake; on 27 March 1941, Gjems-Onstad was in a Swedish police cell.

SOE W/T agent Erik Gjems-Onstad with B2 set.

Gjems-Onstad had no experience of armed combat. So, after landing in the UK, he joined the Norwegian Independent Company 1 (*Kompani Linge*) and undertook British military instruction. Then he transferred to SOE for training as an agent and W/T operator. By the end of 1942 he was considered ready to go behind enemy lines, and it was decided to send him to Trøndelag with Odd Sørli, Johnny Pevik and Nils Uhlin Hansen. The arrival of *Tirpitz* in Trondheimfjord had added urgency to the operation.

*   *   *

In his account of LARK BLUE Erik Gjems-Onstad offers little detail about the crossing from Shetland; perhaps his experience as a youthful merchant mariner enabled him to take it all in his stride?

The third time Odd and I attempted to get to Norway from Shetland we succeeded in landing on the evening of March 14th, having spent in all a fortnight at sea [excluding the time spent ashore recuperating] making the three attempts. We had, however, altered our original course and as it was difficult to land at the place where it was planned and as one of the crew had some friends at the place where we ultimately arrived, we went ashore there and met Petter Løfsnes, a merchant on Bjørøy. He was a good man and willing to help but gave the impression of being a little nervous.[16]

As with other agents, they were helped by the friendly skippers and crews of the many ferries that ply the west coast of Norway:

On March 16th we left Bjørøy by coastal steamer *Bjørnør* to Namsos. The captain, Roman from Trondheim, was very nice and anxious to help us in every way. He arranged about most of our luggage, including two W/T sets to Trondheim, we ourselves were only carrying our personal equipment. The third W/T set was brought by Johnny [Pevik] and Nils [Uhlin Hansen]. Captain Roman said that none of his crew were Nazis or 'contaminated' and on the other boat *Kysten* which covers the same route he could vouch for the captain.

We arrived at Namsos at noon and went by train to Trondheim in the afternoon. At Grong [in Medjå] frontier police inspected our legitimation [ID] cards. They made a thorough examination of the cards and asked for 'grensepass' [border passport] but this was not necessary for a through journey here. We arrived in Trondheim at 8 p.m. on March 17th.

The men were carrying ID cards hot off the presses at SOE's forgery mill –
see the example above – so it would have been a relief when the police moved
on down the train. They reached Trondheim safely; but where next?

> It appeared that the organization had not arranged ... a room for
> me, so for the first few days I stayed with one of the members of the
> organization. Then I moved to a farm just outside the town. But it was
> impossible to install the [radio] station there permanently as I had no
> key to my room, and all the people on the farm thought while I was
> staying there that I was an ordinary office clerk, and no one had any
> suspicion that I was doing illegal work .
>
> At the beginning, therefore, the working conditions were difficult
> but after a few weeks Odd put me in touch with [an] N.T.H.* student
> [Svend B. Svendsen] who had his own room, and here I installed the
> W/T (Station A).
>
> According to plan I was to establish three stations, one in Trondheim,
> one some miles east or west of the town, and one on the north side of the
> fjord, and transmit alternatively in order to avoid D/F'ing. It appeared,
> however, that the boat across the fjord only ran a few times a week and
> it was difficult to get hold of any private boats. It would therefore be
> very difficult to have a station on the north side of the fjord. Just at that
> time the traffic restrictions on the railways were put into force, and as the
> position was rather vague and further restrictions might be expected, I did
> not want to be dependent on a car, boat or railway to get to my stations.

Erik spent a lot of his time pounding the streets looking for the perfect
locations for his radios (and somewhere to live). However, he also found
time to help Johnny Pevik and Nils Uhlin Hansen with the dangerous task
of shifting no less than five tons of arms and explosives from one of the outer
islands to the city. But getting the radio stations established was his priority,
and this was proving to be increasingly difficult:

> During Easter, restrictions and controls were established making it
> very difficult to get to or leave the town. On account of all this I had
> a conference with Odd, and we decided that the easiest would be to
> establish the [radio] stations in or near the town.
>
> It was extremely difficult to find a room in Trondheim to live and
> [another] room for the station, but in the beginning of May I managed
> to establish No. 2 station (Station B). Station B was also placed in a

---

* *Norges tekniske høgskole*, the Norwegian Institute of Technology. It is estimated that the students and
faculty at NTH included 130 resistance supporters.

room belonging to a student. The aerial arrangements were excellent here, and we made an extension from an old outdoor aerial, down through the [flue] pipe to the stove in the room, and this seemed very satisfactory. But after a few weeks it was discovered by accident. The roof was being repaired and the workman found the extension and told the owner of the house about it. The latter became hysterical and threatened to report the student and myself for listening to the W/T – that was the finish of Station B.

After this I had a very difficult time as the person who [was looking after] Station A had gone away for some time and while he was away I did not want to use the station more than absolutely necessary. I looked at several places and in the beginning of July I found a place which could be used (Station C). Station C was in a flat in the town, and had a good outdoor aerial. The owner was, however, rather nervous and the arrangement was somewhat clumsy. I nevertheless kept Station C going and had the W/T there until I left, although I used it very seldom towards the end. From Station C I had good contact, only once or twice did I fail to get contact.[17]

On 25 May 1943 Erik Gjems-Onstad obtained a *Grenseboerbevis* (Border Pass) in the name of 'Egil Strand', born 20 January 1917. His real date of birth was 22 February 1922. (*Norwegian archives*)

Because Odd Sørli had wider responsibilities, Gjems-Onstad increasingly took over the leadership of Operation Lark and of the armed Milorg resistance units in the area. SOE and Milorg had always worked closely together, but at this stage in 1943, according to Gjems-Onstad, they had become fully integrated.

In spite of the pressure on him to keep up the frequency of signals to London and Stockholm, Gjems-Onstad was always conscious of the need to take care of his personal security:

> During the spring and early summer I stayed on the same farm and they had no suspicion. I considered, however, three months at the same place quite sufficient and besides I wanted to live in a place where I could listen, especially after it had been arranged that I should listen in every day. It was very inconvenient to be absent from the farm every day. I therefore started looking for another place to live, but it appeared very difficult especially as I had to find a family who were [relaxed] enough not to report on letting a room.
>
> In the beginning of July I therefore moved to one of the members of the organization and told the family that I had rather 'odd habits'. I could then work in peace, listen and encode the correspondence via Sweden which I have done entirely alone the whole time. By moving to this family the problem of company was solved. Even though I had sometimes visited Odd at the hut outside the town, had done the encoding and took a correspondence course on Odd's recommendation, it was rather lonely at times.

The idea of being able to undertake a correspondence course whilst trying to stay hidden from the Gestapo is inspiring. He does not mention what he was studying, but I suspect it may have been law; Erik became a lawyer – like his father – and a judge after the war. He may have been bored, but he had two stations (A and C) humming with traffic and a third (D) which he used for listening. This period presented an opportunity for him to think through the operating procedures he had to follow as a radio agent:

> The arrangement that I was not to answer Home Station when they called if I had nothing to report was ideal for me, as I could use Station D at home where I only had a small indoor aerial.* In this way I avoided appearing at the places from which I was transmitting ... I think it would be an advantage to state during the calling period how many

---

* Home station radios were far more powerful than the portable sets used by agents. Their signals, therefore, could be picked up by smaller aerials than those needed for transmission.

messages will be sent, in order to let the agent know at once if he will have to listen. This can be done by for instance putting in Q.T.C. 3 in the calling period if 3 messages are to be transmitted.* I think it might also be advantageous for recent messages to be always transmitted before older ones, to enable the agent to switch off as soon as the older messages are being transmitted. This is chiefly for the reason that it looks rather suspicious when a man locks himself regularly in his room, and the chances of his being discovered are naturally greater the longer he stays in the room.†

As previously mentioned, the arrangement with the 3 W/T sets was difficult to accomplish on account of the lack of rooms. Another danger is that when handling several sets it is necessary to get in contact with more people, and more danger of being mixed up in the work of the organization. I think the best would be to have two sets: one to be used as a good station with regular contact, and the other to be kept in reserve or for use at home for reception as I did, provided the arrangement is made that it is not always necessary to answer the Home Station. In order to diminish the danger of D/F'ing … it might be better to change the crystals more frequently. [Thus making life more difficult for the Funkabwehr's direction-finding teams. See Briefing Chapter 8.1 below.]

When Odd Sørli came up with an idea that promised more action, Erik responded with enthusiasm; he needed a change of scenery:

I had by now got used to conditions and everything [was going] well. When therefore Odd suggested starting an organization in Kristiansund N,‡ I was [eager] to join in and we began making plans. Soon after, Odd left for Stockholm in order to report and receive new instructions …

In the beginning of September [1943], Odd told me to arrange for a W/T set and Sten gun to be sent Kristiansund N. [Operation LARK BROWN.] For this purpose I had been given two addresses there, one of them with a password. I sent a man known as Knut Berg by coastal steamer to Kristiansund N. He got in touch with the man at Averøya using the password. The man was rather surprised at first, but I got the

---

* 'QTC' is the international radio Q-code for 'I have … telegrams for you'. See Briefing Chapter 8.3 below.

† The messages were numbered sequentially. Using Gjems-Onstad's suggested system would enable the agent to stop listening as soon as he heard the number of a message he had already received.

‡ *Kristiansund* is on the coast in the county of Møre og Romsdal 140km to the south of Trondheim. There is a town called *Kristiansand* on the south coast of Norway, and even the locals get them confused. A longstanding convention has arisen to name them Kristiansund N and Kristiansand S for north and south.

impression that he had full confidence in the courier, who asked him to keep the [set] and try to find a room for two men who would arrive some time in the autumn. The contact explained to Berg how he had organized a military group and also produced some interesting plans in case of invasion. He said that the only thing he lacked was arms and contact with England. From messages received later it appeared that he had made investigations about Knut Berg and that he had connections with the [Secret] Intelligence Service. I think, however, that he and his group will be of more use to our organization than to the Intelligence Service.

Gjems-Onstad's poaching of this unnamed asset of SIS in Averøya might seem cheeky, but the organization of military groups was more in the remit of SOE than MI6. Indeed, the reason Odd Sørli wanted to send Erik to Kristiansund was to get a fighting unit started in the area; it looked as though they now had a head start. But before he could relocate, he had unfinished business in Trondheim:

It was intended that I should train a new W/T operator at home instead of having a new one brought over [from the UK] when I left Trondheim. It appeared, however, very difficult to find anyone who was willing and could spare the time. I got in contact with a student [at NTH] who was an amateur W/T operator with a speed of 20 [words per minute in Morse]. He was in addition a W/T technician. He was willing, but it was very awkward for him to listen in daily and he had to leave town during the holiday seasons.

When Odd arrived at the beginning of October with instructions and a message that I was to leave for Kristiansund N as soon as possible, I was not able to do so at once but sent a message [to London] asking for a new W/T operator for Trondheim.

At that time the new arrangement with daily broadcasting and ordinary skeds four times a week was put into force. This was not difficult for me, but it would not be possible for anyone doing ordinary work.

Restrictions in the schedules led to limitations in wireless communications with SOE Scandinavia's HQ at the British Legation in Stockholm. However, Operation LARK had a useful fall-back. A railway line ran all the way from the mining town of Meråker just inside the Norwegian border south to Stockholm. Obviously, the border police and the Germans thoroughly checked the credentials of anyone making that journey – but the crew manning the train were not checked or searched. It is thought that friendly engine drivers and conductor-guards carried Lark messages and documents on every return trip between Meråker and the Swedish capital.

A serious setback for Erik's smoothly-running radio operations came in October 1943, when one of the stations was compromised by an attempt to assassinate the notorious Gestapo agent Henry Rinnan.

The members of Rinnan's group, known as Sonderabteilung Lola (Special Section Lola, but called 'Rinnanbanden' by Norwegians) systematically tried to trick Norwegians into betraying themselves by claiming to be members of the resistance. They would then be beaten and tortured, before being handed over to the Nazis. Rinnan had his

Gestapo collaborator Henry Rinnan.

own permanent office in the Misjonshotel (Mission Hotel), the Gestapo's headquarters in Trondheim, and a telephone on which to receive tips from informers: the number was 6505 extension 4. Considering that Rinnan's 50-strong gang was later found guilty of causing the deaths of over a hundred Milorg resistance fighters and SOE agents, and torturing hundreds more prisoners – many of them totally innocent – it is hardly surprising that he and his associates were considered fair game for

assassination. In September 1943 a team of four SOE agents, Johnny Pevik, Knut Brodtkorp Danielsen, Ole Halvorsen and Frederick Brekke (Operation WAGTAIL), were sent in from Sweden with the objective of reconnoitring the Namdalen railway north of Trondheim as part of a plan to sabotage it. However, Odd Sørli re-tasked them to carry out an assassination attempt on Rinnan.[18] The gunmen, led by Halvorsen, caught up with the Rinnan gang on 7 October but ended up shooting the wrong man. In the aftermath, Frederick Brekke and Johnny Pevik, Arthur's brother, were arrested. Johnny was imprisoned and tortured for over a year before being hanged in the cellars of the Mission Hotel.

SOE agent Johnny Pevik, born Oregon, USA, 18 February 1913. Killed by the Gestapo, Trondheim, 19 November 1944.

Erik and Odd Sørli were still planning his move to Kristiansund N, but the situation in Trondheim now got even worse, as he explained in his report:

Odd went to Oslo on October 16th and on the 17th I met the wife of the man with whom he had stayed and she told me that her husband had been arrested that morning. She thought that he was suspected of having a W/T receiver. On October 20th the family of Odd's fiancée were arrested, and at Odd's home the police made enquiries as to whether he had been back. According to the information we now have, it is most likely that the man with whom Odd stayed was arrested in another connection, but that he nevertheless revealed the fact that [Odd] stayed with him and mentioned the name of Odd's fiancée and the sister is as far as we know also free, but the fiancée and her brother are still under arrest. They know nothing of the members of the organization.

In the course of these arrests I had no fear for myself nor for the W/T stations, but in order to be quite safe, I went into hiding, though I arranged it in such a way as to be able to keep up the contact.[19]

The circumstances were now so dangerous that SOE decided Erik's situation in Trondheim was untenable, and he was ordered to leave Norway and head to Stockholm. Characteristically he held off for as long as he could, continuing the training of an NTH student to take over and suggesting he (Erik) relocate to Kristiansund N instead of Sweden:

Both these suggestions were rejected, and I hid the W/T sets and made arrangements to the effect that the W/T operator can take over in case he is told to do so – in that case he will be using the Lark Green plan and the silk code marked B. He must however leave Trondheim during the Christmas holidays, i.e. from December 1st until the beginning of February, so it will be necessary to wait [for transmissions during that time] until he comes back.

The code marked A and all the plans for Kristiansund N, with the Lark Brown plan, I have concealed, so everything is in order, Kr.8,000 which I received from Odd for work in Kristiansund, I left with the organization in Trondheim.

In the beginning of October I trained a man in my original code which is being used for the correspondence via Sweden and the code with Stockholm, and when I got orders to leave for Sweden, it was an easy matter to clear out. I left Trondheim on October 28th in the afternoon.

He made his way to Meråker without being troubled by German patrols and then crossed the border at night over the 1,000m (3,280ft) Store Kluken mountain range. Arriving in Storlien on the evening of 29 October, he handed himself in to the Swedish frontier police, claiming to be a refugee. 'At Storlien I was interrogated and searched,' he recorded. 'The search both of myself and of my luggage, was very thorough.' They released him on 1 November, and three days later he reported to the British Legation in Stockholm.

* * *

First to recognize Erik Gjems-Onstad's service in the war against the Nazis were the British; he was made a Member of the Order of the British Empire (MBE) in 1941. Another six medals followed from the Norwegian and British governments, making him one of the most decorated heroes of the conflict. In the early years of peace he combined service in the Norwegian Home Guard with a day job as lawyer and judge. He then moved into politics – right-wing politics – with an anti-immigrant, anti-Muslim flavour; clearly, the German occupation had put him off the idea of immigration. He died in 2011.

Henry Rinnan and forty-one members of his pro-Nazi group were tried, convicted and sentenced in September 1946. Ten were condemned to death, the rest to long prison sentences. Rinnan himself, convicted of personally murdering thirteen people, was shot by a firing squad on 1 February 1947.

Henry Rinnan under arrest, shortly after running into a door …

5.5 Operation RYPE: the OSS versus the Nordland Railway

NO GERMANS WITHIN TWENTY MILES STOP WE MUST HAVE MORE AMERICANS TO DO JOB STOP.*

William E. Colby

William Colby graduated from Princeton University in 1940 and went on to study at Columbia Law School. He had been there a year when the US entered the war, and he volunteered for the army, eventually transferring to the OSS.

Founded on 13 June 1942, the Office of Strategic Services (OSS) was charged with gathering intelligence and carrying out special operations. It was not by chance that the OSS embraced these sometimes conflicting briefs: President Franklin D. Roosevelt had ordered William J. Donovan (its first director) to organize a service based on the Secret Intelligence Service (MI6) *and* the Special Operations Executive (SOE). In its early months the OSS was toothless. With few agents of its own, it got most of its intelligence from the British via British Security Co-ordination (BSC), a group set up by MI6 in New York City in May 1941. In fulfilment of its objective to encourage the US to join the war against Germany, BSC was more than willing to help the nascent OSS. When Japan's attack on Pearl Harbor brought America into the conflict, the need to boost the manpower and capabilities of the OSS became urgent.

SOE immediately gave access to its global short-wave radio network and provided the OSS with helpful technical information and equipment. Fortuitously, BSC was also able to offer a convenient training facility it had set up in December 1941. This was 'Camp X', more correctly SOE Special Training School 103. Its location was perfect: on the north-west shore of Lake Ontario (between Whitby and Oshawa), it was in Canada but just over the border from New York state. Not only was it convenient, it also counted as an overseas posting for US servicemen and women and thus attracted extra pay. The training was just what was needed for OSS recruits: intelligence and subversion; explosives and sabotage; lock-picking; radio communications, Morse code and encryption/decryption; unarmed combat and the 'art' of silent killing. The scheme was so successful that the first 900 OSS agents were trained at SOE's Camp X. Later, specialist American radio operators were taught in the UK at a dedicated school (STS 53c) in Poundon, Buckinghamshire.

---

*   Contained in a message sent from Operation RYPE, Jævsjø Lake, Norway to London, 18 April 1945. The 'job' was to destroy the railway bridges between Jørstad and Valøy.

SOE Camp X, Lake Ontario, Canada, 1943. Not even the Canadian prime minister was aware of its real purpose.

Over the following three years the OSS grew in independence and was able to deploy agents to China, SE Asia, India, Ceylon (Sri Lanka), the Dutch East Indies, Australia and, of course, Europe and the Mediterranean. With an eye to SOE's national sections, the OSS started to set up what it called 'operational groups' (OG) for Italy, Greece, Yugoslavia, France and Norway. The first ethnic Norwegian recruits (drawn from the 99th Infantry Battalion) were trained at Camp Hale, Colorado from the summer of 1943 and transferred in December that year for further training at Forest Lodge, part of STS 26 near Aviemore in Scotland. But rather than shooting Germans they were left kicking their heels; their first mission did not come until the summer of 1944, when they were deployed to France in support of D-Day operations.

But once France had been freed, the officers and NCOs of the OGs were at a loose end again. Fifty men with fluent language skills were selected to

Alert German troops
southbound on the
Nordland Railway,
1944.

form NORSO I (Norwegian Special Operations) and NORSO II, a smaller
reserve unit. Now twenty-four years old, Major William E. Colby, who had
served in France as a Jedburgh,* was made commanding officer. And they
were finally given a mission. After the liberation of France and the Low
Countries the Allied commanders were even more concerned that the
150,000 German troops in the Trondheim-Narvik area of northern Norway
would be redeployed to their homeland to delay the inevitable downfall of
the Nazis. It was the winter of 1944/45 and the roads were snowed in. The
Royal Navy and RAF Coastal Command now controlled the maritime routes
down the Norwegian coast, removing that option for the Germans.

All that remained for the movement of troops and armaments was the
Nordland Railway, which had been built by the Germans using Soviet

---

* See Chapter 6.3 on Operation JEDBURGH.

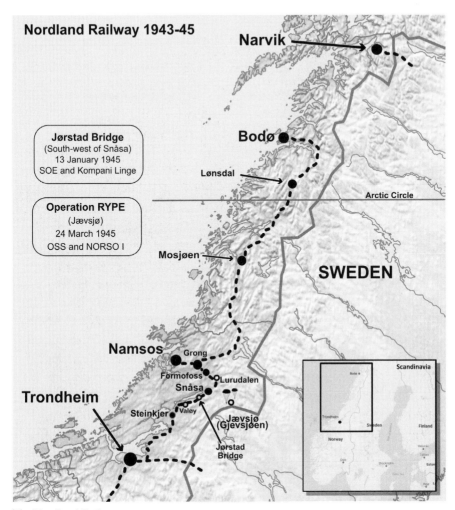

The Nordland Railway.

prisoners of war as slave labour; over 1,000 died as a result of cold, starvation and exhaustion between 1942 and 1945. Sabotaging the line and blocking the Wehrmacht's exit became the object of Operation RYPE.

Colby wrote an account of Operation RYPE in the form of an article, but this only came to light after peace broke out. The CIA said this about it:

Recently [c.2010?], while researching some old CIA files, a CIA historian chanced upon the following account by Maj. William E. Colby of behind-the-lines OSS sabotage operations in Norway during World War II. In November 1945, the War Department's Bureau of Public Relations posed no objection to the article's publication. There is no record, however, that the article was ever published. The first page of the memoir is missing. As Major Colby begins his story, he and his team are being flown to their drop site in Norway.[20]

In November 1945 Colby was still in the OSS; he was destined to become director (in September 1973) of its successor, the CIA. Page 2 of his memoir starts as follows:

> The eight planes continued north, across the North Sea, over the stark fjords and the white mountains, then up the Norway-Sweden coast [sic] past Trondheim, Namsos – almost to the Arctic Circle. By now, night had fallen and the moon was coming up. Below, a faint mist was spreading, taking the sharpness off the rocks, but meaning trouble later.
>
> Then it was midnight, and the pilot called to say that we were 25 miles off course over neutral Sweden. I told the men, and they began to buckle on their white equipment. The pilot veered left and angled earthward.
>
> Now I could see the swath of shaved forest demarcating the two countries. 'This is it,' I told the pilot. Paulsen and Aanonson pulled up the trap door, and I went through into the awful quiet that closes in when the engines recede. Then there was the cold and the wonder if there are friends below – and above. Dimly, I counted the others slipping into the air – one, two, three – formation perfect, five seconds apart.
>
> Then my chute opened, now the others'.
>
> At 500 feet, the underground's landing fires pierced the haze, and with them came the sure knowledge we were at the rendezvous. Step one had come off according to plan; but it was the last thing to go right until we blew up the Nordland railway.

This reads a lot more like an action-packed thriller than a magazine article. The idea of Colby and his Norwegian comrades flying *past* Namsos 'almost to the Arctic Circle' is puzzling. Their drop zone, Jævsjø [Gjevsjøen], was a lake 300 miles *south* of the Arctic Circle and *south-east* of Namsos (see map above). And the major's ability to look out of the plane on a winter midnight over remote Scandinavian countryside and tell both pilot and navigator, 'This is it' is astonishing. Only when they were at 500ft, swinging from their parachutes, could they see the signal fires through the mist covering the ground.

Explaining the justification for the raid, Colby says, 'Large-scale operations were eminently possible south of Trondheim by this time, but SHAEF [Supreme Headquarters Allied Expeditionary Force] had been warned that such landings would risk utter extermination of the trigger-fingered Norse underground. As a result, sabotage was to keep the descending armies bottled up until the heart of Germany stopped.' Frankly, this is nonsense. It is improbable that the 'Norse underground' – by which I assume he means

Milorg – would, accidentally or otherwise, get in the way of an Allied invasion force. Milorg was in regular contact with London; its commanders would have been well aware of any such planned incursion and would have eagerly deployed their forces in its support. Colby goes on:

> That is why, in March of this year [1945], 35 tight-lipped, white-clad, tall, somber men climbed into eight converted B-24s at Harrington [RAF Harrington, home of the USAAF 801st Bombardment Group], southern England [actually in the East Midlands], and flew off into the clear mid-afternoon sky, their giant craft pointed north [initially to RAF Kinloss in north-east Scotland for refuelling].
>
> Inside the Liberators' spacious but uncomfortable cabins, they said nothing, revealed no excitement. They simply sat still and waited with the patience of men matured by long, bitter winters or by the quiet sea …
>
> However, their names read like heroes from some Norse saga – Paulsen, Johansen, Iversen, Eliasen, Oistad – as indeed they were, for the bulk of them had been stranded off Norwegian ships in the early war days and one way or another found their way into the US Army.
>
> Lieutenant Langeland had been a ship's radio man. Sergeant Listeid had been a seaman. Raivio, a Lapp, had fought the Russians in Finland and escaped to America as a ship's crew member. Sergeant Andreasen had been a first mate and talked of nothing but the sea.

801st Bomb Group (Special Operations) B-24D Liberator 'Miss Fitts' takes off from RAF Harrington. Note the black paintwork.

The 801st Bomb Group – the 'Carpetbaggers' – didn't do bombs. This joint USAAF/OSS squadron was set up to support special operations in occupied territories. The 801st BG's B-24s were stripped of their nose gunner, and belly turret and bomb shackles were replaced with British-designed restraints designed to hold C-type supply canisters. Oxygen bottles and back-up radios were removed. The interior used red lighting to preserve night vision.

USAAF personnel loading jerry cans of fuel into C-type drop containers. An estimated 60,000 littered Europe by the end of the war. Photograph probably taken at RAF Harrington, 1944.

However, Operation RYPE didn't start well:

Of the eight planes that set out, only four were able to make their drops. One ship, named Lief for S/Sgt. Lief Oistad (aboard in charge of four corporals), wound up 50 miles inside Sweden, scattering personnel and equipment over an unidentified lake. The men were interned after barely escaping a full-dress skirmish with the local gendarmes. We were heavily armed.

The transports that succeeded in dropping at Jaevsjo [Jævsjø] also succeeded in spreading the party and materiel over a 36-square-mile area, some of the stuff kilometers into the surrounding woods. Many packages had no static cords attached and plummeted to Earth without chutes, burying themselves in the snow …

That first bitter cold night (it was 20 below there, 1,950 miles south of the Circle) was spent gathering up the packages with their colored chutes and hiding them under trees and under snow.

Major Colby's geography left a lot to be desired. They were about 1,950 miles south of the *North Pole*, not 1,950 miles south of the Arctic Circle – that would have placed them in Sardinia rather than Scandinavia. Perhaps it was fortunate that this fanciful article was never published?

A more reliable account of Operation RYPE's arrival in Norway was written later by the group's W/T operator, Lieutenant (then an NCO) Borge Langeland. Norwegian-born Langeland, a former merchant marine radio officer, picks up the story the following morning, 25 March 1945. He desperately needed his radio:

Major William Colby and Lt. Borge Langeland at the end of the war. (*US Army archive*)

There had been no sleep during the night and everyone was kept busy, with equipment that had to be found, unpacked and stored. The radio transmitter and battery were found, but no generator to charge the battery. It was found the next day deeply buried in the snow. It had been thrown out of the plane from about 600-foot altitude without a parachute but, fortunately, it landed in a deep snow drift and was only slightly damaged.

The radio station consisted of a British type B-Mark 2 radio transceiver [probably an SOE Type 3 Mk II, usually called the 'B2'] that was powered by a 6-volt wet cell battery, fitted in a small suitcase for easy transportation. The transmitter had crystal control for each frequency. Five or six different frequencies were assigned to the station to be altered for each scheduled transmission ['sked' – see Chapter 8.3]. This little unit was used for all radio communication with England during the entire mission.[21]

Once he had assembled his radio, Langeland tried to make contact with London:

Radio communication with England was difficult at times due to atmospheric conditions and other circumstances. The first few days' transmissions were made out on the open ground in the daytime and from a pup tent at night. A rock was tied to a piece of wire which was thrown up in a tree to make an antenna and, at night, the radio operator had to lay on his stomach in the pup tent with a flash light in one hand and send or write down the received message with the other. Later, a more comfortable station was set up at the Jaevsjø farm house … However, despite these circumstances, communication was maintained with England nearly every day.

But on 25 March his signals remained unanswered. At noon on the 26th, however, he got through and sent Operation Rype's first message:

ONE OF TWO FIVE STOP PLANES BILL, SAETHER, GLENN, EINER ARRIVED STOP OTHERS NOT REPORTED STOP EQUIPMENT BADLY SCATTERED AND MUCH WILL BE LOST STOP DETAILS LATER STOP CORRECT RECEPTION WITH EURICA STOP MUST HAVE AT LEAST TWO MORE PLANE LOADS BEFORE ATTACKING OBJECTIVE STOP CONDITIONS FAVORABLE FOR RECEPTION TONIGHT.

A few notes about the format of these messages: the signals are numbered consecutively by each station and tied to the date of transmission for clarity. So 'ONE OF TWO FIVE' means 'Our message number one sent on 25 March' (Langeland had started sending it on the 25th but only succeeded in getting it through on the 26th). It was unusual for messages to include punctuation – commas, full stops (periods) and question marks don't encrypt – but Langeland has included them for clarity. He also added this comment about the chore of encoding and decoding:

All radio messages had to be encoded before they were transmitted and, of course, all messages received had to be decoded after they were received. This was a slow and tedious procedure since they had to be coded and decoded letter by letter. No machine was used.

Home base had tried to send RYPE a message on 25 March but cancelled it when they received Langeland's message. So the first message he received from London was numbered '2':

WE HEAR YOU STOP THREE PLANES RETURNED, ONE DROPPED SWEDEN NEAR BORDER STOP REPORT YOUR CONDITION STOP TWO OF TWO SIX.

He was through to the home station at last! But now a long message had to be sent 'reporting their condition'. It probably took a long time to encrypt:

TWO OF TWO SEVEN STOP RECEIVED YOUR TWO STOP STAYING AT JAEVSJOEN [Jævsjø] REPEAT JAEVSJOEN FARM STOP ESTABLISHING DUMPS AROUND THE LAKE STOP REQUEST FOOD BE SENT TO SWEDISH SIDE OF LAKE AS ARRANGED IN STOCKHOLM STOP MANY PACKAGES LOST STOP DROP WAS SCATTERED OVER EIGHT KILOMETERS STOP SEND TWO CONTAINERS BRENS, ONE CONTAINER [M1] GARAND MANE RIFLES, GASOLINE GENERATOR BAKER MARK TWO [B2] RADIO AND BATTERY, MEDICAL KIT TWELVE PAIR SKIIS AND SLEEPING BAGS, SPARE CLOTHING STOP SEND SGT KYLLO, SGT AUSEN AND HAROLD ANDERSEN TO OPERATE BASE STOP RPT KYLLO, AUSEN, ANDERSEN STOP NEED MORE MEN FOR BRIDGE JOB STOP WONDERFUL WEATHER STOP NO ALARM BY GERMANS YET BUT ARE MOVING TO WOODS TO AVOID VACATIONISTS UNTIL MONDAY STOP HOPE TO LEAVE FOR BRIDGE THEN STOP SEND SALT, PEPPER AND CONDENST [sic] MILK.

[Sent 27 March 1945]

This was almost certainly written by Colby who, as we will see, never composed a signal without including demands for more men and weapons to be sent *instantly*. He was very pushy for a 24-year-old officer of limited experience, and certainly ignored the fact that his was not the only combat unit in the field. The reply from the home station is terse:

NOTHING TONIGHT STOP CONTINUE "AREEVE" WEATHER REPORTS STOP SENDING FOUR PLANES SOONEST STOP THREE OF SEVEN.

And Langeland duly transmitted a report of the local weather:

THREE OF TWO EIGHT STOP BAROMETER 2725 TEMPERATURE PLUS 6 DEGR. CELCIUS, VISIBILITY 10 KILOMETERS, OVERCAST, ALTITUDE OF CLOUDS 4500 FEET, WIND CALM, NO PRECIPITATION THE LAST 24 HOURS.

[Sent 28 March 1945]

These reports, sent on a daily basis, contained information that was critical for the pilots of incoming Carpetbagger B-24s. For example, the barometric pressure was needed to calibrate the aircraft's altimeter, and the altitude of the cloud base determined whether they could fly at the right height for the parachute drops.

It was not until the following day that the home station told Operation RYPE what happened to the team dropped over Sweden by mistake:

LEIFS PLANE DROPPED FIVE MEN IN SWEDEN NOW INTERNED STOP EXTENSIVE PUBLICITY, GERMANS MAY SEND PATROLS STOP "KNUTS" CODE AND KRYSTALS SAFE WILL BE DELIVERED TO YOU BY H.G.W.S.T. COURIER STOP ORDERING PETROL GENERATOR FOR YOU IN SWEDEN STOP REQUESTING STOCKHOLM TO MAINTAIN TWO WEEKS FOOD LEVEL STOP NOTHING TONIGHT STOP FIVE OF TWO NINE.

[Message received 29 March 1945]

Apart from the obligatory de-lousing – being scrubbed naked by female nurses of the Swedish Army – their time on the wrong side of the border was not too painful. The five men were given the equivalent of US$300 each and $5 a day each to spend as they wished in the nearby town of Falun in Dalarne county. Of course, most of this was spent in a local bar. But even that soon became boring, and one day Knut Andreassen put down his aquavit and muttered, 'This damned war isn't going to last much longer. We have to get out asses out of here because I should hate to sit here when the war ends.'[22]

There was really nothing to stop them escaping so they did just that – probably with the help of SOE Stockholm – to travel the 450km (280 miles) back to the border. It was a journey that was going to take them some time.

Meanwhile, at Jævsjø Farm, Colby and Langeland were still waiting for reinforcements and an air drop of the supplies replacing those lost on 24 March. It was the end of the month before the next attempt:

SEVEN OF THREE ONE STOP THREE PLANES HEARD OVERHEAD STOP MOMENTARY CLOUDS PREVENTED DROP STOP ONLY ONE USED REBECCA STOP WILL HOLD ATTACK UNTIL END OF MOON PERIOD STOP [Weather report follows].

[Message sent 31 March 1945]

Rebecca/Eureka was a British Air Ministry innovation* which made is easier for aircraft to locate reception parties. A direction-finding device installed on the plane ('Rebecca') guided the pilot to a transmitter ('Eureka') marking the drop-zone. In the case of the 31 March drop, it seemed the lead pilot did not entirely trust it.

PLANES RETURNED UNSUCCESSFUL STOP TWO ACCUMULATORS AND BAKER MARK TWO RADIO ORDERED SENT TO YOU FROM SWEDEN STOP TWINKLE† STORES AVAILABLE TO YOU NOW ARE CARBINES, BARS [Browning Automatic Rifles], STENS, PISTOLS, MARLINS, ONE BREN STOP SENDING SPRINGFIELDS TO TWINKLE SOONEST STOP TEN OF ONE.

[Message received 1 April 1945]

Nothing seemed to be going to plan for Operation RYPE; they had not been anywhere near a railway line yet. On 6 April, over two weeks after their arrival in Norway, a courier arrived from Stockholm:

TWENTY OF SIX STOP COURIER ARRIVED WITH BAD NEWS, SWEDISH MONEY AND RADIO PLANS STOP REQUEST OPENING OF COMMUNICATION WITH WAXWING ON TWELVE APRIL TO PLAN FOR LIERNE STOP HAVE FOUND BRENS, ALL RUCKSACKS STOP WILL LEAVE MONDAY FOR BRIDGE STOP SEND SECOND GROUP HERE STOP WILL NEXT MOON BE THE LAST FOR DROP? STOP

---

* Credit for Rebecca/Eureka must go to Robert Hanbury Brown, an astronomer and physicist who worked at the Air Ministry's Experimental Station (AMES) group at Bawdsey Manor.
† Operation TWINKLE was the shipment of supplies (including arms) to Stockholm in the diplomatic bag for onward delivery to Norway or Denmark.

USAAF flight engineer Sgt. William T. Alexander with a B-24D of 801st Bomb Group 'Carpetbaggers' in 1944, showing the Yagi antenna (above the 'A' in 'PLAYMATE') for a Rebecca receiver.

DETAILED REPORT AND RECOMMENDATIONS LEFT VIA STOCKHOLM TODAY.

[Message sent 6 April 1945]

The bad news was about the B-24, which had crashed in Orkney on 24 March. The plane first experienced technical problems on the flight from RAF Harrington to RAF Kinloss, but had decided to push on after refuelling. When the problems recurred over the North Sea, the pilot turned back, hoping to reach an airfield in Orkney. He crashed. Sadly, the jumpers had taken their parachutes off when they heard the flight had been aborted; they all died. Finally, Langeland decoded the message they were waiting for:

FOUR PLANES COMING TONIGHT STOP TWO WITH PERSONNEL AND REBECCAS, TWO WITH SUPPLIES BUT NO REBECCAS STOP DAWN DROP ABOUT ZERO THREE THREE ZERO GMT LILLEFJELL STOP "P" FOR PETER BBC MESSAGE FOXTROTT I MASTETOPP STOP SEVENTEEN OF SIX.

[Message received 6 April 1945]

A torch (flashlight) was to be used to signal the letter 'P' in Morse – two long, one short – to the aircraft overhead. The flight would be confirmed by the BBC broadcasting the message '*Foxtrott i mastetoppen*' ('Foxtrot on the mast-top') in the personal announcements after the evening news in Norwegian. But disaster struck again:

TWO TWO OF SEVEN STOP THREE PLANES HEARD OVERHEAD AND IN EURIKA BUT NOTHING DROPPED STOP POSSIBLE ONE PLANE CRASHED ABOUT FIFTEEN MILES FROM HERE STOP PATROL OUT TO INVESTIGATE STOP WEATHER WAS BAD AS IT ALWAYS IS HERE STOP.

[Message sent 7 April 1945]

The next message from the home station informed them that the plane 'Jones' had failed to return to RAF Kinloss. It was later confirmed that the aircraft had crashed into a mountainside, killing all eleven people on board instantly.

Colby had written an angry signal complaining they were unable to meet their objectives without reinforcements. He even specified that 'We must have more Americans to do job.' In the end he had to make do with a few Norwegians. Langeland described their first success in his report:

On April 8, the group left Jaevsjø farm on a mission to blow up railway bridges between Jørstad and Valøy. [A stretch of line between Trondheim and Grong, near Namsos: see map above.] At that time there were 15 Americans* in Norway. Leif Olstad and his four men were still in Sweden and Stiansen had gone to Stockholm for medical care. Lt Helgesen, the Norwegian liaison officer who came from England with the group, was still there [in Norway] and he had recruited four Norwegians from the Home Forces who participated in the attack. Three Americans were left to guard the base at Jaevsjo, so it was a small force who set out for the railroad on that day. In addition to his weapons and ammunition, every man carried a heavy rucksack on his back with explosives and provisions …

Great plans had been made to capture a freight train at a small railroad station north of Steinkjer, to run it a few miles to a large bridge. This bridge had been closely inspected a few days earlier by one of the Norwegian members of the party, Lt Harold Larsen. In civilian clothes, he walked up to the bridge and bummed a cigarette from the German officer in charge of the guards, all the time observing the location of

---

* Langeland is probably referring to *Norwegian*-Americans.

the guards, both on and off duty, barbed wire fences and machine gun nests. The bridge had a guardhouse at each end. The plan was to stop the train on the bridge, take out the guards on each side, place the explosive changes and back the train off, then blow the bridge and proceed back to the station where the train was captured, blowing a few smaller unguarded bridges on the way back. However, planning something and doing something is not the same thing, as we soon found out.[23]

What Larsen, Sæther and Langeland soon found out was that they could not just walk up to the railway track and start planting explosive charges. The Germans had cut back the trees and foliage for 200m and set up observation posts with a clear view up and down the line. The three scouts were spotted before they got anywhere near the track, and a troop of Wehrmacht soldiers were soon chasing them. They ran for the hills, before reporting to Colby that his plan would not work. But Harold Larsen – one of the Norwegians Colby said he didn't need – had another idea.

Larsen had reconnoitred a bridge at Tangen and found it to be relatively unguarded. So, on 15 April, Operation RYPE had its first success. The bridge was blown, and they cut the telegraph and telephone lines running alongside the track.* The group then escaped south of Jævsjø into Sweden, before circling back to their base at the farm on the north bank of the lake. That took them three days, and the first thing Langeland did on arrival was signal London:

Msg. Nr. 25. Sent 4/18/45.
TWO FIVE OF ONE EIGHT STOP BLEW TANGEN BRIDGE COORDINATES ZERO FOUR ZERO SEVEN SUNDAY MORNING STOP WITHDREW TO WOODLARK AND THEN TO JAEVSJON STOP NO CASUALTIES NO CONTACT WITH GERMANS STOP COMPLETE REPORT LEAVING BY COURIER [to Stockholm] STOP OISTAD GROUP ARRIVED THANKS STOP …
[Message sent 18 April 1945]

Their five 'misplaced' comrades had finally made it from the detention camp at Falun, just missing the sabotage of Tangen Bridge. But Colby now had reinforcements, and they had arrived in time for Operation RYPE's next

---

* This was in keeping with an SFHQ edict that telecommunications were to be sabotaged as a means of forcing message traffic on to radio, where it could be intercepted by the 'Y service'. Colby and the Operation RYPE team would be unaware that the Allies were reading the Nazis' encrypted radio messages.

and final assault on the Nordland Railway. They only had to wait a few days. Colby takes up the story:

On Monday, 23 April, the unit left Jaevsjø Farm and pushed through soft snow to Seisjoen Lake, going via Lillefjeldet and Seisjoen. There, we broke into a hut and passed the night. Tuesday, we moved north via Andorsjoen Lake and Goas Lake and broke into a hut at Skjorsjohaugen ...

Next morning, a reconnaissance party of myself, Technical Sergeant Langeland (now a lieutenant) and our excellent local guide, Hans Lierma, skied six hours until we met our old acquaintance, the Nordland railway, where it snakes through Snåsa.

It was vastly quiet as we three reached the area. Nothing moved, except the shimmer of sunlight on virgin snow, but Helgesen's spies had told us there were 112 Germans guarding the 5-mile strip under observation ... We counted off the spots we would attack and slipped quietly back to our rendezvous – a hut at Skartnes that the main body had broken into and where it now was waiting.

At moonrise, we quit the shack, 24 men divided up into eight teams, each carrying 30 pounds of rail demolition [explosives]. As was our custom, it was midnight when we deployed along the right of way ...

The men fanned out for 2.5 kilometers and set the bombs. The plan was to detonate at 0005 on a green signal flare from me or, failing that, five minutes later. The nearness of an unsuspected German guardhouse prevented the flare plan and, at 0010, one tremendous crescendo rocked the valley. It was not one explosion here, one there, but the whole works right on the nose. Frightening coordination ...

We ran. Someone fired at my team, but we ignored him. In the distance, a Garand rattled. It was Sæther, hoping to get one of the hated enemy.

The unit assembled at the hut, fresh, joking, exuberant as freshmen despite 18 hours of solid going. There was no rest time, only 50 miles of fairly decent terrain to cover. We were at Jaevsjø Farm in 16 hours, retreating without a break.

The Germans forced Russian slaves to patch up the ruined railway, but it never was much use to them after that. As it worked out, we had completed the mission.[24]

As soon as they got back to the farm, Langeland signalled London with the news:

THREE TWO OF TWO SIX STOP TWO HUNDRED
EIGHTEEN RAILS EQUALLING TWO AND ONE HALF
KILOMETERS OF RAIL DESTROYED BETWEEN LURUDAL
AND LANDSEM MIDNIGHT LAST NIGHT STOP NO
CASUALTIES SLIGHT CONTACT WITH GERMANS STOP
HAVE WITHDRAWN TO JAEVSJO FARM STOP PLANE
JONES DISCOVERED PLUKKEFJERN FJELL COORDINATES
FIVE EIGHT ZERO SIX STOP WILL VISIT STOP ...
[Message sent 26 April 1945]

The number '218' is probably a guess. It is hard to believe they had the time or inclination to actually count the number of track sections destroyed. London's reward for the success at Skartnes was to redeploy twenty of Colby's Norwegian fighters to other operations. 'Other strange things happened,' he wrote. 'We practically lost contact with headquarters and our food ran out. My frantic pleas brought only orders to remain in hiding.' It seems he had changed his mind about the capabilities of the Norsemen; he later asked if Norwegians could be put on the OSS payroll. With reduced numbers, he may have had to cut back on the lookouts posted around the farm:

> Then the Germans hunting us came perilously close. One five-man enemy patrol stumbled on the camp. They were armed with machine pistols. We almost talked them into surrender, but characteristically one started shouting as soon as we lowered our guns. We eliminated the entire detail with tommy-guns, but one Norwegian courier was wounded in the stomach.[25]

Could these few sentences suggest another reason why Colby's 'article' was never published? It sounds ominously as if he is confessing to a war crime, since killing captured soldiers in uniform breaches the Geneva Convention. Borge Langeland's report does not mention the incident at all, but in 2012 an article appeared in a Norwegian daily newspaper, Dagbladet:

> On May 2, the Norwegian-American force at Jævsjø farm was discovered by five German soldiers who had been sent into the terrain to look for them.
> The explanations of what actually happened to the five Germans are different and very varied. However, anyone who has subsequently commented seems to agree that the Germans were soon surrounded and disarmed by the Americans.[26] [Author's translation]

The article then goes on to quote an interview with a documentary film-maker who had found an eye-witness to the shooting:

The journalist and TV producer Ola Flyum,* who has for many years been the author of books and reports about the war in Trøndelag, tells *Dagbladet* that he has succeeded in getting a television interview with an eyewitness.

'The last of the seven [resistance fighters] from the local area who participated in Operation Rype agreed to tell his story just before he died,' says Ola Flyum ...

Flyum confirms the Americans were trying to put a veil of silence on what had really happened. 'The participants agreed to shut up. I think it was the Americans who did the shooting themselves,' says Flyum ... 'As far as I have been able to bring it to light, the Americans first tried to force the Germans to dig their own graves. But this was high in the mountains, and it was in winter, so it was impossible. After they were killed, they were buried in the milk cellar under the sheep barn,' says Flyum.

Several witnesses have said that immediately after the Germans were shot, they were asked by the US commander to urinate on the bodies. Whether Americans did this is still an open question.[27]

There is no suggestion that the Germans were SS or Gestapo; they were just ordinary soldiers, now disarmed. Hitler had committed suicide on 30 April, and the unconditional surrender of the Nazi regime became effective on 8 May 1945, only six days after the incident. Hitler's infamous 'Commando Order' had required his military to summarily execute any soldiers or agents caught operating behind German lines. But Colby must have known that the Red Army was at the gates of Berlin and Hitler was already dead by his own hand. Illegal or not, it was a cruel and unnecessary act and certainly did nothing to further 'the entire reputation of America and its future in the Baltic area'.[28]

On 12 May 1945 Colby was ordered to take the RYPE team to Steinkjer, where they remained before going on to Trondheim. Upon their arrival in the city they accepted the surrender of the remaining Wehrmacht troops and celebrated with a parade through the city centre, Stars and Stripes rather than the Norwegian flag to the fore. The local people turned out in strength to applaud the arrival of the first foreign flag not emblazoned with a swastika. Major Colby was honoured with the Silver Star and Norway's St Olaf's Medal. Later, all members of the team received Bronze and Silver Stars, and Operation RYPE was acclaimed as a major success.

---

* Declaration: Ola Flyum is a friend and colleague of the author.

The NORSO soldiers of Operation RYPE parade in Trondheim, May 1945. Note the huge crowd, with some people watching from the rooftops. (*CIA archive*)

But was Operation RYPE really such a great achievement? Both Major William Colby and W/T operator Lieutenant Borge Langeland give the impression that they were leaders of a very special independent irregular warfare unit dropped into Norway to fulfil the major strategic objective of stopping the movement of German troops from Finland to the north back to their imperilled homeland. That was not the case.

During 1944 Finland's military had gained the upper hand in the Lapland War and driven the Germans across the border into northern Norway. There were no regular Allied forces available to stop them heading south to join the war in mainland Europe, so that job fell to the under-armed Milorg. SOE – then overseeing the activities of Milorg – got the agreement of the Swedish intelligence service to establish bases within Sweden to try and redress that problem. But, ironically, there were problems with rail connections to these locations, and it was decided that air-drops were the preferred option. In fact, two bases and three raiding parties set in the north opposite Narvik were mainly funded by the OSS, which also stocked them with 2.5 tons of weapons and materiel. A further six support bases were established along the border with the county of Nordland.[29]

So, the big picture included SOE, Milorg, the Norwegian intelligence services and the OSS NORSO Operation RYPE. SOE was sending the weapons and explosives Colby was demanding to Milorg. Although the young American major was sniffy about the capabilities of the resistance fighters, they were sabotaging the railways long before he arrived on the scene.

The aftermath of the 7 October 1943 sabotage by Milorg of a German troop train at Ryghkollen, 40km south-west of Oslo. Most of the carriages are below the bank, some in the water.

On 13 January 1945 a local SOE and Kompani Linge unit destroyed the rail bridge at Jørstad, a little south of Snåsa. This was three months before Major Colby and Operation RYPE blew up the Tangen Bridge. If the Norwegians were good at destroying railway lines and bridges, the Germans were, arguably, even better at repairing them. Tangen Bridge was operable again even before the RYPE team got back to its base at Jævsjø Farm.[30]

Six hours after the destruction (on 13 January 1945) of the Jørstad Bridge near Snåsa, a German troop train was derailed, killing over seventy people (including two Norwegians) and injuring another hundred. Local people helped the survivors.

In his controversial pre-war pamphlet 'The Art of Guerrilla Warfare', Colin Gubbins (founder of SOE) wrote this about sabotaging railways: 'It is not sufficient to shoot at the train. First derail the train and then shoot the survivors.' In the aftermath of the troop train crash at the Jørstad Bridge, rail workers – many of whom were XU intelligence agents – and local people rushed to the scene. They had gone, not to shoot the survivors, but to get them out of the wreckage and administer first aid. This was both a humane and an intelligent decision; no retribution was exacted against civilians for the destruction of the bridge in the first place.

In fact, the official history of Norwegian State Railways (NSB) lists no fewer than *eighty-nine* instances of rail sabotage in the first five months of 1945 alone. It is uncertain whether that number includes the destruction of NSB's own administrative headquarters in Oslo. On 14 March 1945 an SOE team led by Gunnar Sønsteby and Arthur Pevik (previously with Operation LARK) seized and destroyed the city centre building with 80kg of dynamite. The result was as shown below.

The morning after the 14 March 1945 destruction of the Norwegian State Railway's administrative headquarters in the centre of Oslo.

Chapter 6

France: 'Votre place n'est pas ici!'

6.1 Georges Bégué: 'Esculape n'aime pas le mouton'

Landed OK. Contact with Frederic. Frederic introduced me to Henri Renan at 54 rue des Marins, Chateauroux. Renan will be my mailbox.
First message of Georges Bégué, SOE W/T Operator, May 1941

Georges Bégué distinguished his early service with the Special Operations Executive in three ways: he was the first agent to be parachuted into occupied France (overnight on 5/6 May 1941); he was the first W/T operator to be inserted; and he conceived the idea of sending messages to agents and resistance fighters via the 'personal messages' ('*messages personnels*') which followed the evening news in French on BBC Radio Londres. M. R. D. Foot quotes the following examples: '*Esculape n'aime pas le mouton*', '*La chienne de Barbara aura trois chiots*' and '*La voix du doryphore est lointaine*'.[1]

Bégué, the son of a railway engineer, was born on 22 November 1911 in the picturesque town of Périgueux in the Dordogne, 110km east of Bordeaux. His father's work took the family to Egypt. When he came of age he went to England to study engineering at the University of Hull. (The port of Hull in the 1930s must have come as quite a contrast to Périgueux – and would have been nothing like Egypt, come to think of it.) He worked hard; in addition to learning engineering he picked up enough English to acquire a wife, Rosemary. When he was called up for military service in the French army he opted for a signals regiment and learned how to be a W/T operator.

On the advent of war he was recalled to the army but, instead of serving as a signaller, he was tasked with using his English to liaise with troops of the 44th Division of the British Expeditionary Force. When France fell, Bégué stayed with the British and was evacuated to England from Dunkirk. His time with the British may have influenced his decision not to join de Gaulle's Free French military, and he signed up instead with the Royal Corps of Signals as a private soldier. While training at Catterick Camp in North Yorkshire in the summer of 1940 he met Thomas Cadett, formerly a foreign correspondent with *The Times* (later joining the BBC). At the time Cadett was a member of SOE and he instantly saw Bégué's potential as an agent for F section.

SOE F section W/T operator Georges Bégué in French army uniform.

Baker Street agreed, and the Frenchman with a Yorkshire accent, now bearing the field name of 'George Noble', was put through a very short version of the SOE agent's course. He was already a trained soldier – in both the French and the British army – but he almost certainly needed to learn the art of jumping out of perfectly good aeroplanes at STS 51 (Dunham House, Altrincham) or STS 51b (Fulshaw Hall, Wilmslow), both close by RAF Ringway, now Manchester Airport. He would also have had instruction at Beaulieu on how to operate as a behind-the-lines agent. His training as a W/T operator would have been truncated to cover just the use of whichever set he was to be issued with – a 'B2' for his first sortie.

On the moonlit night of 5 May 1941 an RAF Whitley dropped Georges Bégué 'blind' into a field between Valençay and Vatan (about 200km – 124 miles – south of Paris, in the unoccupied Vichy zone); there was no reception committee there to meet him. Held in his head was a 'poem code'; connected to his harness was a 'B2' wireless. The additional weight of the set may have given him a hard landing, but B2s rarely worked after being dropped with their own parachute and, of course, they sometimes got lost.* But the radio was essential – the lack of reliable communication with London was preventing SOE from establishing co-ordinated networks ('*réseaux*' in French) in that part of the country. Burdened with the radio

---

* Today's paratroops carry their heaviest packs strapped to the front of their harnesses. The pack is released on a long strap just above the ground so the total weight is delivered in two smaller instalments.

An SOE agent 'goin' thro' the 'ole' of an RAF Whitley converted medium bomber. Note the static line.

and his clothes, he set off on a long trek into the night to find an isolated house, the home of Max Hymans ('Frédéric'), a local leftist politician and member of the Resistance. It was dawn by the time he got there. Hymans was not at home and, when they did meet, his first reaction was to distrust the unexpected visitor; it was some time before Bégué convinced his host he wasn't a German agent provocateur. What helped was that fact that Hymans was a friend of a friend of Thomas Cadett. Finally, his contact decided he was genuine, and Hymans took Bégué and his transceiver to a more permanent location in Châteauroux, 30km (19 miles) south of Vatan. There he was to be looked after by a pharmacist called 'Renan' and a garage-owner by the name of 'Fleuret'.

Bégué didn't waste any time; he got the wireless connected up and sent his first signal to London on 9 May 1941. Happy that everything was secure, F section told him they would send three more agents immediately. He went to the designated drop-zone nearby and on the night of the following day, 10 May, he heard the engines of a Whitley overhead and saw two parachutes descending. Swinging below them were Pierre de Vomécourt ('Lucas', a minor French aristocrat) and 'Bernard'. The third man, Roger Cottin ('Albert'), was delivered two days later. Bernard didn't last long. Shortly after handing over a supply of cash to Bégué he was arrested by the Vichy French police and eventually changed sides, becoming a civil servant in the Vichy government.

While they recruited team members they received air-drops of agents, arms and other supplies; the first two arrived after four attempts on 13 June close to Philippe de Vomécourt's château of Bas Soleil, 16km (10 miles) east of Limoges. (Philippe was the brother of Pierre de Vomécourt.) For six months, Bégué transmitted an average of three messages a day; he knew this was a dangerous level of activity but compensated by keeping the signals short. He must have realized, however, that he was in trouble; the Funkabwehr had picked up his transmissions almost immediately and were jamming them after a few days. The Milice, the Vichy paramilitary police, had been alerted to the presence of a W/T operator in the area of Châteauroux, and direction-finding vans soon joined in the search. That, though, was not what caused him to be arrested.

Lieut. Noel Burdeyron in French Army uniform,1940. He later became SOE agent 'Gaston' and organizer of the 'Autogiro' network in Paris.

Priority one for the remaining agents was the establishment of a much-needed *réseau* in Paris: 'AUTOGIRO'. Pierre de Vomécourt was the network's organizer, and Georges Bégué went north with him, continuing in his essential role as W/T operator. Marcel Clech was a second radio agent.* Also in the team were Noel Fernand Raoul Burdeyron† ('Gaston', or 'Norman Burley'), Christopher Burney (Burdeyron's assistant) and Raymond Flower. Burdeyron, the network's *third* radio agent, soon distinguished himself in single-handedly derailing a German supply train by removing a single rail. It proved to be AUTOGIRO's only successful attack and earned Burdeyron a Mention in Dispatches.

Only five months after Georges Bégué's arrival in France, the inexperienced group suffered its first – and terminal – setback. Early in October 1941, a number of SOE agents walked into a trap set by the Milice in Marseilles and

---

* This former London taxi-driver was later captured and executed at Mauthausen concentration camp.
† Previously head waiter at London's Dorchester Hotel, which is where SOE's senior officers may have first encountered him.

over ten were arrested; someone was talking. Bégué himself was apprehended on the 24th of that month, also in Marseilles. The whole group was interned in the notorious nineteenth century Beleyme prison in the town of Périgueux, Bégué's birthplace. They were still in this dreadful institution in March 1942 when, for no clear reason, Hugh Fullerton, military attaché at the US Embassy in Vichy lobbied the government to have them relocated to the equally filthy and unheated Mauzac internment camp, not far to the south of Périgueux. A former army camp, its huts were mainly used to accommodate Roma, communists, homosexuals and deserters. It may be that the Americans were acting on behalf of the British, and it could have been known that Beleyme was a much easier place from which to escape.

A sympathetic French guard helped them assemble a radio so Bégué could send a signal from inside the camp. In the small hours of 16 July 1942, using a duplicated key, ten SOE agents and the guard slipped through the gate and away into the darkness. A short distance away, they were picked up by a truck driven by a French agent and taken to a well-concealed shelter in a forest 40km (25 miles) to the east. For a week they kept their heads down, undetected by Milice search parties. Starting on 23 July, they were taken in smaller groups to Lyon and into the care of the 'VIC' network, which specialized in getting downed Allied airmen over the Pyrenees to Spain.* VIC's experienced agents guided them safely over the border, but they were all arrested on a train to Barcelona by the paramilitary Guardia Civil. They ended up in another camp, this one at Miranda de Ebro, a 5,000-bunk facility built to house the political enemies of the fascist dictator, Franco.

Negotiations to secure their release took some time, and it was October before Georges Bégué arrived back in the UK. Maurice Buckmaster, head of F section, immediately grounded him; he was far too valuable a resource to be sent back to France. He was awarded the Military Cross and appointed Signals Officer for the section. Later, he was awarded the MBE and received the Légion d'Honneur and the Croix de Guerre from the French. He died in Falls Church, Virginia in 1993 at the age of eighty-two.

6.2 Eccentric Lives: Denis Rake and Nancy Wake

> *He states that he has no fear of death and I believe him.*
> SOE instructor, about Denis Rake, 1941

The very nature of the perilous job dictated that it would attract a variety of devil-may-care eccentrics, and Nancy Wake probably heads the list of such

---

* See also Chapter 6.2 'Eccentric Lives' below.

recruits to SOE. If she had a rival for the title, it would be her radio operator, Denis Rake.

Nancy Wake was born in Wellington, New Zealand in 1912 and was of part-Māori descent. When she was only two years old, the family (including her five sisters) moved to Sydney, Australia. Her father soon departed the scene, leaving her mother to struggle bringing up a lively brood of girls. Nancy left school at sixteen and disappeared from home. The lack of excitement and glamour in her life depressed her; it was the third time she had run away.

She took a job as a trainee nurse at the health clinic of a gold mining community in the outback, but that only lasted two years. Back in Sydney, working for a Dutch shipping company, Nancy came into money; she inherited £200 from an aunt, something like Aus$15,000 at 2020 value. In December 1932 she lashed out on a first class cabin in a passenger ship across the Pacific to Vancouver, Canada, arriving in New York in time to experience the speakeasies and rotgut liquor of the final year of Prohibition. She was still only eighteen.

Before her money ran out, Nancy moved to London. Switching from hotels to a boarding house, she decided to become a reporter like her estranged father. She joined a journalism course – or taught herself journalism, or passed herself off as a journalist, depending on the source. She lied her way through an interview for a posting as a Middle East correspondent, claiming she was

Nancy Wake's forged identity card, 1942. Reputedly, she could drink a man under the table. It is not reported what might have happened next.

an experienced traveller in the region and could even 'write Egyptian'. She got the job, but her employer may have smelled a rat – and in 1934 sent her to Paris to gain some experience.

It is unclear whether she ever developed a talent for reporting, but she certainly had a gift for landing with both feet on any spot with great nightlife.

She learned French, toured the countryside during the day looking for stories and partied hard at night in the bars of the Rive Gauche. Regarding the language lessons, she wrote:

> I never worried too much about all that bloody feminine/masculine stuff, all the le this and la that – it would give you the shits – but it wasn't too long before I could communicate what I wanted to say, and I got better from there.[2]

To her credit, she expanded the scope of her writing into the field of politics, in particular the rise of Adolf Hitler and the spread of National Socialist ideology. With friends she took a field trip to Austria and there witnessed, for the first time, the Nazi persecution of the Jewish community: 'Roving Nazi gangs [were] randomly beating Jewish men and women in the streets.'[3]

'It was in Vienna', she wrote, 'that I formed my opinion of the Nazis. I resolved there and then that if I ever had the chance I would do anything, however big or small, stupid or dangerous, to try and make things more difficult for their rotten party.'

And she certainly lived up to that resolution.

In 1937, Wake's financial problems were solved when she met a prosperous French businessman, Henri Fiocca. They married on 30 November 1939 and were living in Marseille on the Mediterranean coast when the Germans overran the north and west of the country. She became a courier for the Resistance, working undercover as an ambulance driver and becoming a guide for downed British, Polish and Canadian airmen attempting to escape back to Britain via Spain and Portugal.[4] Nancy was suspected by the authorities of involvement with the Resistance and, if she hadn't been married to a wealthy French industrialist, she would have been arrested on a whim. The Gestapo and the Vichy French police held off from detaining her but put her under surveillance, opened her mail and monitored her telephone calls. They even put a reward of 5m francs on her head; but her ability to stay ahead of them earned her the code name 'White Mouse'. As she recalled:

> A little [face] powder and a little drink on the way, and I'd pass the [German sentry] posts and wink and say, 'Do you want to search me?' God, what a flirtatious little bastard I was.

Early in 1942, the escape network Nancy was working for suffered a setback when its 33-year-old Scottish organizer was arrested. He was Captain Ian Garrow of the 51ˢᵗ Highland Division. Garrow had been with the British Expeditionary Force when France was invaded. His unit was unable to get to Dunkirk and most ended up as prisoners of war. But Garrow went on the run, established contact with the Resistance and made himself useful by helping other soldiers and airmen back to Britain.

Nancy paid for a lawyer to represent Garrow during his trial before Vichy judges; but to no avail. In May 1942 he was sentenced to three and a half years in prison at Mauzac-et-Saint-Meyme-de-Rozens on the Dordogne River, some 100km inland from Bordeaux. She sent him letters and food while plotting his escape. A guard she had bribed gave Garrow a uniform and, on 8 December 1942, he put it on and mingled with other guards ahead of a shift-change. According to Nancy, he should really have had no chance: 'He was too tall, too handsome to be anything but a British

Nancy Lake, Capt. Ian Garrow (centre) and Nancy's husband Henri Fiocca. The photograph may have been taken in May 1941, when Garrow was living with the Fioccas at 13 rue des Phocéens, Marseilles.

officer.'[5] But he walked out of the prison unchallenged. Resistance fighters were waiting for him and got him to a hiding place in Toulouse.

It was not a good time to hang around. German troops had occupied Vichy France in response to Operation TORCH, the November 1942 Allied invasion of the French territories in North Africa. A determined team of helpers smuggled Garrow to the Pyrenees before waving him off at the border. From there he followed the footprints of the many escaping flyers he had helped reach the British consulate in Barcelona. By 4 February 1943 he was in Gibraltar and, two days later, on a plane heading for England. Having acted as Garrow's courier, Nancy replaced him as head of the network.

But Nancy's own luck (if that's what it was) ran out when her husband, Henri, was also arrested. The Resistance had to assume he would be tortured to force him to disclose his wife's whereabouts; it was time for her to leave France, too. This proved challenging. The plan was to send her by the same route over the Pyrenees used by Garrow. But it took six attempts over many weeks to ensure that she was safely across the border. She did not arrive in London until June 1943, but she instantly focused on getting back again. She wanted to continue the fight against the Germans and be closer to her husband.

Her first port of call was the Free French Forces, where she was interviewed by a 'Colonel Passy' (André Dewavrin). Nancy was stunned when Passy turned her down. No explanation was forthcoming, but the most generous excuse was perhaps that, as a French-speaking foreigner, she was considered more suitable for SOE. If that was the case, Passy could have at least given her the telephone number of the redoubtable Vera Atkins. Atkins was No. 2 to Maurice Buckmaster, head of SOE's F Section, and was in charge of the recruitment of agents to be sent into France. She was mightily impressed by Nancy and later described her as 'a real Australian bombshell. Tremendous vitality, flashing eyes. Everything she did, she did well.'[6]

Although it was Vera Atkins' intention to recruit Nancy as a courier – SOE was looking for French-speaking women for that role – it soon became clear that she had far more to offer. Her training reports, probably from F Section's STS 5 at Wanborough Manor near Guildford in Surrey, indicated that she had 'excellent fieldcraft' and was 'a very good and fast shot'. She also 'put the men to shame by her cheerful spirit and strength of character'.

That 'strength of character' came to light during Nancy's W/T operator's training. While on this course she met radio specialist Denis Rake, who was monitoring the progress of recruits through their training. He was someone with a background almost as colourful as her own. One thing they had in common was that both had fathers who were newspaper reporters. Rake claimed to have been born in 1901 in Brussels to *Times* correspondent Francis Rake and Belgian opera singer Emma Luart. In itself, this would have been remarkable, because Emma was only nine years old at the time. In fact, his mother was one Margaret Jones – another thing Nancy and Denis had in common is that both were inveterate liars. However, one source claims his Welsh mother was a soprano with the Opéra de La Monnaie.[7] The same source suggests that when he was still a toddler he was given to the Circus Sarazini, who employed him as a child acrobat in performances around Europe. Nine years later, the outbreak of the First World War put an end to touring and the circus returned Denis to his mother. When his father died in 1915, mother and son moved to London.

At the war's end Denis, then aged sixteen, returned to Brussels, where a British diplomat seduced him and whisked him off to Athens. Their relationship did not last long, and Denis was soon paired up with a royal prince. When the Greek press found out, the young Englishman went on the road again, this time to Venice.

His return to Britain marked the start of the first period of some stability in his life. From 1924 to the outbreak of the next war Denis worked in London's West End, performing in plays and musical comedies. In 1939 he left the stage and put his perfect French to good use by joining the Royal Army Service Corps (RASC) as a translator. His unit became part of the British Expeditionary Force (BEF) posted to the Bordeaux region.

When the Germans invaded Northern France, Denis's unit was ordered to relocate to Saint-Nazaire on the southern coast of Brittany for repatriation. There they boarded the Cunard cruise liner *Lancastria*, one of nineteen vessels which had been sent to the port to evacuate as many as possible of the BEF troops who had failed to escape through Dunkirk and the Pas de Calais two weeks earlier. Some 8,000 soldiers were crammed aboard, with a few dozen civilians. But twenty minutes after the *Lancastria* left harbour on 17 June 1940 she was bombed by the Luftwaffe and sank, with the shocking loss of over 4,000 men, women and children.* Denis Rake was one of the survivors. It may seem odd that someone just plucked from the sea after such a nightmare should be transferred from the army to the Royal Navy Volunteer Reserve, but that's what happened to Rake. A few weeks later, after being posted as an interpreter to a French minesweeper, the *Pollux*, he was in the freezing water once more, clinging to a piece of wreckage. He couldn't swim.

The combination of his claimed teenage radio training and fluent French meant that a W/T operator's role with SOE F section was the obvious next step for Wake. Supposedly, in the summer of 1941, he overheard two men in a pub talking about a secret organization that was putting agents behind enemy lines:

> Calling on a well-placed friend to pull some strings for him, Rake's enquiries led to the War Office, then to an interview with Lewis Gielgud (elder brother of actor John Gielgud), the recruiter for SOE's French section.[8]

One has to speculate that the 'well-placed friend' might have been Sir John Gielgud himself; he was an actor and could well have met Rake in London's theatreland. He was also gay, but not as overtly as Rake:

> In the autumn of 1953 the newly knighted actor was at the height of his fame and about to direct himself in a prestigious West End production when he was arrested in a public lavatory in Chelsea. Gielgud was charged with 'persistently importuning men for immoral purposes', a crime that transgressed the social taboos of the era and threatened to ruin him.[9]

---

* Historically, the biggest loss of life in the sinking of a single British ship.

Although a police officer had tried to disguise the recently-knighted actor's identity by naming him as 'John Smith' on the charge sheet, he was recognized in court by a newspaper reporter. Gielgud pleaded guilty and was fined £10.

Although homosexual acts were illegal at the time, Lewis Gielgud passed Rake on for assessment. Whoever interviewed him took the view that the candidate was 'a trifle effeminate' and 'a drug addict' because of his dependence on sleeping pills.[10] It may well be that his sleeping problem was caused by what is now called 'post-traumatic stress disorder'.

Denis Rake in uniform of the Royal Navy Volunteer Reserve, c. 1940.

Any hope that Denis Rake would allay the fears of his interviewer and distinguish himself in training soon disappeared at SOE's boot camp. He refused to undertake any explosives training and did the minimum on the firearms part of the course. He also rejected the idea of undertaking anything too physical – a strange decision for someone who allegedly spent nine years of his youth working as a circus acrobat. He quit SOE after a few weeks of training but was enticed back, on condition that he gave up the sedatives and with the promise of a pass on the commando training.

Early in 1942, with strict warnings about security ringing in his ear, Rake boarded a flight to Gibraltar. On the night of 13/14 May he and another agent, Charles Hayes, arrived off the coastal resort of Juan-les-Pins between Cannes and Nice. They had sailed there in a felucca, one of a class of a wooden fishing or cargo boats with single or double masts and lateen (triangular) sails. The two agents were ferried ashore in an inflatable dinghy and headed off in different directions.[11]

After failing to convince his primary contact of his bona fides he headed for a bar in the centre of Antibes. He had been told to look for a man in a beret, sitting at the back, reading a copy of *Nice-Matin* and smoking a short, black cigar. The man in the beret was 'Clément', a resistance agent who was to accompany Rake 300km (190 miles) north to Lyon.

There he was taken to meet Virginia Hall, a W/T operator who had completed SOE's tough training in spite of her left leg having been amputated below the knee after a 1933 hunting accident in Turkey. The French called her '*La dame qui boite*' ('The lady who limps'). Hall, an American from Baltimore, arranged for Denis to lodge with a prostitute. Such arrangements with brothels and ladies of the night were common; you got a bed and were not required to complete the *fiche* used by hotels to register a guest's presence with the police. But Rake's radio connection with the UK did not work well, and he was relocated to work with the SPRUCE network's radio operator, Edward Zeff. They sent a regular stream of useful messages to England during the day. At night, supposedly, Rake sang at Lyon's *La Cigogne* cabaret club. It seems you can take the short-wave radio operator out of showbiz, but you can't take 'cabaradio' out of the clandestine agent …

Rake's work for SPRUCE didn't last; after a few weeks he was betrayed. Virginia Hall had introduced him to a young agent recently parachuted into France. But the youngster made the grievous mistake of telling a Vichy-supporting relative he had been in England. The relation immediately denounced him to the police. Under interrogation, he told the cops about a British radio operator called 'Justin' (Rake's field name). Hall discovered what had happened and alerted Rake to the fact that the Gestapo must have his description; he needed to get out of France immediately. It was the finale for show-stopping performances at *La Cigogne*.

SOE radio agent Virginia Hall somewhere in the French countryside, 1943.

Rake, however, was reluctant to leave; there was still work to be done. He insisted on staying in the country but said he would move on to another network in need of a W/T operator.

Hall told him that SOE agents Edward Wilkinson and Ben Cowburn* had recently set up a new circuit in Paris but were unable to go operational until they could add a radio specialist to the team. She gave him his only means of making contact with Wilkinson, a photograph, and the name of a bar where he might find him, the Café Napoléon.

Rake headed north to the demarcation line. He was stopped by a German soldier at the border with the occupied zone and had to bribe him with most of the cash he was carrying to get through. Once in Paris, it took five nervous visits to the Café Napoléon before he made contact. Wilkinson was relieved to see him. When he asked where Rake had been staying for nearly a week, he replied that he had met an anti-Nazi SS officer in a restaurant and was staying at his apartment. According to a French source, '*C'était le coup de foudre*' ('It was love at first sight'). Wilkinson was appalled at this blatant breach of security and demanded Rake quit a liaison that was putting the whole circuit at risk. Of course, Rake might have been lying or, at least, exaggerating, and the encounter is mentioned in Maurice Buckmaster's memoirs as no more than a casual meeting. However, Buckmaster's book on the history of F section makes no mention of Rake's homosexuality at all.[12]

German Funkabwehr D/F team operating from a Paris rooftop, 1943. (*Bundesarchiv*)

SOE agent Edward Wilkinson ('Alexandre'), c. 1941. He was executed on 7 September 1944 at Mauthausen concentration camp in Austria.

---

* Later famous among SOE agents for putting itching powder in the underwear of U-boat crews.

There was another problem – Rake didn't have his radio with him. The wireless set had been sent via another route and had failed to arrive. With no other option available, Rake and Wilkinson travelled back to Lyon to get a spare radio from Virginia Hall.* With another circuit organizer, Richard Heslop, he again faced the challenge of getting through to the occupied zone.

When they reached the demarcation line, Rake complained of feeling tired and ill from the journey. They decided to find somewhere to stay and to attempt the border the following day. Rake checked into the Café des Faisans; Heslop and Wilkinson found rooms in another place nearby. They arranged to meet up the next day, but when Heslop and Wilkinson arrived at 11.00 the following morning they were arrested by the Vichy police. Rake had been given away by the café manager and was being detained in his room. The two agents were furious, assuming that Rake had betrayed them.

All three were transferred to the prison at Castres for questioning. Conditions in the jail were dreadful, and Rake caught dysentery. He was brutalized during questioning, and one particularly vicious interrogator smashed the bones in his foot. After three months' solitary confinement the men were transferred south of Lyon, to a prisoner-of-war camp at Chambaran. It was a fortuitous move: the French commandant was sympathetic and told them his guards would look the other way if they wanted to escape. Once out of the jail, Heslop and Wilkinson headed north back to Paris, still believing Rake had ratted on them to the police. Rake teamed up with some British NCOs and went south-west to the Pyrenees.

The hard trek over the mountains was a nightmare for Rake, in agony from his broken foot. On arrival in supposedly neutral Spain they were arrested by the 'Benemérita', Franco's notorious paramilitary Guardia Civil, and thrown into a prison at Figueras, just south of the border. Next stop was the Miranda de Ebro concentration camp 50km (31 miles) inland from Bilbao. It took some months for the British Embassy to secure his release, and he finally arrived back in the UK in May 1943.

Denis Rake was a wreck. He needed surgery to insert a metal plate into his foot; fractured bones in the foot can take three months to heal – but longer if you have been walking over mountainous terrain. He was also mentally exhausted by the rough interrogation and maltreatment he had suffered in France and Spain. His rejection by fellow agents Wilkinson and Heslop had damaged his morale, and he had a nervous breakdown. After recuperating

---

* The UK awarded Virginia Hall the MBE in 1943. She joined the OSS in March 1944. After the war she was awarded Distinguished Service Cross (US) and the Croix de Guerre (France).

from surgery he was given light duties as a 'conducting officer', mentoring recruits through their courses and reporting on their progress at SOE's 'finishing school' at Beaulieu.

It was here that Nancy Wake happened on Rake being berated by another female recruit for 'being rude to her'. The angry woman insisted she was going to report Rake and demanded the New Zealander support her. Nancy refused, insisting she had heard nothing. Now Nancy became the focus of the woman's ire and was told that she would be reported too – for being a drunk. Nancy ended up being fired – a decision that was quickly overruled by Maurice Buckmaster when he found out. She was soon back in uniform and heading to Scotland for training in explosives, weapons and silent killing.

After graduation, Wake boarded a converted Liberator bomber and was parachuted into the Auvergne region (125km, 78 miles west of Lyon) on 31 April 1944 on her first operation. SOE knew her by the code name 'Hélène', and her cover name in France was 'Madame Andrée'. Jumping from the plane with her were Major John Farmer and the hangover from her farewell party. From Auvergne they headed south, 750m (2,500ft) up the mountains of the Massif Central, to the spa town of Chaudes-Aigues, where they were to meet up with the STATIONER circuit and the local Resistance. April 1944 was a critical time for SOE's plans to severely disrupt Germany's ability to respond to the D-Day invasion.

However, their intelligence was bad. The organizer of STATIONER, Maurice Southgate, had been arrested, and his role taken over by Pearl Witherington, a courier born in Paris, the daughter of British parents. If that wasn't bad enough, they discovered from Witherington that 'Gaspard', the leader of the local Maquis, was unfriendly. He had said that he didn't want to work with the British and that the two new arrivals were useless because they hadn't brought a W/T operator with them.

Outside the building, Wake and Farmer discussed what they were going to do next; Gaspard had about 10,000 fighters under his command but the man seemed determined to cut off his primary supply of materiel. Wake and Farmer overheard the Resistance members speculating about how much money the SOE agents had with them. One suggested someone should seduce Wake, steal the money and then kill her. Nancy was livid and went back inside, no doubt to teach the men a few new expletives in both French and English. Where the hell was the radio agent?

They moved on, 8km (5 miles) to the west, to make contact with a Resistance group commanded by Henri Fournier. Here they met with a much warmer reception, and Fournier found them a secure hotel in the pretty village of Lieutadès, where they could rest and wait for their missing W/T operator to turn up.

It was well into May 1944 when Nancy spotted her friend Denis Rake getting out of a car in front of the cemetery. (The church is directly opposite the village bar.) She and Farmer were angry with him. They knew he had refused to be infiltrated by parachute – more damage to his fractured foot would have rendered him useless. Instead, he had been flown by Lysander to the nearest available landing site, which was near Clermont-Ferrand, much further north. They accused him of having gone off with someone he fancied, but he protested that he didn't know where his colleagues had disappeared to after escaping the malign attentions of Gaspard. Although Wake and Farmer were furious with Rake they were extremely relieved to see him.

Fournier was even more excited; Gaspard's idiocy was his good fortune. He had not been expecting a radio operator to arrive out of the blue, but now he would be in contact with the UK at last. He set to and drafted lists

SOE agent Nancy Wake with the Maquis, France 1944.

of the weapons and explosives they needed. Nancy encrypted the detailed requisitions, and Denis Rake's thumb and forefinger were soon working his Morse key. Within days the team was manning the carefully chosen dropping-points, and listening out for the distinctive sound of four Pratt & Whitney radial engines. This told them to light the signal fire before ducking into cover; no one wanted one of the heavy containers dropped by the RAF's Liberators to land on their head. The supply drops were so successful that a repentant Gaspard turned up, begging Nancy and Dennis for a share of the new weapons.[13]

They even took delivery of a new arms instructor to help with the training of recruits. By the time the Germans started pouring more troops into the region it was too late. On 6 June 1944, Operation OVERLORD had begun, and Allied forces were taking control of the beaches of Normandy. In co-ordination, the Resistance forces of the Massif Central had sabotaged key railway junctions, destroyed several factories and cut many underground telephone cables in the area.

6.3 Operation JEDBURGH: Overlord and the Reivers

The disruption of enemy rail communications, the harassing of German road moves and the continual and increasing strain placed on German security services throughout occupied Europe ... played a very considerable part in our complete and final victory.

General Dwight D. Eisenhower,
Supreme Allied Commander, May 1945

The planning for D-Day had started early in 1942, some six months after the collapse of the disastrous Molotov-Ribbentrop Pact and the Nazis' invasion of the Soviet Union. Roosevelt and Churchill did not hurry to meet Stalin's demands for the opening of a 'second front'; they were already fighting on other 'second fronts' in the Western Pacific and North Africa and, arguably, it would have been a huge mistake to go too soon.

By the spring of 1943, plans to cross the English Channel in force were well advanced. It was decided in April that French Resistance forces should play a key part in disrupting and diverting the German military from the rear. But how? The French underground was too fragmented, under-trained and under-equipped to be left to its own devices. SHAEF decided that Allied support teams needed to be inserted at the same time as the execution of OVERLORD – acting too soon would risk revealing the timing and location of the landings. Operation JEDBURGH was named after the

Scottish border town notorious in the fifteenth and sixteenth centuries for the activities of lawless raiders known as the Border Reivers; both English and Scots, they plundered both sides of the frontier. (It should be said that many historians insist the choice of name for the operation was entirely random.)

Selection and training of the three-man JEDBURGH teams got under way in good time. In the second half of 1943 the units with most experience of irregular warfare were the SOE and the Royal Marine Commandos (both in Europe), as well as the Special Air Service (SAS) in North Africa. But it was impossible to keep the Americans out of the mix, and the best OSS agents were put through selection. The essential third member of each team would be French, not just for political reasons, but because of their language skills and local knowledge; they were mostly recruited from the Free French BCRA (*Bureau Central de Renseignements et d'Action*, Central Bureau of Intelligence and Action). It was further determined that two of the team would be officers and the third an NCO trained as a W/T operator. In all, 300 men served as 'Jedburghs' or 'Jeds'.

These were very much rules of thumb; some teams were duos, others comprised four or more. They also varied in the mix of nationalities. Long after the war, Sir Richard Brook of SOE said this:

> These teams were in theory tripartite but in practice mainly bipartite. The tripartite concept meant three members from three different participating countries. The original idea, for example, mandated that a Jedburgh team working in France would have one American, one British, and one French member. Likewise, a team working in Italy would be composed of an American, a British, and an Italian member. In practice, however, only 10 of about 100 Jedburgh teams had members from three participating countries. Jedburgh teams were frequently unable to find a local representative. In many cases, particularly because of U.S. preference, the Jedburgh teams had one British and two American members or one British and two French members.[14]

At the time, Richard Brook was regional director for France and the Low Countries at Special Force Headquarters (SFHQ). One can only speculate why the OSS was averse to working with the French. Could it be because French communists were at the heart of the Resistance?

Totally indispensable to the operation were the B-24D Liberators of 801st Bomb Group, the 'Carpetbaggers', and the Lysanders of RAF 138 Squadron (Special Duties). The Carpetbaggers had the range and capacity for the insertion of men and equipment by parachute; the Lysanders had stealth and

A Special Duties RAF Lysander, an aircraft of great character. Note the long-range fuel tank below the belly and the permanent access ladder. Extraneous equipment like machine guns was stripped out, increasing the aircraft's range.

The training staff at ME65 Milton Hall, 1944–5. Identities are unknown, but they all seem to be wearing British Army battle dress.

a short landing and take-off (STOL) capability enabling them to exfiltrate agents from the field.*

A training school was set up in Cambridgeshire at (another) stately home, Milton Hall (ME65) near Peterborough. The house, stables and extensive

---

* In late 1943 the SOE had access to twenty-three Handley Page Halifax B Mk II Series 1 (Special) converted four-engined bombers for dropping agents and stores and towing gliders. These were considered barely enough to support existing operations.

grounds were all available for the broadly based programme aimed at raising all the recruits to the same level of skills needed if they were to work closely together. Shown above is a rare photograph of Milton Hall's directing staff (trainers). The size of the facility is a good indication of the commitment made to the irregular warfare dimension of D-Day.

Sgt. Arthur Brown, Operation JEDBURGH W/T Operator, 1945.

Instruction started with two weeks of tough commando training at bases in northern Scotland. This was not a problem for the many SAS operators recruited to Operation JEDBURGH, but others not considered fit enough for the rigours of behind-the-line operations would be 'returned to unit'. The rest were transported south to Milton Hall, where they received further firearms and sabotage training. The standard-issue personal weapons were the Colt .45 semi-automatic pistol and the M1 carbine.

During their courses the W/T operators were sent to STS 54b at Belhaven School in Scotland[15] for practice in long-range communications. This took the form of exchanging messages with STS 54a at Fawley Court, just north of Henley-on-Thames, some 390 miles distant. One of the radio agents was Arthur Brown from the Royal Tank Regiment. He later recalled:

The training at Dunbar from March 1944 onwards was, I believe, largely a confidence building exercise to enable W/T operators to test the kinds of radio equipment they would be using in the field, and over the same distances. The rotation of the 100 or so Jed operators through Dunbar was done in groups for about a week or ten days per group.[16]

Arthur Brown, a Londoner who had not been in combat before but was rated highly competent, became Tommy Macpherson's radio operator (see below).[17] Another Jed who went to Belhaven School was Ron Brierley. He wrote this about his experiences:

Small groups of us occasionally went to Belhaven when we were stationed in Scotland on exercises – we worked our radio scheds back to

[STS 54a at] Henley, simulating the distances we should have to cover from France. I went there on two occasions but only for a few days at a time and memory is pretty vague.

I do know I was there at New Year 43/44 with a small group – we went into Dunbar in the evening and had a high old time – afraid we were a bit 'over the top' and got into bother with the police – one of my pals 'Cobber' Cain was locked up for the night – something to do with a policeman's helmet – which they didn't appreciate. There was quite a fuss – the telephone lines were buzzing and we were all quite glad to get back to Milton [Hall].[18]

In 1944 Ron Brierley was sent to Brittany and Doubs (east of Dijon) on JEDBURGH operations. His war wasn't over when France was liberated; the SOE sent him to the Sittang Valley in Burma (Operation REINDEER) and then to Sumatra.

Operation JEDBURGH agents on the range with Colt .45 automatics, Milton Hall (apparently in the walled garden), 1944.

'Jed' trainees practising the receipt of Morse signals. Milton Hall, 1943–4.

These small teams were to be deployed across France (and later the Netherlands and Denmark), so keeping in touch with SFHQ in London would be essential. All agents received wireless telegraphy training, not just those designated as radio operators – if the latter were killed or captured, the whole team would become incommunicado. It takes a lot longer to teach someone how to operate a short-wave radio, send and receive Morse, encrypt and decrypt messages, than it does to strip and clean a Colt .45 or corrupt a supply of tank engine oil.

So, much of the course was dedicated to the operation and maintenance of JEDBURGH's chosen 'Jed Set', the Type B Mark II, the workhorse 'B2'.

They were issued 'code books' printed on silk with the 500 phrases they would use most often in signals replaced with four-letter codes, to save Morse keying time. One-time pads (OTPs) for the encoding of messages were also on silk to aid concealment and destruction. The use of OTPs reflects the growing influence in such matters of SOE's chief cryptographer, Leo Marks. From the start, General Charles de Gaulle's Free French had refused point blank to use any code system of British origin. Curious about the method they were using, Marks broke it, but was forbidden by SOE from telling the French. The code turned out to be a slightly modified version of the unsafe poem codes being used by SIS; consequently the French would be given no say in encryption matters.[19]

Jed groups were given the code names of boys or medicines, and Team 'Hugh' was first out of the blocks late on D-Day 1. Their destination was

The CO of Milton Hall bids farewell to newly-graduated American JEDBURGH agents prior to their transfer to a nearby airfield.

A nervous-looking Jedburgh team (wearing parachutes) waiting to board a B-24D Liberator of the Carpetbaggers. (*CIA archive*)

Châteauroux in central France, appropriately the same location where Georges Bégué made his historic entry as the first W/T operator into France three years earlier. In the seven months to the end of the year, a further ninety-two teams arrived in fifty-four *départements* of France. They would be dropped under cover of darkness and met mostly – but not always – by a local resistance group.

On D-Day+3 SHAEF General Eisenhower transferred control of the Operation JEDBURGH teams already in the field to the French. This was a political move to placate de Gaulle, but it is unlikely that real operational control passed from SF Headquarters in London.*

Those early drops were a nightmare for the Jeds' W/T operators. According to M. R. D. Foot, a lot of the radios were damaged as a result of faulty packing.[20] This was precisely what the Paraset was designed to avoid, and it might be argued that the time between the start of JEDBURGH training and D-Day – about a year – was sufficient to get another production line opened.

*   *   *

Baker Street tended to select experienced hands for JEDBURGH, probably to counterbalance the relative inexperience of the OSS candidates. One exception was a tall, handsome and genial 18-year-old called John Sharp. The son of a Scotland Yard detective, he grew up in South-West London. Sharp had been in the Green Howards regiment long enough to be trained as a gunner, driver and radio operator on a Bren Gun Carrier, when he volunteered for 'special duties'. (Each tank and armoured fighting vehicle has a radio operator lurking inside it.) Only after he was accepted did he realize he had become a member of SOE.

After training at Wanborough Manor his first assignment was as W/T operator to two-man JEDBURGH team 'Isaac' headed by 51-year-old Lieutenant Colonel Sir James Hutchinson, the son of a Scottish shipping magnate. A baronet, Hutchinson was one of quite a few minor British and French aristocrats who served in SOE and SIS. Hutchinson spoke French fluently, whereas Sharp had never been out of England before. On the night of 10/11 June 1944 Team Isaac was dropped into France at the second attempt from a Stirling bomber† they were sharing with a 10-man SAS team

---

* However, once the Normandy beachhead had been established, de Gaulle sacked all the British SOE agents in France. See *Les Réseaux Bordelais* below.
† The Short Stirling was the RAF's first four-engined heavy bomber, entering service in early 1941. It was replaced by the better-performing Handley Page Halifax and Avro Lancaster in 1943. The Model IV was a version adopted for parachute-dropping and glider-towing.

SOE W/T Operator Sgt. John Sharp (second left) meets local Maquisards during JEDBURGH Operation Isaac, Morvan, June 1944.

on a different mission. Their intended destination was Morvan, in the hills 75km west of Dijon. The first attempt had been cancelled and, in view of the appalling weather, this one should also have been aborted. The pilot and his navigator hadn't a clue where they were and saw no signal from the ground. Descending from 3,000ft, the twelve men were scattered over several square miles far from the Maquis reception committee. Hutchinson broke his toe, and Sharp was left swinging from a tree.

As the SAS soldiers disappeared into the night, John Sharp and his commander managed to extricate themselves and headed into the hills overlooking the valley where they had landed. At daybreak the two men had an excellent view of the Vichy Milice collecting the containers of their equipment – including Sharp's two radio sets. Later in the day, the Maquis arrived and – no doubt emboldened by the recent D-Day landings in Normandy – fought a bloody battle with the Milice over the spoils of the disastrous insertion. Very short of food, with the burly young radio agent supporting his older commander, Team Isaac headed towards one of their predetermined rendezvous points, travelling by night and lying up during the day.

SOE W/T operator Sgt. John Sharp connecting the battery to his radio set, France, 1944. Note the aerial.

Three days later, they encountered a Madame Nitler, who took them into her house, served up a hot meal and sent a message to the Maquis. The resistance fighters were delighted to see them and were even able to provide Sharp with a replacement radio, which he described as 'a lightweight agent's suitcase set: very nice'.[21]

Under Madame Nitler's care it wasn't long before Lieutenant Colonel Hutchinson was able to attend a series of meetings with the leaders of all the local Maquis groups to record their area of operation, how numerous they were, what attacks they had carried out against the enemy and the weapons and explosives they needed. In the meantime, Sharp had familiarized himself with the new radio – he had been trained on the B2 'Jed-set' – and used his first transmission to let SFHQ they had arrived and were open for business.

The young W/T operator edited his commander's overlong signals as he encoded them. Impressed by what they were receiving, London upgraded Isaac to Operation VERVEINE. The first sign that Eisenhower had given command of behind-the-lines operations in France to de Gaulle was when a French colonel turned up saying he was now the new *chef*. He was not particularly helpful, but Hutchinson was experienced and competent enough to work round him most of the time, using Sharp to call in airstrikes against trainloads of German troops trying to reach Normandy.

On one occasion the French colonel told them they had to arrange the destruction of a series of bridges over the River Loire. But Hutchinson and Sharp were under orders from SOE *not* to blow the bridges as they might be needed by advancing Allied forces. Sharp signalled London questioning the French plan, but while they waited for a reply, the Germans blew the bridges themselves, abandoning thousands of their own soldiers to be taken prisoner. In September 1944 the two members of Operation VERVEINE got back to the UK.

The following year, John Sharp joined SOE's Force 136 operation in the Far East and soon found himself teaching the basics of W/T operation to insurgents fighting the Japanese in the Arakan region of western Burma (now Myanmar). He was Mentioned in Dispatches and later awarded the Military Medal. In 2017, belatedly, the French awarded him the Légion d'Honneur. He died on 14 August 2019.

* * *

Views on the effectiveness of Operation JEDBURGH vary. Given that ninety-three teams were deployed, it would have been absurd to expect a 100 per cent success rate. However, a case could be made that the antics of Edinburgh-born 'Tommy' Macpherson alone, in delaying the arrival of the 2nd SS Panzer Division ('Das Reich') in Normandy, were sufficient justification for the whole venture.

On D-Day the elite Nazi division's 15,000 men and 209 tanks, half-tracks, self-propelled guns and support vehicles were stationed in Valence-d'Agen, a short distance north of Toulouse in South-West France. They were commanded by SS-Gruppenführer Heinz Lammerding. No one expected a JEDBURGH team – even with the support of substantial resistance forces – to be able to stop an SS division in its tracks. But that was the challenge given to Tommy Macpherson.

After a sojourn with the Queen's Own Cameron Highlanders Macpherson had transferred to 11th Commando and started an action-packed grand tour off the coast of Libya. He was captured and spent the next two years as a PoW or escapee in Italy, Austria, Yugoslavia, Germany and Poland, before reaching Sweden by boat across the Baltic.

Tommy Macpherson and others landed at RAF Kinloss in North-East Scotland on 4 November 1943; he had been on the run for two years and was awarded the Military Cross. His resourcefulness did not go unnoticed and he was, within a matter of days, recruited to Operation JEDBURGH and ordered to report to Milton Hall for training. His course ran from January to March 1944, and on graduation he was promoted to the rank of major. He was to command Team Quinine, which comprised 18-year-old Lieutenant Michel de Bourbon ('Aristide'), and a British radio operator, Sergeant Arthur Brown. It was revealed after the war that de Bourbon was actually 'Prince' Michel de Bourbon-Parma who, in the unlikely event of the 1789 Revolution being reversed, would have been a distant claimant to the French throne.

SOE agent Lt. Tommy Macpherson, Queen's Own Cameron Highlanders and 11th Commando. Probably 1943.

After dark on 8 June 1944 Team Quinine was dropped into a field north of Auriac to be met by a Maquis reception committee. It took a while for the maquisard meeting them to get over the fact that Macpherson had chosen to jump in the most inappropriate parachute attire – his regimental kilt. It was fortunate the drop had taken place at night. Any puzzlement was soon overcome by the gift of arms and explosives which had descended with them.

The best way to move tracked fighting vehicles is on flat-bed rail cars, and Das Reich assumed this would be the way they would reach Normandy in good time. Tracked vehicles (especially tanks) are slow, consume huge quantities of fuel and damage roads; equally, asphalt roads damage tanks. Forcing Das Reich off the railways and on to the Route Nationale 20 (RN20) running from Toulouse north through Limoges and Châteauroux would slow the column down and make it more vulnerable to attack. SFHQ's strategy for dealing with the threat from this SS division – hardened in battle on the Eastern Front – was brilliant.

SFHQ had just the man for the job. Tony Brooks had been born in Essex but raised in France and Switzerland. When the Germans invaded, he escaped via Spain to Britain intending to join the British Army; but at seventeen years old, he was too young to sign up, and so travelled straight back to the Jura mountains south-east of the city of Dijon to work in the family business. While he had been away, his aunt had been helping Allied soldiers and airmen get home to the UK. That looked more exciting than office paperwork, so he helped with the repatriation efforts for over a year. In May 1941 it was noticed that the Milice was paying far too much attention to Brooks' activities, and he headed for the Pyrenees again. Back in London, he was recruited by SOE who, on 9 April 1942, commissioned him as a second lieutenant and promptly sent him off for training.

At the beginning of July that year – now codenamed 'Alphonse' – he was parachuted back into France near the favourite delivery-point of Limoges. After making contact with SOE's *in-situ* agents he helped to set up the

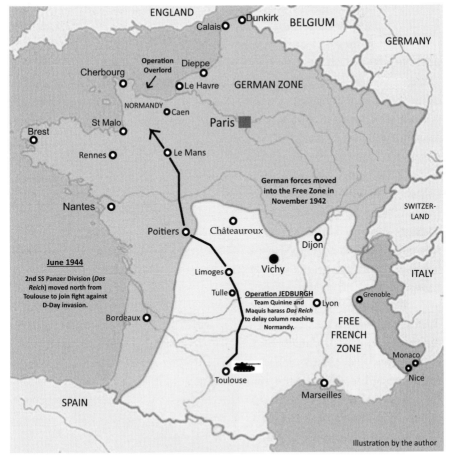

France, June 1944. Operation Jedburgh teams sabotaged rail cars and tracks forcing 2nd SS Panzer Division on to the road north from Toulouse. Roadblocks and bridge attacks delayed their arrival by 2–4 weeks. (*Map by author*)

PIMENTO network covering southern France. An important part of his brief was to win the support of railwaymen, working through their trade union.[22]

Over the following two years Tony Brooks showed such determination and courage that he became head of the network. Early in 1944 his *réseau* successfully sabotaged trains being moved by the Germans from Marseille to Dijon, and the SOE now let him know that he needed to do the same job on the lines running north from Toulouse.

The secret of his success was to drain the oil from the axle brakes of the low-loader rail cars and replace it with a sticky concoction of carborundum and abrasive provided by London. The rail workers of the PIMENTO network provided the location of every low-loader in the area, and Brooks then dispatched teams – including two sisters aged sixteen and fourteen – to sabotage each one. The disabled carriages would seize up after a few miles and block the tracks, the damage could not be fixed quickly and the cars were often stuck in locations such as tunnels and cuttings where it was difficult to unload the tanks.

Once Tony Brooks had forced the armoured convoy on to the roads, two other SOE units were in place to harass Das Reich. Team Quinine was poised to the east, an American-led team to the west. Tommy Macpherson started with the simplest of obstacles: large tree trunks placed across the road stopped the column and were too heavy to be pushed aside by armoured cars. There followed a two-hour delay while the Germans brought up a bulldozer from the rear. The next time, Macpherson booby-trapped one of the trees with anti-tank mines and neatly added a crippled bulldozer to the blockage. In a further twist, Macpherson had a resistance fighter with a Sten gun hidden in the trees. As the SS column got ready to set off again, he emptied a magazine at them and ran off into the woods before they could figure out where he was. Yet more delay ensued.[23]

SOE agent Major Tommy Macpherson CBE, MC & Two Bars, TD, DL.

SOE Radio Operator Sgt.
Arthur Brown DSC, LdH.
1944/5.

Lammerding's officers kept looking for opportunities to get back on the railway, but the SOE's rail workers stayed ahead of the game, blowing bridges and track wherever they could. Arthur Brown's regular radio contacts with SFHQ ensured they were kept supplied with all the explosives, timers and detonators needed. Brown spoke no French, so at times he must have felt out of the loop; the best he could do was to keep up with Macpherson, lugging the heavy 'B2' and making sure it didn't get damaged. After rigging the aerial at each stopping-point he would brew some tea.[24]

After a few days, the ploy of denying the SS use of the railway was beginning to pay off. The head of the column had only travelled 80km (50 miles) and the tracks had started to come off the vehicles, causing even more delay. Maquis commanders told Macpherson that no fewer than 60 per cent of the Panzer tanks and one third of the half-tracks had broken down, disabled by the tarmac they were travelling on.

In a radio signal to his HQ, General Lammerding reported he was facing a familiar problem; it would take four days to get the tanks mobile again, but he was out of spares and, with the railway rendered inoperable by 'terrorists', it would take some time to get them.

Using the Resistance, Macpherson now started to destroy the road bridges, and progress for Das Reich became agonisingly slow. He had done the job commendably and, when the division reached Tulle, 250km (155 miles) north of its starting-point near Toulouse, it left his territory and he handed over to other resistance groups.

By rail the 2nd SS Panzer Division should have been able to reach Normandy in 72 hours. In fact, it was seventeen days before the first tanks limped into the region, and weeks more before the rest of the column was able to engage the forces of Operation OVERLORD; the D-Day beaches had already been secured.

Tommy Macpherson, the trusty Sergeant Arthur Brown and his 'B2', and all the Maquisards they could muster continued to harass the Germans occupying central and southern France. By 1945 Macpherson had been promoted to the rank of major and awarded the CBE, *three* Military Crosses, the Croix de Guerre three times, and the Légion d'Honneur. His exploits continued after the war with MI5, MI6 and the Foreign Office. He was eighty-five when he died. Arthur Brown was awarded the Croix de Guerre for his service in France. During his time in the Far East with Operation DILWYN he was Mentioned in Dispatches and he was awarded the DSC on his return.

SOE W/T operator Roger Landes.

6.4 Les Réseaux Bordelais: 'wireless operators were precious'

Undoubtedly, there were other W/T operators like Sergeant Arthur Brown. They would struggle to keep up with the team organizer, make sure the batteries were kept charged, code and decode diligently and try not to mangle the Morse. They would even brew the tea. Roger Landes was not one of these.

Born in Paris on 16 December 1916, Landes was the middle son of three. His father, Barnet Landes, was a naturalized Briton of Polish-Jewish descent, his mother was a 'White Russian'. After fleeing the Tsarist pogroms, Roger's great-grandfather had founded a jewellery business in Hatton Garden, the hub of London's diamond trade. His father set up a similar business in Paris, and Roger studied architecture at the *École Nationale des Arts Décoratifs*. In 1938, when the family business failed, they all moved to London and Roger found work as a quantity surveyor with London County Council. In March 1941 he was conscripted, fortuitously as it turned out, into the Royal Corps of Signals.

He was talent-spotted by someone browsing personnel files for potential candidates for SIS or SOE. Roger Landes had three of the most important

ENGLAND
Calais○ ○Dunkirk BELGIUM
GERMANY
FARMER
Dieppe
Cherbourg Le Havre ○
○ ○ *SALESMAN* *MUSICIAN*
AUTOGIRO
St Malo Paris ■ *JUGGLER*
Brest ○
○ *CHESTNUT*
○ Le Mans

P R O S P E R

BUTLER
Nantes ○ *ARTIST* *DONKEYMAN* SWITZER-
LAND
Poitiers○ ○
Châteauroux
FRANCE 1943 Dijon○
SPRUCE
Main SOE Networks Limoges○ Vichy *GREENHEART* ITALY
○Tulle *PIMENTO I*
Grenoble○
Bordeaux Lyon○
FREE
FRENCH
PIMENTO II ZONE
Toulouse Monaco○○
○ *SPINDLE* Nice
PRUNUS ○
SPAIN *WHEELWRIGHT* Marseilles○
ITALIAN
ZONE

Some of the SOE networks in France, 1942–3. Code names in *ITALIC CAPITALS*. (*Map by the author*)

attributes: military training; fluency in a foreign language; skills in W/T operation and Morse. His immediate transfer to SOE was requested by the head of F section, Maurice Buckmaster, and he was sent off for training.

Seven months later, after sunset on 31 October 1942, Roger Landes was happily swinging under a parachute over central France; it was his *seventh* attempt to make the drop. Now code-named 'Aristide', his orders were to work as radio operator for Claude de Baissac ('David'), organizer of the SCIENTIST network. Descending from the same aircraft was a second W/T operator, 27-year-old Gilbert Norman, code-named 'Archambaud'. Norman was born in Saint-Cloud, near Paris, to a British father and a French mother. Educated in both countries, he was bilingual. On the outbreak of war he joined the Durham Light Infantry and was commissioned but, like

Landes, promptly pinched by SOE. While his colleague headed south to the German-occupied hinterland of Bordeaux, Norman journeyed up-country to join the PROSPER network, which sprawled across France from Brittany to the eastern frontier. Its organizer was Francis Suttill.

It was originally intended that Landes should also join PROSPER, but that plan was changed when, in July 1942, SCIENTIST's intended radio agent Harry Peulevé experienced a heavy parachute landing and fractured a leg. Network organizer Claude de Baissac had met Landes during training; he liked the young man and put in a special request for him to be sent as Peulevé's substitute.

Roger Landes' distinguishing feature was that he had no features that distinguished him at all. He was short and slightly built; perhaps a bit weedy. Proof of this 'invisibility' came on 3 August 1943 when visiting a house where he kept one of his B2s. The house belonged to a Madame Jardel, who bravely allowed him to transmit from the maid's room. He parked his bike in the garage, removed the radio from under the bed and keyed his messages. As he was getting ready to leave he was interrupted by Madame Jardel's daughter, who told him her mother had been arrested by the Germans earlier that day. The house had been searched, but the radio set remained undiscovered. In spite of that, Landes decided to take the radio with him. Then the girl announced that someone had been watching the house since they had taken her mother away. Out of the window he could see a fair-haired man in civilian clothes standing a little way down the street on the opposite side. But why hadn't the watcher seen him arrive? Landes concluded that he must have gone to the local café or taken a comfort break. He resolved to brazen it out.

He perched the case containing the radio on the bicycle's pannier rack, donned his *béret Basque* and pushed his bike out of the garage towards the German. He bid the man a cheery '*bon jour*', but as he passed him the radio fell off the rack. It seems that the dumbest of SD's* assets must have got the job of watching houses, for this one helped Landes recover the case, perched it back on the bike for him and watched the agent pedal away.[25]

* * *

In the following months de Baissac and Landes worked hard together to develop SCIENTIST into a circuit second only to PROSPER in the north. On its eastern limits it had easy access to the '*zone non-occupée*' (ZNO) – Vichy France – and at its west to the Bay of Biscay.

---

* SD: *Sicherheitsdienst*, the intelligence agency of the SS and the Nazi regime.

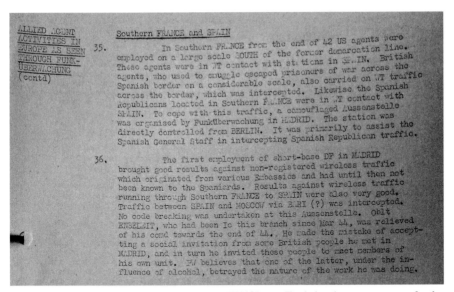

Comments of Oberst-Leutnant Mettig of OKW/Chi on Funkabwehr interception of radio traffic between southern France and Spain, September 1945.

To the south was the Spanish border, high in the Pyrenees, and the agents of SCIENTIST inevitably had to assist the passage of escaping servicemen over the mountains. The planning of this – ensuring couriers in Spain were aware of their imminent arrival – demanded advance radio contact. Also, when communications with the UK were difficult, it was easier to relay traffic through Barcelona or Madrid. This would explain the radio transmissions detected by the Funkabwehr.[26]

Mettig's claims about 'large scale' operations by the US in the ZNO should be taken with a pinch of salt. The OSS only made a significant impression on France with the launch of Operation

SOE W/T operator Major Gilbert Norman.

JEDBURGH in the summer of 1944. Much of the traffic must have been the busy SOE escape networks.

SCIENTIST was far too big for just one W/T operator. In May 1942 a new agent, Henri Labit, was parachuted 'blind' into the region. It was a Sunday and he was unable to find a bus heading into Bordeaux. Instead, he boarded a service to Langon, which crossed the demarcation line between the ZNO and the occupied northern zone. At a checkpoint he was ordered off to have his papers examined; he was carrying his radio in a suitcase. When two Germans instructed him to open it, Labit told them to open it themselves. As their attention was diverted, he pulled out his pistol and shot them and five other soldiers, before making a run for it. The gunfire drew in other troops who gave chase. When he realized he could not escape, the 21-year-old bit on his cyanide pill and died instantly.

More bad news came through in the summer of 1943. Radio agent Gilbert Norman, PROSPER's organizer Francis Suttill and a courier called Andrée Borrel had been arrested on 24 June and taken to the notorious headquarters of the SD at 84 Avenue Foch in Paris. Norman had been caught red-handed: he had his radio with him. The Germans saw this as an opportunity to try a *funkspiel* ('radio game') and they forced him to send fake messages to Baker Street. As

Resistance fighters in SCIENTIST country, SW France, c. 1942.

well as trying to get the British to accept misleading intelligence, it was hoped that SOE's replies would betray other agents. *Funkspiel* had been refined in the Netherlands by Abwehr Section IIIF under Major Hermann Giskes. He called it Operation NORDPOL ('North Pole'); the Allies called it '*Englandspiel*'.

The head of cryptology at SOE, Leo Marks, first became suspicious of these messages as a consequence of the way he and his FANY radio operators tackled the problem of 'indecipherables' – signals which could not be decrypted because of errors made by W/T operators in the field. During the training of agents a careful record was made of the mistakes they made in encoding. This information provided useful clues about the errors in illegible messages. It was a system that worked.[27] Hermann Giskes' team comprised professional and very competent radio operators who definitely did *not* make mistakes. So, over a short period of time, every one of SOE's agents in the Netherlands suddenly stopped sending 'indecipherables'. In Marks' opinion that was impossible, and he sounded the alarm.

His superiors at SOE did not believe him and refused to take action. Even when two agents escaped back to England and reported that the whole network had been compromised, they were arrested on suspicion that they had been 'turned' by the Germans. As a consequence, some fifty-four courageous Dutch agents were caught and executed by the Nazis. It was an unforgivable disaster – and now it was happening in Paris.

When the SD forced Gilbert Norman to compose a message they could send to SOE, he tried to warn London he had been captured and was working under duress. The Funkabwehr knew he had to include a security check to confirm the message was genuine. However, the check was a two-part action along the lines of 'make a mistake in the tenth and twentieth characters of the signal text'. Norman made the first mistake but not the second. Instead of this being taken as a warning, he received a message telling him to do his positive check correctly. The Germans tricked F section into sending two agents to investigate what had happened to PROSPER; one of them was captured. Norman was eventually sent to Mauthausen concentration camp and was killed there on 6 September 1944.

* * *

By the time de Baissac was recalled to the UK on 16 August 1943, Roger Landes had proved he was the obvious choice to take over leadership of the *réseau*. Second only to the challenge of disrupting the German occupation was the need to ensure that political infighting within SCIENTIST did not obstruct that priority objective.

Landes' network embraced the *Organisation Civiles et Militaire* (OCM) on the right of the political spectrum and the *Francs-Tireurs et Partisans* (FTP) on the left. The latter's base was among Bordeaux dock workers, while OCM's membership comprised right-wing former army officers and civil servants. These included André Grandclément, the son of an admiral who had served in the army between 1928 and 1934, when he was invalided out after a bad fall from a horse. He had established the OCM network in South-West France in 1941.

Until summer 1943 Grandclément was more than happy to accept the support of SCIENTIST (under the leadership of both Claude de Baissac and Roger Landes), which provided him with radio links to London and frequent deliveries of much-needed arms, ammunition and explosives

French Resistance leader and double agent André Grandclément.

for the supposed 40,000 *résistants* under his command. In the period to April 1944 Landes had used his radio to co-ordinate 143 drops at a rate of four per month.

But disaster struck in August, when the Gestapo arrested Grandclément's wife. Searching his house, they discovered a card index revealing the identities of many OCM leaders, and hundreds were arrested within days. Grandclément himself was detained in Paris. The local Gestapo chief offered to release him, his wife and his comrades if he showed them the locations of the arms dumps SCIENTISTS had helped the group accumulate. He told them, and later gave them a guided tour of the locations.

With the knowledge of the Germans, Grandclément contacted Roger Landes and suggested they meet at the house of Bordeaux police inspector, Charles Corbin. Landes agreed but went to the rendezvous with another radio operator, Marcel Defence ('Dédé le Basque'),* both armed. When the turncoat revealed his intentions, an angry Landes drew his gun. Perhaps it was the presence of the police officer and his wife and daughter that caused him to re-holster the weapon and let Grandclément depart in his Gestapo car. It was to prove a big mistake.

---

* It is unclear why Defence was known as 'Dédé le Basque'; he had a Scottish mother and a French father.

Without weapons and explosives SCIENTIST was impotent. Grandclément identified Roger Landes to the Germans, and they put a price on his head; it was time for him to head into Spain, and police officer Charles Corbin went with him. They left on 1 November 1943 and crossed the Pyrenees to face the usual sojourn in Franco's Miranda de Ebro camp. Landes finally reached England (by air from Gibraltar) on 15 January 1944; ten weeks of his valuable time lost. Shockingly, he was greeted by MI5 and accused of being a double agent. The absurdity of this was soon noted, and he was presented with the Military Cross.

* * *

Not bearing any grudges, Roger Landes was soon demanding to be sent back to France. The head of F section, Maurice Buckmaster, was unhappy with the idea, concerned that he might be too recognizable by the Gestapo in Bordeaux. It was March 1944, PROSPER and SCIENTIST had been lost and SOE now needed to prepare the ground for Operation JEDBURGH. There would be more, smaller *réseaux* (see map below), and overall control would come under command of SHAEF to ensure it worked in support of OVERLORD.

Landes convinced Buckmaster he was the man to set up the ACTOR network covering the area from Bordeaux south to the Spanish border. Its orders were to attack and destroy all communications available to the enemy: rail, roads and landline telephone and telegraph systems. The imminence of D-Day was no secret to the French or to the Germans (they just didn't know where it was going to take place).

On 28 February 1945 Landes and his fellow passenger, French-Canadian radio operator Allyre Louis Sirois ('Gustav') from Saskatchewan, were at RAF Tempsford in Buckinghamshire. As darkness fell, they climbed on board a Halifax of 138 Squadron with their kit and settled in for the uncomfortable two-hour flight south. Sirois was to move on to Toulouse, where he was to work for Captain Rechemann, a British-trained Frenchman. But the curse of Landes continued to plague him. After repeated overflights his pilot, Flight Lieutenant Johnson, could see no Morse signal from the ground and turned north again for Tempsford.

They tried once more the next evening, and this time a flashing torch confirmed he was over the landing zone at Marsac, 60km (37 miles) north-west of Toulouse as the crow flies. But it was windy, and the pilot was concerned about flying as low as 500ft; he climbed to 1,000ft, and the two agents jumped through the hole in the belly of the aircraft. Sirois went first,

SOE networks in France after the fall of PROSPER and SCIENTIST. The names of the networks are shown in *ITALIC CAPITALS*. The Nazis took over the 'free zone' in November 1942 and the Italian zone in September 1943.

closely followed by his radio and then Roger Landes. But as Landes got closer to the ground the wind caused him to swing violently. He pulled hard at the suspension lines trying to stabilize his descent, but it was too late, and he hit the ground hard. Unable to get to his feet and in great pain, it became obvious he had been seriously injured.[28] The shock had badly jarred his spine, and there was a sharp pain in one of his ankles.

Among the reception committee was a burly farmer called Arthur. Landes told him to leave and get clear of the landing ground; the sound of the Halifax's four engines would have attracted the attention of the Germans or the Milice. But Arthur leaned down, pulled the diminutive agent up into a sitting position and slung him – fire-fighter style – over his shoulders. The

SOE W/T operator Roger Landes dressed to jump. Note the parachute by the door behind him.

SOE man then suffered the indignity of being carried across the fields to a reception base that had been set up at a farm.

Someone at the farm had the good sense and grace to start cooking omelettes, while Arthur struggled to get Landes' boot off. The ankle was swollen and painful to the touch. Omelettes consumed, Arthur bound up the damaged ankle, slung Landes over his shoulders again and set off to carry him the *five kilometres* to the village of Marsac. Roger Landes was not a big chap, but he must have weighed a lot more than a newborn calf. The reaction of Madame Daubeze when they turned up on her doorstep has not been recorded. She was a member of the local resistance group and lived in the house with her mother and two daughters; her husband was a guest of the Germans at a prisoner-of-war camp.

As they got Landes on to a bed, another member of the reception committee arrived with his suitcase. Landes looked at it in horror; the case had dropped into a pond and was sodden. But it wasn't a radio this time. When Landes opened a concealed compartment, his hosts gasped as he started to peel off bundles of cash. Madame Daubeze and her family carefully pegged it to indoor washing lines in the hope it would dry. There was a million francs there. Meanwhile, Allyre Louis Sirois (Gustav), who had landed with his radio and both legs intact, had been whisked off to Toulouse. The network there was awaiting the arrival of Captain Rechemann, who was in the process of being inserted by sea.

Seeing Landes' ankle, Madame Daubeze promptly grounded him. When the doctor arrived he declared that the unfortunate 'fall' had wrecked the tendons in his lower leg but no bones had been broken. The remedy was cold compresses to get the swelling down, and three weeks of bed rest. It could have been a lot worse; the agent was now far more worried about the danger his presence was imposing on Madame Daubeze, her family, the doctor and the local *réseau*. The concern was well-founded; 24 hours after his arrival the same Halifax made the journey from RAF Tempsford and dropped supplies. Heavy aircraft overhead two nights in succession concerned the Germans enough for them to start house-to-house searches throughout the village.

That wasn't the only hazard. Although the local *réseaux* were doing their best to make the enemy's control of the region as uncomfortable as possible, the level of arrests was high. This attrition was mainly caused by the continued aid being given by the hated traitor André Grandclément and his wife, Lucette. This contrasted starkly with the care being heaped on Roger Landes by the Daubeze family. Every time he tried to get out of bed, they pushed him back, careless of their own safety. But the enthusiasm with which the Wehrmacht started its search of the village soon petered out and, when they reached the Daubezes' street, they gave up. However, bad news now arrived: the doctor and Madame Daubeze's brother-in-law had both been arrested on 6 March. Landes was appalled, believing he might have been the cause, but he was reassured that this wasn't the case. The doctor had given medical care to a group of injured American flyers who had been trying to reach Spain. When they were later captured they told the Germans who had patched them up.[29]

When the German patrols in Marsac thinned out, the redoubtable Madame Daubeze started to take her guest for walks under cover of darkness. Maybe her idea was to convince him that he should stay in bed, but it didn't work – as his ankle healed he became even more determined to get to Bordeaux and start work reorganizing the networks and renewing the attacks on enemy communications. On 14 March she finally gave in; the doctor's prescribed six weeks of bed-rest had barely lasted a fortnight. Landes bade farewell to the brave Daubeze family and limped off for a 30km (19 miles) walk south-west to the village of Auch to make contact with a truck driver who had agreed to take him a further 75km (47 miles) south to Adé, just outside Lourdes. From there he would be able to catch a train 200km (124 miles) north-west to Bordeaux.

Everything went to plan, and Roger Landes stepped off the train at 12.30 pm the following day. He mingled with the crowd of arriving passengers and strolled out of the station unaccosted. His first port of call the following day was Madame Jacqueline Desport; she was able to bring him up to date on all his other contacts. Not immediately available were a man who had died of a heart attack and another who, after sabotaging two flying boats in the harbour, had taken to the hills with the Maquis. Quite a few others had also joined the Maquis, leaving Landes short-handed.

Once he had identified the location and size of any active groups which could form the foundation of ACTOR, he knew exactly what had to be done next. The first arms drop took place at the end of March at a location south-west of Bordeaux to a reception committee drawn from a group of 300 resistance fighters and commanded by Christian Campet ('Lancelot'), a police inspector. The next delivery came ten days later; the RAF Halifax made one pass to drop containers and a second to drop two men. It was a belated start for Roger Landes, but by D-Day members of ACTOR were blowing up rail track and points, cutting overhead power lines and telephone cables and demolishing bridges up and down South-West France.

A key factor in the success of these operations was the negotiating skill Landes used to persuade the local Maquis – or *Forces françaises de l'interieur* (FFI) as

Bordeaux Maquis leader Leon Dussarat.

de Gaulle had renamed them – to co-operate in combined operations. Not only did they co-operate with SOE, they began to work with each other. As always, the offer of arms drops was a great inducement. In response to an approach by Landes in early April, Maquis leader Leon Dussarat agreed to combine his forces of 700 maquisards and arrange no fewer than fifteen drop zones. Good radio contact with London enabled air deliveries to start in a matter of days. The RAF needed to confirm the drop sites were viable, and each was then given a code name, a letter (to be signalled in Morse with a torch) and a phrase in French to be used by the BBC in its *messages personnels* to signal the date of the flight. This arrangement enabled Roger Landes to stay out of the operational loop for each shipment; the less physical contact he had with the Maquis in the hills, the better.

The plan worked smoothly until 30 April, when the parachutes on a drop of twelve standard C-containers and eight other packages failed to deploy. The wireless sets were wrecked. A report of this serious incident reached the RAF on 12 May; at that stage of the behind-the-lines attrition against the occupying forces it was not a critical loss, but something had gone very wrong at the packing centre, and the next faulty parachute might be attached to an agent rather than a container. When, at the end of May, Landes informed London he had 1,220 fighters in ACTOR all ready and willing to support the impending invasion in the north, they had no hesitation in meeting his radioed requests for further supplies. He was promoted to the rank of major a few weeks later.

Throughout the summer of 1944 Landes received alarming reports that 'Bernard' – the turncoat André Grandclément – was using a devious scheme to divert Maquis resistance fighters to his own group. He had produced a forged letter, purportedly signed by the former head of the network, Claude de Baissac, in which he claimed to support Bernard's plan to work with the Germans against the Bolsheviks. Roger Landes had become desperate to put Grandclément out of action, and his luck suddenly changed on 26 July, when he got a message from Alban Borde ('George'), the leader of the *réseau* in the city of Bordeaux. A fighter had been given the singular task of hunting down Bernard and killing him. This man, 'Merilhac', had achieved something that had evaded the rest

Bordeaux Gestapo chief Friedrich Dhose. Photograph probably taken on his arrest.

of ACTOR – he had found Grandclément and his wife Lucette living with a young bodyguard, Marc Duluguet, near Arcachon on the coast 50km west of Bordeaux.

The BCRA had already ordered their execution. Bernard may have known about this, so when 'George' offered to help him get to safety in the UK, where he could make the case for his pro-Vichy stance, Grandclément readily agreed. There would be a delay, he was told, while they made radio contact with London and arranged for them to send a Lysander.[30]

The SOE team agreed that Grandclément's treachery had resulted in the death of too many comrades and relatives to justify any action other than the one they were about to take. André Bouillard shot André Grandclément, Christian Campet shot the bodyguard Marc Duluguet and Roger Landes shot Lucette Grandclément in the back of the head with his .45 automatic pistol. As the network's commander he could not order anyone else to do it.

Daylight drop of arms, ammunition and explosives from multiple aircraft in Corrèze, near Tulle, 14 July 1944.

The first thing Landes did on arrival back at Bordeaux was signal London with news of the executions. The response was, 'Good work!'[31]

On Tuesday, 29 August 1944 a newspaper appeared on the streets of Bordeaux. Entitled *Sud-Ouest* ('South-West'), it was published by Jacques Lemoine. The front-page headline read BORDEAUX A FÊTÉ SA LIBÉRATION ('Bordeaux Celebrated its Liberation') above the subtitle *Les dernières troupes allemandes avaient quitté la ville dimanche dans la nuit*

The people of Bordeaux celebrate the departure of German forces, 28 August 1944.

('The last German troops have left the city on Sunday night'). The people of Bordeaux had literally danced in the streets throughout Monday.

ACTOR's W/T operators continued to co-ordinate with SFHQ in London to ensure that the Maquis were able to harass the German

General Charles de Gaulle, leader of the Free French forces, arrives on 17 September 1944 at Mérignac airport for his visit to Bordeaux.

retreat. Roger Landes continued to be a diligent radio operator and, in the interests of safety, continually switched his transmission points between three locations. At the same time, his job as chief of ACTOR was becoming more complicated. More JEDBURGH agents had been parachuted into the region, and even a team of ex-pat Spanish republican fighters had helped to liberate the city.

SOE W/T operator and commander of the ACTOR network Major Roger Landes MC & Bar, LdH, CdeG, aged twenty-nine.

Further to the east, American and French forces had arrived on the Mediterranean coast on 15 August 1944. Operation DRAGOON had left from Corsica and landed on the beaches of Cavalaire-sur-Mer, Saint-Tropez and Saint-Raphaël between Toulon and Cannes. The GARDENER and JOCKEY networks provided the invaders with local intelligence and support, and it took only four weeks for them to meet up with General George S. Patton's forces near Dijon.

As the fighting ended, French politics took over. Charles de Gaulle saw votes in claiming a victory that was not solely his, and news came through that he was due to fly in for a visit on 17 September 1944. Local resistance groups buried their differences for a while, and Roger Landes graciously took on a new role as British liaison officer to the FFI. He was invited to attend official events and dusted off his British Army uniform bearing the crowns of a major on the epaulettes.

But when Landes was eventually introduced to de Gaulle, the general peered down at the small Paris-born Briton and said, 'Vous êtes Anglais? Votre place n'est pas ici.' ('You are English? Your place is not here.') The men and women who had fought alongside 'Aristide' to resist the Nazi occupation of their country looked askance. De Gaulle then made matters worse by ordering Landes to leave the country within 48 hours. Word of the incident quickly spread among the ordinary folk of Bordeaux, and some 4,000 people gathered in the street in front of Landes' base at the Hôtel de Bordeaux. Most of them were members of the FFI, still armed to the teeth and shouting, 'Aristide au balcon! Aristide au balcon!' Landes resisted the urging of his aides to wave from the balcony, rightly believing London would be unhappy if he stirred up rebellion against France's next president. Instead, he went to his wireless location at Rue de Guynemer and reported the situation to SFHQ, asking for advice. Getting no immediate reply, he set off on a tour of the region, meeting many of the *résistants* for the first time. They expressed gratitude for his efforts; de Gaulle was not popular in this part of France.

The general's ingratitude extended to other British officers he came across, including George Starr (WHEELWRIGHT) and Peter Lake (FOOTMAN); it was an insult to all those many SOE agents, male and female, who had been tortured and killed by the Gestapo. In fact, de Gaulle had sacked all British officers serving in France and French officers who had co-operated with the SOE and SIS. His objective was clear: Britain was to be denied any credit for liberation from German rule.

Landes eventually arrived back in London on 10 October 1944. Maurice Buckmaster took one look at him and sent him to hospital. He thought he had a liver complaint and had lost over 12kg since D-Day, but he recovered after a period of rest. In any case, the Japanese were a long way from surrendering, so he volunteered for SOE's 'Force 136' operating in the Far East. In Malaya he taught Chinese guerrillas how to encode and decode messages and transmit and receive them on radio sets.

Back in the UK, a year on, Roger Landes received a bar to his Military Cross. Decades later, when the French were trying to right the injustices meted out by Charles de Gaulle, he was awarded the Croix de Guerre and the Légion d'Honneur.

Chapter 7

Signing Off

This book is an expression of admiration for the young men and women who travelled to war in the dead of night. Their means of transport – boat or aeroplane – would inevitably announce their arrival behind the front line. Those W/T operators who evaded immediate capture with a functioning radio then broadcast their presence on frequencies constantly monitored by the enemy.

Throughout the whole war there were many fewer radio agents than troops who splashed ashore on any of the five Normandy beaches at dawn on 6 June 1944. At one level they performed an essential but purely utilitarian function: to maintain regular contact with their home base. But many went beyond that to become 'organizers', network leaders responsible for some of the most outstanding *coups de main* of the war. One such W/T operator was Odd Starheim.

In southern Norway Odd Starheim keys a message to his home base in the UK.

By the age of twenty-three Starheim had already served five years in the Norwegian merchant navy as a radio operator. When Germany invaded, he joined the army to fight the occupiers but was captured. He quickly escaped and crossed the border to Sweden. Unable to find anyone to help him reach Britain, he returned to Norway, and from there he hitched a ride on a boat headed across the North Sea. But the appalling weather on 11 August 1940 forced them back. Two days later, they were more successful and reached Aberdeen.

Before his bones had warmed up Starheim volunteered for 'special duties'. The Royal Victoria Patriotic School recommended him to MI6, but there was no chance such a man would go unnoticed, and he was snapped up by SOE. Five months later, a Royal Navy submarine surfaced off Norway and sent the agent and his radio off in a canoe. Starheim paddled hard and bailed frantically for three miles through choppy waters to reach the shore. From there he had a 25-mile trek over snow-covered ground to his local base.

It was early days for covert operations in occupied Norway, so his first task was to recruit scouts to observe enemy warships passing Flekkefjord from their home ports in the Baltic. It was from one of these observers that a new courier brought him a report of a battleship heading out to the Atlantic; it was the *Bismarck*. Over the next few months he radioed a hundred succinct and accurately-coded messages; his years of experience as a merchant marine W/T operator were paying off. 'Who is this boy? I would serve with him anywhere' was scrawled across one of his signals at the Admiralty.

In the summer of 1941 the Funkabwehr was regularly D/F-ing his radio and, rather than risk their major asset falling into the grasp of the Gestapo, SOE brought him back to London. However, by October he was in Norway once more, this time sending intelligence from an apartment in Oslo. Unfortunately, this new base proved short-lived, and he had to escape through a window when German search teams surrounded the building.

The 600-ton ship *Galtesund* worked the south and west coasts, shuttling passengers and cargo between Kristiansand, Stavanger and Bergen. On 15 March 1942, when she made a routine stop at Flekkefjord, west of Kristiansand, five new passengers came on board. They had luggage with them, but that wasn't unusual. What was exceptional was that they had weapons concealed in the bags. Once out to sea, their leader, Odd Starheim, produced a hand gun, forced his way on to the bridge, closed down the *Galtesund*'s radio and gave the captain a course for Aberdeen. The first the owners – and the Germans – knew that something was amiss was when the handling agents at the ship's destination reported her overdue. The Luftwaffe failed to locate her, and three days later she tied up alongside a dock in Aberdeen.

The reaction of the ship's crew and passengers to their unanticipated refugee status is unknown. But in exchange for his audacious action and a cargo of tobacco, chocolate, margarine, explosives and truck tyres, the British awarded Starheim the Distinguished Service Order (DSO).

In March 1943, Odd Starheim's body was discovered on a beach at Tjörn, just north of Gothenburg on Sweden's west coast. On 28 February he had tried to repeat his *Galtesund* exploit by hijacking another coastal steamer, the *Tromöysund*, also from Flekkefjord. But this time the Germans responded more speedily and sank the ship, killing all forty-four people on board, including thirteen SOE agents. The Norwegian War Cross was added to Starheim's DSO.

*   *   *

American W/T operator Virginia Hall helped repatriate many downed airmen and escaped PoWs. Alexander Foot and Alexander Radó of the *Rote Kapelle* ensured that priceless intelligence on Hitler's conduct of the war reached Red Army commanders in Moscow. Martin Clemens, Paul Mason and William Bennett were just three of the Coastwatchers whose invaluable support of the US and Australian military stymied a Japanese invasion of Australia. Through MI6 Atle Svardal kept the RAF and the Royal Navy informed of German warship movements along Norway's coast. In France, Nancy Wake and Denis Rake flirted with gullible Boche officers – but only one of them was serious. Arthur Brown was central to Tommy Macpherson's success in delaying the arrival of the SS Das Reich armoured division at the Normandy beachheads.

As if in defiance of their original life expectancy, many of these gallant individuals lived on into their eighties and nineties.

Chapter 8

Technical Briefings

The purpose of these four briefing sections is to provide the reader with short introductions to the technical aspects of a Wireless/Telegraphy operator's 'day at the office'. They are not intended to make you an expert.

8.1 The Radio Sets

The Leading Edge

The radios developed at the research establishments of SIS and SOE were designed to be as small as possible; not an easy undertaking in pre-transistor and pre-microchip days. Valves ('tubes' or 'vacuum tubes' in American English) were the unavoidable and most unreliable component of all these sets; if they were hot and took a knock they could fail terminally. So replacements were always needed, and sets were built so the agent could remove a faulty component and, without too much trouble, plug in a spare. If he or she didn't have a spare, they were out of business until the next air drop or Lysander touch-down. The other essential components were the plug-in 'crystals' used to generate the precisely timed signal frequencies needed for radio transmission and reception.

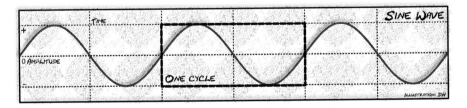

The frequency of a signal is measured in terms of 'cycles per second' or 'Hertz' (abbreviated to 'Hz'). Frequency is related to 'wavelength'. The wavelength of the signal in the above illustration is shown as two intervals. If we double the frequency (from three to six waves) we halve the wavelength. The sets are called 'short-wave radios' because the frequencies they used were in the High Frequency (HF) band of 1.7–30 Megahertz (MHz) – wavelength 176.3–10.0m. Knowing the wavelength was important; 50 per cent was the optimum length of the single-wire aerial for that transmission. If an agent is transmitting at 30 MHz, his antenna needs to be 5 metres long.

A commonly used radio, the Mk VII Paraset, operated on a range of 3.0 to 7.6 MHz. The range of the human ear is between 20 and 20,000 Hz (20 kHz), so the listener would only know a signal was present if it could be heard through a speaker or headphones.

Continuous Wave (CW)

Sets could handle either Morse code or voice or both. Each has advantages and disadvantages. Morse works by switching the constant carrier wave (CW) on and off. The Morse key (sometimes called a 'telegraph key') is a fancy switch.

When the key, the control at the right (above), is gripped between thumb and forefinger and pressed down (*never* tapped), a contact is made and the carrier wave is transmitted until the key is released again. The knurled knobs are used to adjust the distance of travel to suit the preferences of the operator. This is how the dots and dashes of Morse are created: short and long depressions of the key. CW sets use less power, are more compact and are faster than voice for sending encrypted messages.

Voice radio is more complicated than CW. Instead of the carrier being switched on and off, it has to be modulated (bent) to represent the sound waves of the human voice as received through a microphone.

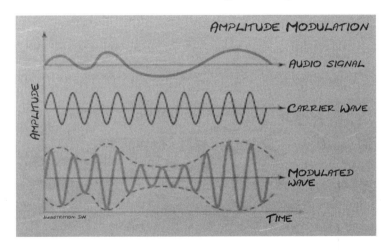

Of course, at the receiving end, the radio has to extract the audio signal from the modulated carrier and present it through a pair of headphones or a speaker (the latter not a wonderful idea for an agent working in some unsuspecting host's spare bedroom).

Trop Scatter

The *range* of portable short-wave radios is an important consideration. The distance from the coast of central Norway to the receiving stations in the English Midlands is some 1,200km (750 miles). From the former Yugoslavia to the same receivers it is over 1,800km (1,100 miles). How does a 6-volt DC set producing only 5 watts of power cover such distances? The troposphere comes to the rescue.

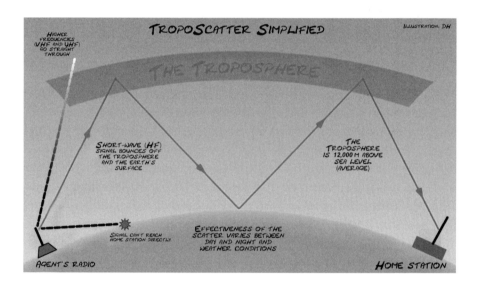

The troposphere covers the whole planet at an average altitude of 12,000m (39,000ft). Signals in the High Frequency band of 1.7 to 30 MHz bounce off the troposphere back to Earth (preferably to something fairly smooth like an ocean) and then up again. This cycle can repeat over huge distances. The schedules ('skeds') given to agents would take account of the time of day and give the best frequencies for each transmission. (See Chapter 8.3 below)

The Components

So, what are the main components of a short-wave radio? A useful illustration is a CW/voice set called a 'Teleradio'. This was used by the Australian Coastwatchers, and each component came in its own very visible box.

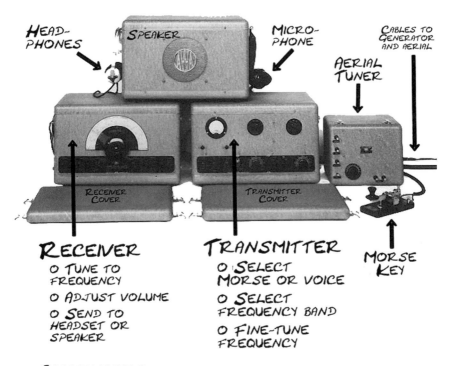

HEAD-
PHONES

SPEAKER

MICRO-
PHONE

CABLES TO
GENERATOR
AND AERIAL

AERIAL
TUNER

RECEIVER
COVER

TRANSMITTER
COVER

RECEIVER

O TUNE TO
FREQUENCY

O ADJUST VOLUME

O SEND TO
HEADSET OR
SPEAKER

TRANSMITTER

O SELECT
MORSE OR VOICE

O SELECT
FREQUENCY BAND

O FINE-TUNE
FREQUENCY

MORSE
KEY

AWA COASTWATCHERS RADIO SET

ILLUSTRATION: DH

Amateur radio enthusiasts ('radio hams') call big sets 'boat anchors'. The Amalgamated Wireless (Australasia) Ltd (AWA) Model 3B shown above was more of a 'boat sinker'. The boxes were all made from steel and had covers to protect the dials during transportation. The dimensions of the two main boxes are identical: 41cm wide, 26cm high and 26cm deep (14 by 10 by 10 inches). The whole set weighed over 100kg (220lbs) – think in terms of five suitcases each right on an airline's economy-class baggage limit. And don't forget the 12-volt lead-acid battery ('accumulator') needed to power the set. That would add a further 18kg (about 40lbs); plus another 18kg if you are prudently carrying a spare. Mains electricity supply was scarce on the Pacific islands, especially on the summits of jungle-clad mountains, so the Coastwatchers recharged their batteries with a 'portable' petrol (gasoline) generator which, according to Commander Eric Feldt, weighed 32kg (70lbs).[1] And fuel was needed for that, of course. The total weight was 168kg (370lbs), plus the weight of the jerry cans of petrol at about 20kg each including the can.

Cartoon from Alex Perrin's book *The Private War of the Spotters.*

Australia's and New Zealand's Coastwatchers did not develop the Teleradio themselves – they inherited it. The set had two characteristics which distinguished it from the radios being developed in Europe. First, it was able to handle both Morse and voice traffic. The latter proved to be a great advantage when sending urgent signals; for example, when Coastwatchers needed to alert other islands to squadrons of Japanese bombers passing overhead in their direction. But the ability to pick up a microphone and switch to voice had an impact on the size and power demands of the Teleradio. Protection against damp, fungus and mildew were far higher priorities than portability. The rule of thumb was that it took about twelve sturdy islanders to reposition one of these sets.

A powerful multifunctional radio in a fixed location was a luxury developers in Europe could not afford. Portability had to be very high in the list of design criteria.

Developed in 1941 by Major John Brown of SOE, the Type 3 Mk II (below, usually called the 'B2') was small for its day – especially when compared with the Teleradio. It sent at frequencies between 3 and 16 MHz (CW) at 20 watts and had a range of over 1,000km. But it still weighed 15kg in a cardboard suitcase. Trying to carry it through a village as though it

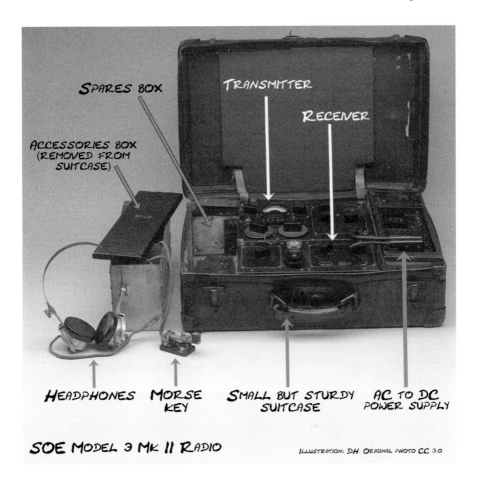

SPARES BOX

TRANSMITTER

RECEIVER

ACCESSORIES BOX
(REMOVED FROM
SUITCASE)

HEADPHONES   MORSE   SMALL BUT STURDY   AC TO DC
KEY   SUITCASE   POWER SUPPLY

SOE MODEL 3 Mk II RADIO   ILLUSTRATION: DH. ORIGINAL PHOTO CC 3.0

just contained your laundry would be difficult. Later models such as the 'A3' (Model A Mk. III) got the weight under 10kg, with a narrower frequency range of 3.2 to 9.55 MHz and reduced power output of 5 watts.

The Mk VII Paraset was developed by the Royal Signals Special Communications Unit at Little Horwood and at SIS Section VIII Whaddon Hall. It was known as the Paraset because it was designed to improve the chances of surviving a drop by parachute. It is often described as an SOE radio, but although SOE certainly used it (the Norwegian agent Oluf Reed-Olsen had one), it was originally developed for MI6. Its official name was the 'Whaddon MkVII'.

The lightness of the Paraset made it the 'must have' radio for SIS agents, but there was a cost to be paid. The transceiver had to be physically switched between transmit and receive and, according to M. R. D. Foot, the noise this created would cause interference to any other sets within 100m.[2] Also, it was impossible for the agent to hear the Morse he was sending. The signalling

The 'A3' (Model A Mk. III) radio set in an attaché case. Note the 12in wooden ruler at front.

An SIS/MI6 Mark 7 Paraset radio concealed in a small suitcase. (*Photo by Timitrius – Flickr: CC BY-SA 2.0*)

range was not as good as the 'B2' or its smaller successor, the 'A3' (see the comparison table below).

COMPARISON OF RADIOS	SOE Type 3 Mk II 'B2'	SOE Model A Mk III 'A3'	SIS Mk VII 'Paraset'
Transmit	3–16 MHz	3.2–9.55 MHz	3.0–7.6 MHz
Receive	3.1–15.2 MHz	3.2–5.25 MHz	3.0–7.6 MHz
Power	20–30 watts	5 watts	4–5 watts
Range	800–1,000km	> 800 km	700km
Weight	15kg	< 4.1kg (ex-PSU)	2kg (ex-PSU)

Comparison of SOE and SIS radio sets. 'PSU' = Power Supply Unit.

The signalling range was very much a function of the care taken by the W/T operator to get the length and orientation of the aerial right. (See section on Aerials below.)

SOE and SIS each tended to be most enthusiastic about the radios they had developed themselves. In the summer of 1943, when SOE started the training of the agents for Operation JEDBURGH, the preferred short-wave set was the 'B2' – now nicknamed the 'Jedset'. (See Chapter 6.3 France above.)

Size did matter. Much ingenuity was invested in finding ways to conceal radios in transit. The smallest were hidden in bundles of kindling, at the bottom of babies' prams and even in hollowed-out books. But the suitcase was the commonest and considered the most convenient means of transport.

Radio set concealed in bundle of kindling. (*UK National Archive: HS 7/28*)

Aerials

The aerials used by short-wave radios were about as simple as they could be: an extended piece of insulated wire about half or a quarter of the wavelength of the frequency being used. For example, the wavelength of 8MHz is 37.5 metres, so a half-length antenna needs to be 18.75m. The length did not have to be dead accurate, because the radios included a control that enabled them to be fine-tuned.

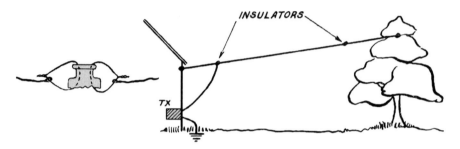

Illustration of an externally-rigged aerial from the manual for the SOE Type A Mark 1 radio. (*Marion Hearfield. www.johnhearfield.com/WSA/WSA.htm*)

SOE's early Type A Mark 1 radio was based on the British Army's Wireless Set No. 18 Mk III and could handle both CW (Morse) and voice communications. On the outbreak of war in 1939, Norman Hearfield was working as a radio technician in Leeds. He immediately joined the RAF and was issued with the Type A Mark 1. He kept it. Decades later, his son John found the operator's manual in his father's files and decided to publish it.

An illustration from the manual (above) shows how an antenna could be rigged horizontally, outdoors where possible. It stresses the importance of ensuring the aerial is insulated and even suggests an ingeniously improvised insulator using the neck of a bottle. The radio's suitcase includes 60ft (18m) of aerial as standard and recommends using a minimum of 25ft. Earthing is important, and the drawing

An insulated wire antenna extending up the trunk of a tree. (*UK National Archive HS 7/49*)

shows the transmitter earthed in preferably moist ground. Antennae can also be deployed vertically, as shown in the photograph opposite.

Any external aerial is going to risk revealing the W/T operator's location to a sharp-eyed enemy searcher. The options for concealment are limited, but one possibility was to disguise it as a washing line.

A wire antenna concealed inside a braided clothes line. (*UK National Archive HS 7/49*)

Aerials can also be extended indoors, but you would probably need to be in a dance hall to accommodate 18 metres. Helpfully, the Type A Mk 1 manual has another schematic (see above) showing a possible indoor radio installation.

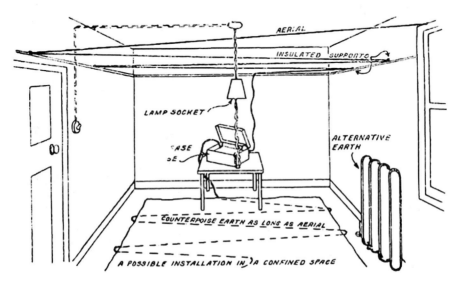

Illustration of an internally-rigged aerial from the manual for the SOE Type A Mark 1 radio. (*Marion Hearfield. www.johnhearfield.com/WSA/WSA.htm*)

Clearly, this is not something that can be set up in haste; nor would a quick escape from marauding Funkabwehr troops be possible. Also, the rigging of the aerial is dependent on the presence of picture rails – not a common feature of modern homes.

Vertical Delivery

This book contains many accounts of the RAF (and the USAAF) inadvertently delivering W/T operators and their radio sets to two different locations. Reuniting the agent with his beloved B2 or Paraset then became an onerous task, especially if the moon was the sole source of light. The proximity of enemy patrols sometimes forced agents to vacate the scene in haste, leaving them to watch from a distant treeline as the enemy harvested the sets.

The SOE had a practical solution: tie the radio to its operator. In his excellent 1960 book[3] agent Ben Cowburn described how this worked when dropping from a converted Whitley bomber into France in early September 1941:

> Only the wireless-transmitter which one of my fellow-passengers was taking had its own special packing. It hung in a foam-rubber-lined bag from the roof of the fuselage directly above the exit-hole in the floor. It was to be attached by strops to its owner's rigging, so that both George (all wireless-operators were known as 'George' in those days) and his transmitter would go down together under the same parachute …
>
> Inside the fuselage with us were the R.A.F. sergeants who were to act as dispatchers. They brought refreshments and gave us information. In particular, it was the dispatcher's job to attach the automatic-opening strop, known as the static line, to your parachute. The principle is that, as operational parachutists are dropped, for accuracy, from too low an altitude to have time to open the canopy themselves, the bag containing the parachute is tethered by means of this strop to a point inside the fuselage. As the man drops away and the strop is pulled taut, it holds back the bag, thus liberating the canopy a short distance below the plane …
>
> George IX, the owner of the transmitter, lay forward of the hole, and I just aft of it, with the four other 'bodies' further along the fuselage. The order of exit was to be: first George and his wireless-set, then myself, then one more man.
>
> We all seemed to have no difficulty in dropping off to sleep as we were advised to do by the dispatcher with the assurance that he would see we did not 'miss our station'. In fact he had to awaken me from a nap to say we were passing over Tours and that we should soon reach the target …

We were losing height and then came the news that the ground-signals had been spotted. George and I moved right up to the opposite edges of the hole with the radio-bag swaying between us. A little red light appeared on the wall. George swung his feet down into the hole and remained poised on the edge by his hands. The dispatcher raised his arm, the engine note changed, and the floor heaved up and down as the captain levelled out at the altitude of 500 feet prescribed for dropping. The red light changed to green, down came the dispatcher's arm, and George and his radio-bag vanished with a crash, leaving nothing but the strop of the static line hanging down through the hole.

Cowburn was next to plunge through the hole and experience the blast of the slipstream and the sharp tug as the static line pulled his parachute open: 'I hit the ground with a crack sooner than I expected,' he wrote. He had been dropped from just 300ft.

The reception committee included 'George I', whom he names as 'George Noble', the first SOE W/T operator to be parachuted into France. George Noble – real name Georges Bégué – had been delivered 'blind' four months earlier. (See Chapter 6.1 above)

8.2 Counter-measures

Signals intelligence

The problem with radio is that anyone with a suitable receiver (able to tune to the same frequency as the transmitter) can hear what is being sent. The objective of signals intelligence (SIGINT) is to receive and record (by hand) all such broadcasts from a zone of interest and decrypt them into clear text that can then be analysed. This is what the Royal Signals Corps Y-service and the Government Code and Cypher School (GC&CS) did in concert at Bletchley Park, and the GdNA (*Oberkommando des Heeres/General der Nachrichtenaufklärung*) did for the Wehrmacht. GdNA was less automated and less centralized than GC&CS. (See Chapter 8.4 Briefing on Cryptology below)

German records of counter-intelligence radio operations reveal that the number of agent-operated stations intercepted in occupied Norway during the period to the end of 1943 was only seventeen. Two of those were identified as being controlled from Moscow and the rest from London. Lieutenant General Albert Praun, Chief of German Army Signal Communications, said this about the performance of the radio-intercept platoons during the invasion and eventual occupation:

The mobile operation of an intercept platoon in the Norwegian Campaign in 1940 suffered from all the defects inherent in inadequately prepared improvised operations. A few radio operators were picked from each of six different [German] units in the West, but no translators or cryptanalysts. The equipment was also inadequate. Later on, there was no shipping space to move the platoon up in time and close enough to the German operations staff and the enemy area which war covered, nor was the platoon given any data or instructions.[4]

There was constant pressure on agents in the field to get their coding procedures right; encryption usually took longer than the transmission itself, but failure to do it properly could render the intelligence illegible at the home station.

General Erich Petersen, Field Marshal Erwin Rommel and General Albert Praun. (*Bundesarchiv*)

German direction-finding

SIGINT activity did not carry the same immediate danger as being detected by the SS and the Gestapo; the likely outcome of being caught with a radio strapped to the back of your bicycle was death. The Germans did not rely on catching agents transporting radios; they were equipped to detect and capture them in the act of transmitting messages back to the enemy in Britain. For this task specialist equipment was needed, sets that would not only detect signals across the short-wave frequency band but also *the direction from which the signal was being sent*. This is known as 'radio direction-finding', RDF or sometimes D/F. Shown below is the Fu.NP.E Radio Direction Finder, a commonly-used set.

RDF sets have antennae which can be rotated. When the aerial is 'pointing' directly at the transmitting radio, the signal will suddenly die; this is known as the 'null signal'. The bearing of the covert set can then be read off in degrees and plotted on a map from the known position of the D/F receiver.

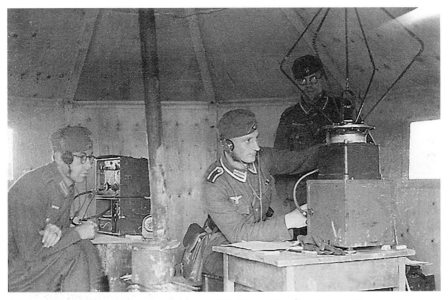

An Fu.NP.E RDF set being operated from a fixed base. Note the shape of the antenna.

The sets can be in fixed locations on land, usually as high as possible, in positions that provide coverage of areas most likely to include an enemy observation post. In the case of Operation ROSKA (see Chapter 2.6), it was assumed to be positioned with a clear view across the fairway leading from

A mobile RP2a unit in a trailer. Note the different configuration of the antenna.

Inside a mobile RP2a station. The dial on the right is the frequency-selector. The operator's hand is on the wheel that rotates the antenna until he hears the signal die. He can then read off the bearing from the scale above the wheel.

the north into Florø. However, in general terms, fixed-location RDF sets would be tasked with monitoring a very wide area of interest. Mobile D/F stations offered much greater flexibility and, if the enemy radio was unwise enough to stay on the air too long, a chance to reposition to obtain additional bearings.

RDF stations could also be mounted on warships and patrol boats. In Norway, the Germans frequently used requisitioned fishing vessels. Direction-finding was also done from the air using Fieseler Storch light aircraft.

The RDF set being used on the aircraft in the photograph above seems to be a PeilG 5 manufactured by Telefunken. The loop antenna could be manually controlled from the passenger seat in the cockpit. But a post-war German report suggested that this apparently excellent idea was useless in the mountains.

A Fieseler Storch Fi 156 landing on a mud track. It appears to be fitted with a D/F antenna below the rear passenger seat. Eastern Front, 1943.

The use of D/F aeroplanes (Fieseler Storch) in Norway was ineffective. One can quote the following reasons: owing to the atmospheric and geographical conditions the aeroplanes could only be used during the summer. Even during this time the Fieseler Storch, (the only one, stationed at Fornebu) could not get a single cross-bearing valuable for the mobile D/F. Besides all [enemy radio] operators were warned to look out for this sort of aircraft.[5]

Allied successes in the breaking of ENIGMA, LORENZ and other codes are well known today. But how good were the Germans at breaking the ciphers used by the Allies? The British planned a post-war operation to interview all prisoners of war who had worked in SIGINT. When the Americans learned about this plan (called TICOM – Target Intelligence Committee), they insisted on becoming involved. The existence of TICOM remained a secret for many years (long after ENIGMA became public knowledge), but most of its interviews and reports are now available.[6]

Countering the counter-measures

Of particular interest is TICOM /I-148, which concerns Norway.

Most TICOM documents are transcripts of interviews with PoWs. Occasionally, however, the interrogators would give their subjects 'homework' and send them off to write their own accounts of designated topics of interest. The effectiveness of this was a function of the prisoner's willingness to

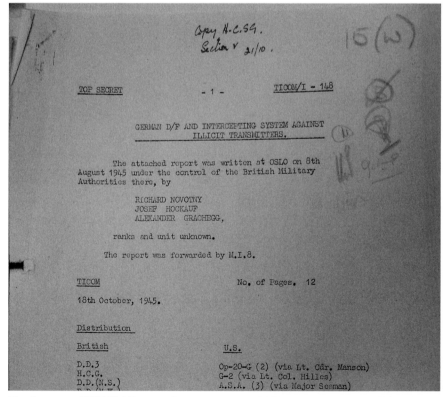

The first page of TICOM/I-148, a German account of RDF operations against SIS and SOE radio agents in Norway.

co-operate; some were unrepentant Nazis, while others accepted the game was up and willingly volunteered what they knew.

TICOM/I-148 was homework given to three Germans detained in Oslo, Dr Richard Novotny, Josef Hockauf and Dr Alexander Grachegg, and they completed it on 8 August 1945. TICOM records their 'ranks and units' as unknown but, given that they shared two doctorates between them, they were probably senior technical staff with academic backgrounds. Their 11-page report seems both thorough and frank about the capabilities and failings of their organization. It begins by describing the organization of the German D/F-ing system:

> Stationary intercepting units specialised for the different illicit networks intercepted practically all illicit and suspected wireless traffic. Intercepting units were connected to long range direction finders either by direct telephone and teleprinter or wireless links. Whenever illicit traffic was intercepted all long range D/F were immediately informed and put into action while the traffic was on the air.[7]

The tendency of short-wave radio to bounce off the troposphere meant that many long-range stations across occupied Europe might be able to hear the illicit signal. However, the shorter the range, the better.

Finding Operation ROSKA

General Praun's post-war report included a map showing the location of RDF stations covering Norway.

In 1940 the two long-range RDF stations in Norway were located near Oslo and Trondheim. These were supplemented by stations at Als in Denmark and Husum in Germany, just south of the border with Denmark. It seems from the report that, surprisingly, no further long-range listening posts were added during the following years. The three technicians' account continues:

> There was a stationary intercepting unit at Oslo and in Trondheim. All illicit transmitters of the so-called Western net (located in Norway, Denmark, France, Belgium and Netherlands) had to be intercepted. Besides, special interceptors had to keep a search watch for the Russian illicit wireless system and all unknown and suspected traffic.

What happened after an illicit signal was detected they described as follows:

> The bearings were immediately reported from the D/F Stations by teleprinter to the central plotting office in Berlin. There the bearings were plotted on maps and the resulting cross-bearings indicating the

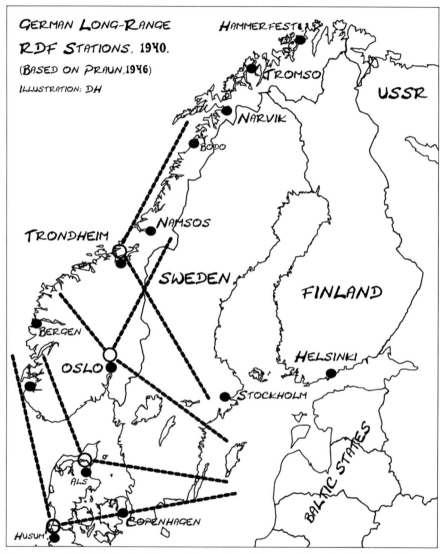

Long-range RDF Stations in Norway, Denmark and Germany. Based on the Praun Report.

approximate location of the illicit transmitter sent to the interception and D/F centres of the respective territories.

The accuracy of the bearings shifted between 30km and 50km and was generally sufficient for the mobile D/F to enter the range of the ground wave. Generally 2–3 D/F cars were simultaneously put into action from different places in order to get a cross-bearing as accurate as possible.

The accuracy of 30–50km would have been enough to pin a transmission down to, say, the Florø area and to exclude Trondheim and Namsos. Along Norway's western coast RDF boats were a much more appealing way of triangulating an illicit radio than moving cars along the difficult roads of the area.

The map that follows is the author's speculation as to how the Germans might have used such vessels to get the fix on Operation ROSKA's radio on 13 March 1945. The position of the RDF boats might not be exact, but the principle applies.

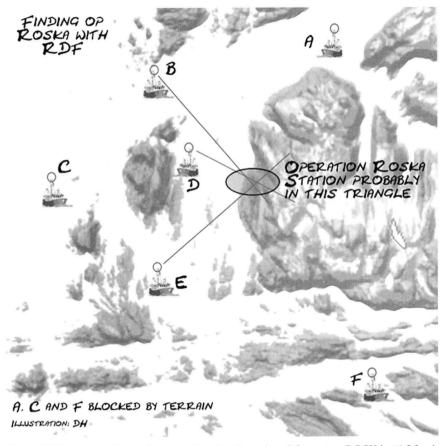

Using RDF-equipped fishing boats to pinpoint the radio of Operation ROSKA, 13 March 1945. (*Speculation by the author*)

This fix would have been good enough to justify putting boots on the ground – and this is exactly what happened, the SS finding Operation ROSKA with disastrous consequences. It is not known whether the searchers possessed portable D/F devices, but it certainly seems they were available:

When the mobile D/F succeeded in getting a cross-bearing with an accuracy of about 1–2km, specialists with small-range D/F mounted in suitcases or in body harness worn under the clothes had to locate the exact position of the transmitter.

Clearly, these short-range D/F units were far more suitable for use in urban areas, where a careful radio operator might have lookouts watching for trucks with tell-tale aerials on their roofs.

Using Berlin as a clearing house for radio intelligence must have slowed the process down, but it did have some advantages:

Every night reports arrived by teleprinter from the HQ in Berlin about frequencies, call signs, schedules and characteristics of new channels, details about channels already known. In addition new types of transmitting plans seized in all parts of Europe were immediately forwarded to all intercepting units. For each channel a special card containing all details was provided which had always to be kept up to date. The interceptors had at their disposal both the card index and a list of call signs. Additionally, messages of wireless channels whose codes were seized were decoded, documents translated, etc.

German radio intelligence operator flashing his portable RDF set.

The German investment in equipment and people dedicated to countering illicit radio operations in Norway was considerable and may, indeed, have far exceeded the number of enemy targets:

The German intercepting and D/F in Norway comprised about 120 experts and 20 girl interceptors at the end of 1944.

In the intercepting station in Oslo were: 5 receivers for intercepting the Western net (4 shifts); 2 receivers for intercepting the WNA-net (4 shifts) and 1 receiver for intercepting unknown traffic (4 shifts). The station in Trondheim was smaller.

The mobile D/F consisted of approximately 20 D/F cars and D/F boats, each for 2–5 men.

In spite of all those 'experts and girls', the report's authors admit they would rather have spent the war occupying a country that was flatter and, probably, less Arctic:

The German interception and D/F organization in NORWAY had to cope with extremely great difficulties.

Owing to atmospheric (northern lights) and geographical conditions transmitters could better be intercepted on the continent than in NORWAY. Transmitters situated on the west coast were very difficult to intercept in OSLO, particularly when using directional aerials. An additional difficulty was the problem of the silent zones (skip distance). From OSLO for example a transmitter operating in the area of ELVERUM [115km to the north] could not be intercepted ...

Owing to great distances the communication system could not be as good in the other parts of NORWAY as it was in the OSLO area. In OSLO the D/F cars could easier operate than in the mountainous country where all unknown cars were regarded with curiosity and sometimes with suspicion. Besides, the D/F cars in towns were able to approach the station much easier than in regions with bad roads ...

In 1944 about 12 illicit transmitters were seized by D/F.

One of the most fascinating sections of the report by Novotny, Hockauf and Grachegg comes near the end. It is entitled 'How the Illicit Operator Could Escape the German D/F'. The section starts with a six-point checklist:

1) The intelligence of the country for which the illicit W/T operator is working, has to check up where the intercepting stations are situated in order to place the W/T station in the dead zone.

2) Interception is difficult when the home station sends messages pretending to be in communication with the outstation, thus deceiving the interceptors who are trying to find the illicit transmitter in vain.

3) If the home station is operating on a frequency exactly 500 k/c higher or lower than the frequency of the outstation, the interference on the frequency of the outstation (when using German intercepting receivers) is such that it is almost impossible to get the signals ... The interceptor, when using his second receiver to intercept the out station, gets such a whistle in his earphone that he cannot take the signals.

4) The use of directional aerials makes intercepting and D/F difficult but can however not completely stop it. Also the use of reflectors hampers the D/F people.

5) W/T stations located near rivers, lakes, in mountainous regions are safer than in open country. If the local interference is not too great, the transmitter should be located near transformers or electrical plants in order to deceive the D/F.

6) Traffic during the night. The interceptors are not so diligent as during day time, also D/F is much more difficult, particularly in mountainous regions.

It is clear from this 'homework' that Novotny, Hockauf and Grachegg were planning totally new post-war careers once they got back to their families in Germany:

Work on high frequencies over 12,000 [kHz], as the common D/F sets only reach the 12,000 limit.

An ideal illicit transmitter is a high speed transmitter with remote control, automatically destroyed by explosives in case the D/F enter the room where it is operating.

This idea seems somewhat radical. Moving radios from one location to another as frequently as possible was challenging enough, but doing it while carrying *plastique* (explosive) and fuses would add a certain edge to proceedings. No suggestions are made about how to time the detonation and, of course, the agent would need to be long out of the door before the explosion.

The next piece of advice is far more down to earth:

When the enemy uses D/F aeroplanes, the W/T operator should not stop the traffic immediately or the aircraft would know the suspected area. The method of deceiving the enemy consists in off-tuning a little. Thus the signals intercepted will fade and the aircraft thinks that it is out of the ground wave.

That is more sensible and easier to achieve, but if the operator off-tunes a little too much, there is a danger that the home station will lose the signal completely and have to ask for a retransmission. They continue:

The W/T operator is exposed to more danger than others and should not have the code. For emergency cases he shall have an emergency code.

It seems each SIS agent had their own emergency Playfair cipher; this probably also applied to SOE operators. (See Chapter 8.4 below: Briefing on encryption) Atle Svardal and Fredrik Persen of Operation ROSKA were caught by surprise and, according to Persen, before they could destroy their logs and paperwork. (See Chapter 2.6 above) If the Germans got their hands on any one-time pads in their possession, this would enable them to send fake signals (the *funkspiel*) up to the point where the home station realized the agents had been captured.

Arguably, it is this paperwork that should be rigged to explode, preferably with an incendiary device. If the radio station was ship-borne, naval officers were under orders to dump encryption materials overboard should they come under attack. One Royal Navy ship failed to do this, and the significant and widespread consequences were later described by Praun:

> In the summer of 1942 a German submarine operating in the eastern Mediterranean captured a ship on which was found a complete set of radio codes used jointly by services of the British armed forces in the Mediterranean theatre from Gibraltar to Egypt. The security of radio communication in this area was a matter of vital concern in safeguarding the British supply-line. The submarine, which had been assigned to other tasks, was immediately recalled after reporting this valuable prize. Because it was then possible to decrypt rapidly all British communications using these codes, German countermeasures at sea and in the air were especially successful for the next two weeks. Then this traffic ceased entirely. The British had become suspicious and did not resume radio operations until six weeks later, after couriers had been able to deliver new codes throughout this far-flung theatre of operations.

Some of Novotny, Hockauf and Grachegg's advice is geographically very specific:

> Operators in the OSLO area should never send longer than a fortnight from the same place, and never return to a place where he had already operated before.

Many people who live in the large cities of Norway – Oslo, Trondheim and Bergen – occupy apartments rather than houses. German radio intelligence had a trick up its sleeve to deal with this:

> When a transmitter is located in a large building with several floors it is possible to find out the floor in which the transmitter is operating by switching off the fuses of each floor successively.

And finally, they advise:

> Guards must be posted in such a manner that they can observe in all directions without being seen themselves. The enemy will come disguised appropriate to the respective region. Small closed lorries and people with suitcases, rucksacks etc, are particularly suspected.

Above all: *Don't transmit for too long*!

British signals intelligence

The British SIGINT service in the Second World War was known as MI8, more usually referred to as the Radio Security Service (RSS). The main RSS D/F stations were: St Erth (Cornwall), Stockland Bristol (at Bridgwater, Somerset), Weaverthorpe (North Yorkshire), Wymondham (Norfolk) and Sandridge (near St Albans), all in England; Thurso, Clayock and Cupar (north of Edinburgh) in Scotland; and Gilnahirk (a few kilometres south-east of Belfast) in Northern Ireland.[8] RSS also had a fleet of mobile stations based around the UK, but these were quickly relocated into Europe after D-Day.

A rare contemporary photo of a British D/F station. This is the RSS station at Thurso in northern Scotland. There appears to be a second station in an adjacent field.

The first three fixed stations were built in the 1930s by the GPO,* probably for the Security Service, MI5. The original model comprised four 10m (33ft) antennae orientated at 0, 90, 180 and 270 degrees, plus a wooden shed for the equipment and operator.

The antennae were fed into the hut, through a radio goniometer (which determined the direction of incoming radio signals) and from there to an HRO receiver. The system needed to be orchestrated from a central RSS headquarters to make sure all participating receivers were listening to the same transmission. This made the job of the operators particularly challenging. The stations were linked by a fixed-line telephone network, over which HQ

---

* The General Post Office was then the public sector body responsible in the UK for post, telegraph and telephone services.

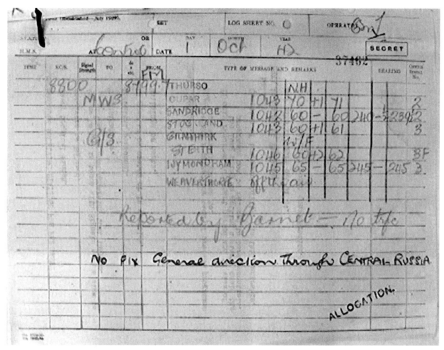

An RSS Direction-finding log sheet. The bearings are in a narrow range (60–71°) making a good triangulation difficult. At the bottom it says, 'NO FIX. General direction through CENTRAL RUSSIA'.

would feed the operators (through one of their headphones) the frequency they should listen to as well as the sound of the transmission itself. After tuning to the target frequency, they had to listen in the other ear as they turned the goniometer to the 'null signal', which indicated the direction of the transmission. This was then passed back to the D/F control room at HQ over the telephone net.

The bearings for each station were then recorded on a form; an example from 1 October 1942 is shown above. Of course, unless you have a very special brain, it is impossible to picture mentally the co-ordinates of a transmitter from numerical bearings such as this. The solution conceived by the RSS was an impressively well-designed map which could be used with a simple ruler, as shown below.

In this example, a fix has been obtained from three DF stations: Cupar in Scotland, Stockland Bristol (at Bridgwater in Somerset) and Wymondham in Norfolk. The map is surrounded by a set of bearing scales, one for each station. Cupar uses the second scale, Wymondham, the fourth and Stockland Bristol, the seventh and final scale. The fix, where the three lines intersect, seems to be near Zagreb in Croatia.

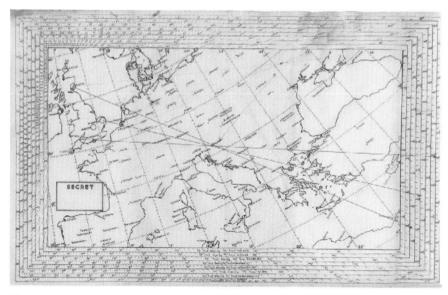

The Radio Security Service plotting map.

A radio message logged by 16-year-old Bob King on the evening of 9 December 1941.

In 1939, at the outbreak of war, the activities of all radio amateurs were closed down; the concern was that they might provide cover for enemy infiltrators reporting back to Germany. That concern proved unfounded – the Germans were hopeless at getting spies into the UK undetected. Of the 120 known to have arrived, thirty became double agents and seventeen were hanged or shot in HM Prison, Wandsworth. All of them were poorly trained and carried badly forged identity papers and insufficient cash. One Spanish agent couldn't even speak English. It was a disaster.

Soon after silencing the British radio amateurs, the RSS started to recruit the best of them to work as 'Voluntary Interceptors' or VIs. Nearly 1,700 were signed up and they provided a valuable service in boosting the capacity of RSS's harvesting of radio traffic in occupied Europe. One of the VIs was a 16-year-old (many were teenagers) called Bob King. He recently told his story on-line.[9] An example of one of his intercepts is shown above.

Under the heading 'R.S.S. Log Sheet', Bob has written 'BERTIE'. This means he is monitoring traffic out of Berlin. The first line shows the Morse Pro-signs he heard. A few lines below that, he reports 'VY HEAVY ATMOSPHERICS', indicating that the signal was difficult to hear. Then he records the thirty five-letter groups of encrypted text for Bletchley Park's cryptanalysts to get their teeth into. A hyphen (-) marks where he was uncertain about the letter he heard.

The remarkable role played by Bob and the other VIs in the war was not made known until years after the revelation that Enigma had been broken.

8.3 Morse Code and Pro-signs

If you succeed, you will soon be covered in glory.
The Chappe Brothers, 2 March 1791

The origins of Morse

Samuel Morse was born in Charlestown, Massachusetts, two years into the presidency of George Washington, when improved communications became vital to the growth of the newly independent nation.

In this context, most Americans are stirred by the romance of the Pony Express. This coast-to-coast relay race of well paid teenagers gripped the imagination of early twentieth century Hollywood, but in reality the service only lasted between April 1860 and October 1861. The challenge of reliable transcontinental communications demanded more sophisticated technology than a *mochila* (backpack) and a six-shooter. The breakthrough had arrived in 1840, when accomplished artist and inventor Samuel Morse was granted US

Patent 1,647 for 'Improvement in the mode of communicating information by signals by the application of electro-magnetism'.

Morse had the foresight to see the potential of electricity flowing along a wire but recognized that its reach was limited to just a few hundred metres. Chemistry professor Leonard Gale of New York University came to his rescue with the 'repeater', a device that captured the signal before it became unintelligible and boosted it for transmission along the next leg of its journey. Using repeaters in a New Jersey demonstration, Gale sent a signal over 16km (9.9 miles).

Credit where it is due: in 1791, the Chappe brothers sent the message, '*Si vous réussissez, vous serez bientôt couverts de gloire*' ('If you succeed, you will soon be covered in glory') over exactly the same distance (16km) using a chain of mechanical semaphore stations. The following year, the French linked Paris with Lille, a distance of 230km (143 miles). A semaphore network covered the whole country decades before the Americans had saddled their ponies.

However, the object of the exercise was not to move electricity around but to propel *information*.

The early days of telegraphy

The 1824 invention of the electromagnet by English physicist William Sturgeon spurred on the considerable ingenuity being applied to the solution

Single needle telegraph instrument from Kennedy, Rankin Electrical Installations (1903 edition), Caxton, London, 1903.

William Fothergill Cooke and Charles Wheatstone's electric telegraph, 1837. CC-BY-SA 4.0 GFDL.

of this problem in the US and Europe. The use of coils to convert the electrical signal to magnetism made it possible to flick a needle left or right, as shown in the illustration above.

This was not very user-friendly, because the operator had to wait for the needle to stop flicking to and fro before he could write down the corresponding letter. However, by making the left click sound different to the right (using one ivory and one metal stop), this simple, robust device became an *audible* instrument.

The most elegant electro-mechanical solution (put to work on early British railways) was devised in 1837 by engineers William Cooke and Charles Wheatstone. This used the polarity of the electrical current (positive, negative or zero) to point a pair of needles at an array of letters. Five needles could point to twenty letters; there was no 'C', but 'S' could substitute for a soft 'C' and 'K' for a hard 'C'. This reduced the number of lines needed from 26 to six. In the photograph above of one of the Cooke and Wheatstone machines you can see how, if the first needle (on the left) points north-east and the fourth points north-west, they intersect at the letter 'B'. The device was easy to use after a little practice. However, it still needed too many wires.

The move to Morse

Samuel Morse's crucial breakthrough was this: he devised a system which only required a single wire to carry a text message over long distances. It needed the simplest of devices at each end and came with considerable versatility, indeed so much so that it would work with no wires at all (but the invention of radio was needed for that). Taken together, these features assured its longevity and universal application.

It worked like this: all you can do with an electrical signal on a single wire is switch it on and off, and the telegraph key was developed to do just that job.

Model J38 'straight-line' telegraph key used by the US military during the Second World War and still popular with radio amateurs today. The key is gripped between thumb and fingers – not tapped.

Depression of the key causes a current to be sent, but it stops immediately on release. This makes it possible for the operator to vary the length of each transmission. Samuel Morse's 'code' makes the job of the operator easy by restricting the length he or she needs to send the 'short' (the dot) and 'long' (the dash). Ideally, the dash should be three times the length of the dot. This, then, makes it possible to represent letters, numbers and punctuation marks as short patterns of dots and dashes.

Once you have agreed the coded representation (recognized by both sending and receiving parties), it can be carried via a number of media: electricity on wires; by radio; using a signal lamp (still used by most navies); revealing and concealing a distinctly coloured shape; or by making a noise (for example with a signal horn or by tapping the water-pipe that runs through your cell).

The dots and dashes are no more than a way of representing Morse on paper. In fact, their use is frowned on because it encourages the learner to think of the code in terms of its component parts rather than as a *shape*. In other

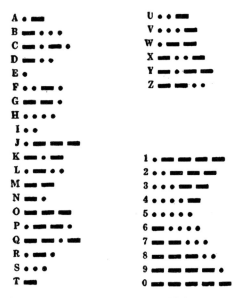

INTERNATIONAL MORSE CODE

1. A dash is equal to three dots.
2. The space between parts of the same letter is equal to one dot.
3. The space between two letters is equal to three dots.
4. The space between two words is equal to five dots.

A 1922 version of the International Morse Code.[10] The current standard (ITU 2009) for word gap is seven units, not the outdated five units as shown. There are ten language-specific Morse codes: Arabic, Chinese, Cyrillic, Devanagari (for Sanskrit and Hindi), Greek, Hebrew, Japanese, Korean, Persian and Thai.

words, if you hear (or see) 'di-dah' don't write down '· −', always write 'A'. It's all about pattern recognition. Seeing or hearing the pattern 'di-dah' needs to trigger the letter 'A' in your brain. Similarly, when sending with a key, seeing a letter must cause the corresponding movement of your hand. This concept is emphasized very effectively in a post-war US Army Signals Corps training film.[11] It even stars a J38 telegraph key and a piano-playing blonde!

You can use a personal computer to learn Morse. The 'DX Zone', a website for amateur radio enthusiasts, includes a page of links to downloadable training applications; there are about eighty of them, mostly free.[12] Once you have found an app you like, the process is then the same as learning a musical instrument or a foreign language − a little practice, often. Even if you can get

```
                              CROW  PLAN
CALL SIGNS.            CROW . . . . . W R O
                      HOME . . . . . W X D

FREQUENCIES.          CROW . . . . . 7163..Y..Main Day
                                     6967..X
                                     3565..W..Main Night
                                     3638..V

                      HOME . . . . . 7393..T..Main Day
                                     6847..S
                                     3510..R..Main Night
                                     3638..P

FREQUENCY CHANGE SIGNALS.
                      NM..Change your transmitting frequency to..
                      LK..Am changing my transmitting frequency to..
                      HG..Here transmitting simultaneously on...and...
                      Examples.
                      NMX..Change your transmitting frequency to 6967
                      LKP..Am changing my transmitting frequency to 3638
                      HGTR..Here transmitting simultaneously on 7323 and
                                                                    3510
SCHEDULES.            TUESDAY...1400., THURSDAY...1145., SATURDAY...1545.
                              These times are G.M.T.
ADDITIONAL CONTACTS.  The signal "QRX" will NOT be used.  Urgent additional
                      contacts are signalled in the following manner:-
                      You put down the time required in four figures,
                      adding as fifth figure the day indicating figure of
                      the day you wish the contact.  This gives a five
                      figure group.  This group is then transposed into a
                      five letter group from the transposition table,
                      either line or a combination of either line of which
                      may be used.

TRANSPOSITION TABLE.  1  2  3  4  5  6  7  8  9  0
                      M  T  A  G  Y  R  C  E  W  O
                      P  X  D  H  U  N  F  B  Z  S

DAY INDICATING FIGURES.Sunday..2.,  Monday..8.,  Tuesday..6.,  Wednesday..4.,
                      Thursday..9.,  Friday..5.,  Saturday..3.
                      Example.
                      If you want a contact on Monday at 1745, the in-
                      dicating figure for that day is 8.  This added as
                      fifth figure gives 17458.  Transposed into letters
                      from the transposition table this gives:-
                      From the first line ... MCGYE
                      From the second line ... PFHUB
                      From the two lines... PCHUE

PROCEDURE.            Normal commercial and "Q" code of signals.
CONTACTING.           Home station will listen on WRO's main frequency
                      for five minutes at scheduled times and will reply
                      for five minutes on Home's main frequency.
                      IMPORTANT.
                      1.  DO NOT CALL US if you have no traffic to send.
                      2.  We will call you at scheduled times if we have
                      very urgent messages for you, so always try and
                      listen.
                      3.  Remember always that the enemy is listening for
                      you, therefore the shorter your messages the harder
                      it is for him to locate you.
                      4.  After initial contact, keep your calls down to
                      the absolute minimum.
                      5.  DO NOT USE ONE WORD OF PLAIN LANGUAGE.


                      6.2.42.
```

An SOE Frequency Schedule (or 'sked') for Operation CROW in 1942. Sometimes called a 'signals plan'.

tuition at your local radio amateur club, these programmes are still the best way to practise daily and get your speed up to the target of twenty words (or five-letter groups) per minute using a straight-line Morse key.

Procedures

Even when fluent in Morse, there was more to learn before a student W/T operator could be let loose on a live radio set. On a specific frequency it is possible to transmit or receive but, unlike a telephone, not both at the same time. Procedures had to be agreed in advance to swap control between the two communicating parties in an organized manner. This is the Morse equivalent of an operator on a voice radio link saying 'Over' when they have finished talking.

These are the steps that had to be followed to send a message. The message will have already been encoded (perhaps by someone else), so the operator will be looking at a piece of paper containing an array of hand-written five-letter groups. They will also have to hand a critical document called a 'sked' or 'signals' plan (see example above).

In order to avoid the likely confusion caused by agents attempting to contact their home bases at the same time, using the same frequency and identifying themselves with identical three-letter call signs, each station was provided with a tailor-made schedule. A copy of this sked was available to the home station. The plan shown was developed for SOE Operation CROW, an ill-fated project in 1942 to establish guerrilla forces east of Oslo fjord and provide them with regular radio contact with the UK. It is worth reading carefully, because it gives a clear indication of what the station should do and what it must not do. Transmission is allowed at fixed times on three days a week, but it explains how that can be varied in emergencies.

1. Once the agent is sure they are sending at the correct day and time they need to set up the antenna (if not permanently rigged) and get the radio ready for sending, tuning it to the frequencies specified in the sked. Using such a plan, operators would know that a 'signals-master' would be listening out for them at the home station.

2. When the radio set was powered-up and tuned to the right frequency, the operator would listen to make sure that the frequency was not already being used by another operator. If it was, they would wait for it to become clear.

3. When confident the frequency was clear the operator would then attempt to make contact with the home station. This was done by sending a Morse sequence that looked like this:

CQ CQ CQ DE ABC ABC ABC AR K

CQ = Call for contact: 'Seek You'
DE = From
ABC = Operator's call-sign.
    Call-signs were in the form 'AQS', 'NJA' and 'ZUA'.
    They should not be confused with Operation Codes such as
        'ERIC', 'ERICA' and 'ROSKA'.
AR = End message (might get dropped if the message is urgent)
K = 'Over'

---

4. The W/T operator then switches from 'transmit' to 'receive' and listens. The abbreviations used conformed to international standards, but the way in which they were used could vary, although they would still be legible to experienced operators. Consider the following real message that was logged as being transmitted at 17:00 Hours on 19 December 1941.

CZE QSA0 PSE CALL=K

    CZE = The sender's call-sign.
    QSA0 = Your signal-strength is zero. (Nothing heard.)
    PSE CALL = Please call.
    K = 'Over'

Later, the same operator sends this:

CZE =SRI QSA0 QRX NEXT NW 5400 73 GB VA

    CZE = The sender's call-sign.
    SRI = Sorry
    QSA0 = Your signal-strength is zero. (Nothing heard.)
    QRX NEXT 5400 = I will call at the next pre-arranged time on
        5.4 MHz.
    73 = Kind regards.
    GB = Goodbye.
    VA = I am closing down.

The significant point here is that CZE is a *German* W/T operator attempting to make contact with his base. He fails and tells them he will make another attempt at a later, pre-scheduled time. No message has been sent; that will be done later – in code. Radio operators working for the SIS 'Y' Service had no trouble interpreting German procedural traffic, and the style differences worked like an 'accent' distinguishing their messages from those transmitted by other nationalities.

5. Usually the response from the home station would come back in seconds and would be in the following terse format:

ABC ABC ABC RST477 GA

> ABC = Operator's call sign
> RST477 = Signal strength (Readability 1–5, Strength 1–9, Tone 1–9)
> GA = Go ahead (may be followed by K, 'Over')

The agent can now proceed to send the encrypted message. The W/T operator's message would look something like this.

ABC QTC 327/95 KA ZJGCA <u>WBAAO DRSDN EGTEA ESEPR ETRAB ERBEY IRNTN RFNEK SEOXZ RDUDV SYNDS OEYNO TNDGS NEIRL OJOCG SEKET YOWTJ TNPPY</u> AR K

> ABC = Operator's call sign
> QTC 327/95 = Message number 327, 95 letters in this message.
> KA = Message starts
> ZJGCA = Designator group (see below).
> WBAAO to TNPPY = The cipher-text (underlined for clarity).
> AR = End of message.
> K = 'Over'

The home station would then acknowledge receipt, and both stations would sign off. Only rarely would the home station ask for the message to be repeated.

The nineteen five-letter groups of the message are preceded by a 'designator group', which tells the home station which key to use to decrypt the signal into clear text. This might indicate a line from a one-time pad if that was the system being used. (See Chapter 8.4: Briefing on Cryptography)

There are a lot of 'Q-codes' and procedural codes, but only a few are used in practice.

8.4 Codes and Crypto

One of the most singular characteristics of the art of deciphering is the strong conviction possessed by every person, even moderately acquainted with it, that he is able to construct a cipher which nobody else can decipher. I have also observed that the cleverer the person, the more intimate is his conviction.
Charles Babbage, *Passages from the Life of a Philosopher*, 1864

Cryptography: a long history

This book started with the observation that the very act of sending information via radio waves makes it vulnerable to being overheard on any radio receiver tuned to the same frequency as the transmitter. But there is a means of defence known as 'cryptography' (or 'cryptology'), the science of 'secret writing'. A message which could be read by an adversary ('clear text') is transformed and transposed into an apparently meaningless string of letters and/or numbers ('cipher text'), which can only be read by someone who knows the set of rules which the sender used to make the message private.

Cryptography has grown in step with technological change, to protect the data and images carried on today's powerful and sophisticated networks from unwarranted intrusion and corruption. But cryptology is not a new phenomenon – far from it. About 4,000 years ago, the hieroglyphic inscriptions on the tomb of Egyptian king Khnumhotep II included strange characters to conceal the real meaning of the obituaries. First to introduce some degree of mechanization to the coding process were the Spartans, who in about 5 BCE devised a system by which a message would be written on a strip of papyrus wrapped around a cylinder like a thick pencil (a '*Scytale*'). Only when the papyrus was wrapped around a cylinder of identical diameter could the message be read. This was a 'transposition cipher', because only the sequence of the letters was changed, not the letters themselves. Meanwhile, the Romans opted for a system of shifting the letters of the alphabet by a pre-designated number of places left or right. So the word 'OCEAN' would become 'RFHDQ' if the key was 'three-places-to-the-right'. And thus things progressed until the 1854 invention of a code used (too much) by radio agents in the Second World War; the Playfair Cipher.[13]

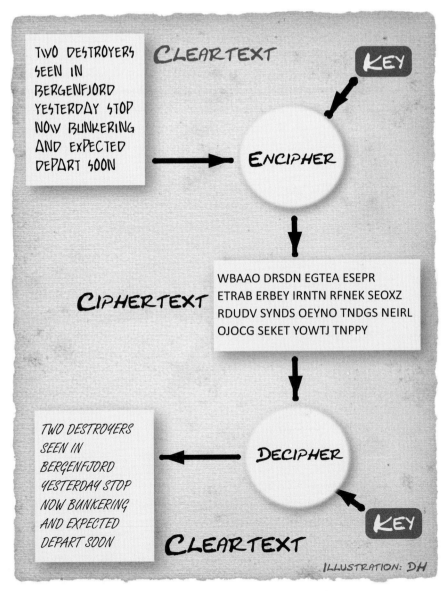

The basic stages of encryption and decryption.

Clandestine agents were unable to use machines to encrypt and decrypt their dispatches. Devices such as the British Typex, American SIGABA and German Enigma[14] were designed for use by radio operators serving in the military and at their respective operational headquarters; they would be equipped with the same device and trained to use it in an identical manner. The sophisticated Lorenz was reserved for communications between the highest levels of the Nazi command structure, including traffic between Hitler and his generals.

However, this approach was not practical for agents working in the field for organizations such as the SIS, the SOE and the OSS. To begin with, machines like the TypeX were far too big. Illustrated below is the TypeX 22, introduced by the UK in 1937. It was based on the commercial Enigma, but with many improvements such as five cipher wheels (the German Enigma never had more than four), two plug-boards (the German Enigma had one) and two 'ticker-tape' printers, enabling single-person operation. Fred Jones, a Royal Navy radio operator, compared the commercial Enigma and the full-specification TypeX:

> The major difference, apart from giving a printout of both plain-text and cipher text, was the requirement for an A.C. mains supply. It was also very heavy. It used to take two strong Marines to lift the beast off its table and carry it to a secure area when we entered harbour.[15]

These machines were considered secure enough to send Ultra traffic to commanders on the battleground, and there is no convincing evidence the Germans were ever able to crack it. They gave up trying in 1943, primarily because, having captured a TypeX in the field, they saw it was a variation of

The TypeX 22 cipher machine. Note the five rotors (above the keyboard) and the two plug-boards (front left and right). The large drums are printers: the one of the left for plain text; the one on the right for cipher text. These are an important means of avoiding transcription errors. Under the document-holder is a 'Morse perforator' enabling messages previously punched on to paper tape to be transmitted at high speed. CC BY-SA 3.0.

the Enigma. This was true, but they concluded it was not worth the effort required to crack it. After all, if Enigma was totally secure – as they believed – TypeX must be totally secure too!

TypeX Mark III: The portable, hand-cranked, version weighing 30lbs (13.6kg). (*Christie's*)

The keyboard gives an indication of the size of the device, and it is clearly not practical for use by an undercover agent. Even the Mark III 'portable' version (shown above) is far bigger than the radio sets being used. This was a mechanical unit; as the left hand typed, the right hand turned the wheel. Imagine also the predicament of an operator under orders to destroy such a machine in the event of capture.

Book codes

The idea of book codes is delightfully simple. Each agent and home station would have an identical copy of the same book or document. (The second text of the Beale Cypher uses the US Declaration of Independence.) 'Identical' means editions in which the pagination was exactly the same.

The Political Warfare Executive (PWE) was set up in August 1941 as a department of the Foreign Office. Its objective was to undermine the morale of German forces (and their families at home) by spreading negative propaganda about the regime through illicit newspapers, leaflets and radio broadcasts. It proposed that their W/T operators employ book codes and described their use with great clarity in the document shown below. (This was for Operation CROW,[16] and space has been left for the code name of the agent and the title of the book to be used.)

The book code system could be used as a source of *keys* used in a process of transposition. This was the case with the *Rote Kapelle*. (See Chapter 4.4 above)

C R O W

175

Book Code used in communications to _____

Name of book _____

Seven figure groups will be used, i.e. 3621409.

Starting from left to right, the first three figures stand for the page of the book, i.e. 362.

If one wishes to refer to page 27, the group would read 0271409.

The fourth and fifth figures in the group refer to the line on the page, i.e. the fourteenth line.

The sixth and seventh figures refer to the word in the line, i.e. ninth word.

The figure 0 will be used in the case of single figures up to nine, to keep the whole group up to seven figures in all.

In spelling a name or word which is not available in the book which has been agreed upon as a basis for this code, the letters of the alphabet will be represented by figures, A being taken as the last figure in the group preceding the word to be spelt. Such words will not necessarily be seven letter groups. It will depend on the length of the word. i.e. "howitzer" would therefore read, if it came after the group given above as as example, as follows:-

16,23,31,17,28,34,13,26.

It must be noted that a comma should be inserted between each number taken to represent one letter. See above example.

PWE description of the use of book codes. HS 2/152. (*UK National Archives*)

After the war, Oberstleutnant (Lieutenant Colonel) Mettig, the head of German army signals intelligence, was debriefed as part of the TICOM project. His interrogator noted these comments:

PW [prisoner-of-war] states that a special weakness of Allied agents' ciphers was the use of books for enciphering. Usually only a minor inroad or other clue was required to reproduce a piece of the cipher text and conclusions could thence be drawn as to which book was used. In the case of one Allied transmission in the summer of '42, five or six French words of a text were ascertained, leading to the conclusion that the cipher book dealt with the Spanish civil war. In view of this assumption, all French books about the Spanish civil war in the State libraries of Paris, Madrid and Lisbon were read with the object of tying in these 5–6 words. The book was found. PW always looked on a great research effort as worthwhile.

The effort invested in this case was considerable. Stage magicians often say they get away with their acts because the audience will not believe how much trouble they go to in order to make their tricks work. (See also Chapter 4.4 for a description of how the Funkabwehr found a copy of the book being used at a radio base in Brussels.)

Manual encryption systems

A different approach to encryption was needed for SIS and SOE agents, something that did not involve much more than pencil and paper. Searches in the UK National Archives reveal that SOE radio operators used *two* 'manual' encryption systems. The following is a quote from SOE's assessment of Norwegian agent Herluf Nygård's training:

> Codes: Accurate and capable. Has a sound knowledge of *both systems* and with further practice should use them effectively. [STS 36: 8 August 1943. Author's emphasis]

Using a wider variety of sources, we can deduce that the two systems were:

- Poem Codes, later replaced by Worked-out Keys (WOKs), a system based on One-Time Pads (OTPs)
- Playfair Codes, probably for use in emergencies

Each is described further below.

Poem codes

It's impossible to consider poem codes and their use by SOE without considering the work of Leo Marks (the son of Benjamin Marks, owner of the London antiquarian bookshop Marks & Co which featured in the movie *84, Charing Cross Road*). When, at the age of twenty-two, Marks was conscripted he trained as a cryptologist. Considered too much of an 'oddball' for GC&CS at Bletchley Park – a place full of oddballs! – he was assigned to SOE. On arrival he was given a test message to decrypt using the key, to see how fast he was. The target time was 20 minutes, but Marks took all day … SOE had forgotten to give him the key, but he had extracted the plain text without it. His brilliance was undeniable, and he soon became head cryptographer.

At the time he joined SOE it was using 'poem codes'. This is a system based on the use of a poem designated for each agent and known to the person who would decrypt their messages in the UK. In simple terms, five words would be chosen at random from the poem for each message. The letters of the alphabet would then be numbered consecutively through the selected words.

Here's an example using *The Eagle* by Alfred, Lord Tennyson (a longer poem would be more secure):

He clasps the crag with crooked hands;	Words 1 to 7
Close to the sun in lonely lands,	Words 8 to 14
Ringed[17] *with the azure world, he stands.*	Words 15 to 21
The wrinkled sea beneath him crawls;	Words 22 to 27
He watches from his mountain walls,	Words 28 to 33
And like a thunderbolt he falls.	Words 34 to 39

Five words need to be chosen for the message; for example:

CRAG SUN WORLD SEA LIKE

The nineteen letters are then numbered according to alphabetic sequence (duplicates from left to right):

C	R	A	G	S	U	N	W	O	R	L	D	S	E	A	L	I	K	E
3	14	1	7	16	18	12	19	13	15	10	4	17	5	2	11	8	9	6

The numbers indicate the order in which the nineteen columns will be shuffled. The clear-text message is then arranged into columns (ignoring the spaces) which are five rows deep.

TWO DESTROYERS SEEN IN BERGENFJORD YESTERDAY STOP NOW BUNKERING AND EXPECTED DEPART SOON STOP

1	2	3	4	5	6	7	8	9	10	11	12	13	14	15	16	17	18	19
T	W	O	D	E	S	T	R	O	Y	E	R	S	S	E	E	N	I	N
B	E	R	G	E	N	F	J	O	R	D	Y	E	S	T	E	R	D	A
Y	S	T	O	P	N	O	W	B	U	N	K	E	R	I	N	G	A	N
D	E	X	P	E	C	T	E	D	D	E	P	A	R	T	S	O	O	N
S	T	O	P	M	A	Z	Y	K	G	J	Y	V	S	T	R	B	L	N

Cells 5 to 19 of the bottom row are filled randomly to complete the grid. The cipher text is then created by transposing the columns according to the numbers derived from the poem: 3, 14, 1, 7, etc.

ORTXO SSRRS TBYDS TFOTZ EENSR IDAOL RYKPY
NANNN SEEAV ETITT YRUDG DGOPP NRGOB EEPEM
WESET EDNEJ RJWEY OOBDK SNNCA

After the message has been prefixed with a code indicating which words have been chosen from the poem (4, 11, 19, 23 and 35), this is what the transmitted message would look like if it were intercepted by the Germans or anyone else listening to the frequency at the time. (Note that, later in the war, a second transposition was introduced.)

A potential problem was soon spotted by Leo Marks. The poems being used had all been published in full. If an enemy cryptanalyst could deduce a phrase from the verse, perhaps only a few words, they could guess which poem it was from. Once they had the full poem, decipherment would become simple. Marks' solution was to create poems which would never be published – and probably never should be. To render the verse more memorable he would make it funny and/or obscene. For example:

> Is de Gaulle's prick
> Twelve inches thick
> Can it rise
> To the size
> Of a proud flag-pole
> And does the sun shine
> From his arse-hole?

In his book, *Between Silk and Cyanide*, Marks claims this poem was written by the FANYs of Grendon. A further innovation was the 'One-Time Poem' (see One-Time Pad, below). This enabled a totally different poem to be used for each message.

But Christmas 1943 was a sad time for the young cryptographer. On learning of the death of his girlfriend Ruth (believed to be the goddaughter of SOE chief, Sir Charles Hambro) in a plane crash in Canada, he sat down and wrote a poem which has become one of the most famous in the English language thanks to its use in the film *Carve Her Name with Pride* (1958).

> The life that I have
> Is all that I have
> And the life that I have
> Is yours.
>
> The love that I have
> Of the life that I have
> Is yours and yours and yours.
>
> A sleep I shall have
> A rest I shall have
> Yet death will be but a pause.
>
> For the peace of my years
> In the long green grass
> Will be yours and yours and yours.[18]

Three months later, Marks gave the poem to SOE agent Violette Szabo as her personal poem code for use when she was in occupied France. She was captured, tortured and killed by the Gestapo in early 1945.

Worked-out Keys (WOKs)

Leo Marks gradually replaced poem codes with more secure techniques, often against opposition from the cryptographers of Bletchley Park, who thought his new ideas too complicated for field agents. He first invented a method called Worked-out Keys (WOKs), the use of pre-arranged transposition keys obviating the need for poems altogether. Even though this was enhanced using a clever device to make the code *look like* a poem code (as a time-waster for German cryptanalysts), it was eventually replaced by invincible one-time pads (OTPs – see below), and these were used until the end of the war.

If the Germans only *suspected* the British were using poem codes, Swedish intelligence (Säpo) knew it for certain. During its April 1943 interrogation of a contact of Peter Tennant (the head of SOE in Sweden using the cover of press attaché), the interviewee revealed that Tennant had tried to teach him a poem he could use to encrypt messages sent to the UK. They were told the poem started, 'The owl and the pussycat went to sea in a beautiful sea-green boat with lots of honey and plenty of money wrapped up in ...' These are (almost) the words of the first verse of a famous 'nonsense poem' by English poet Edward Lear: *The Owl and the Pussy-cat* (1871).

The Owl and the Pussy-cat went to sea
In a beautiful pea-green boat,
They took some honey, and plenty of money,
Wrapped up in a five-pound note.[19]

If it had never been published, the poem would have been perfect as an encryption key: the word 'runcible', which appears later, does not even exist – it was invented by the poet.

The Germans struggled with the codes used by Allied agents. Even though Leo Marks at SOE considered poem codes and book codes too easy to break, SOE agents often used verses by poets they had been introduced to at school: Shakespeare, Keats, Byron, Racine, Molière and (as in my example above) Tennyson. But Lieutenant General Praun wrote this in his post-war report for OSS:

> After the arrest of an agent, it was the task of message evaluation to solve previously intercepted messages with the help of the captured records. Cryptanalysis proper, as practiced in field radio intelligence, was not possible, since the word systems used by the agents were based on certain books – usually novels – which provided the key.[20]

And note the comments quoted earlier of Lieutenant Colonel Mettig, head of German army SIGINT, about the vulnerabilities of book codes.

One-time pads (OTPs)

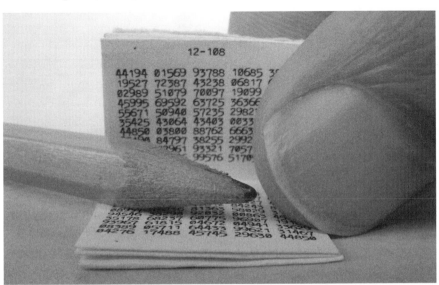

A numerical one-time pad. (© 2009 Dirk Rijmenants, *Cipher Machines & Cryptology*. Used *with permission*)

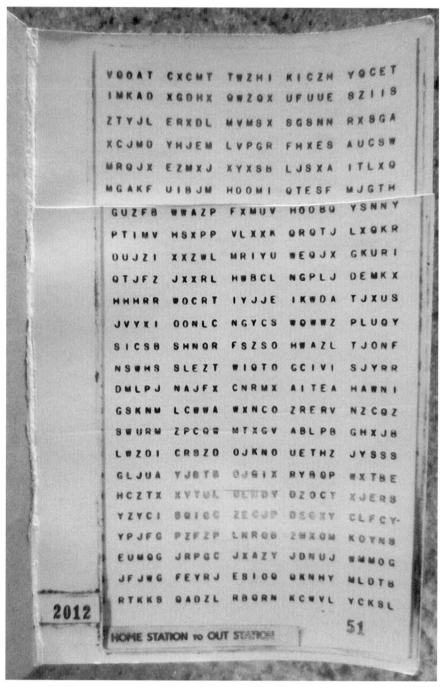

Page from an SOE one-time letter pad ('2012' is the pad number, not the date). (*Clive Bassett, Harrington Aviation Museum*)

OTPs are based on the idea that messages should be encrypted and decrypted using unique and random sequences of letters or numbers as the keys. The keys can be used for substitution or transposition and are issued to the agent in the form of a booklet or pad, from which each key can be torn and destroyed after use. Leo Marks had his one-time codes (Worked-out Keys – WOKS) printed on a special silk from which used keys could be torn. He considered that silk could be more easily concealed under the clothing of agents likely to be 'patted down' when subjected to a random stop and search in the street.

Each page of the one-time pad shown above should be destroyed after use. The purpose of this is not only to conceal it from the enemy but to prevent the agent using it again. The emphasis is on the 'one-time' part of 'one-time pad'.

Shown above is a page from an SOE one-time letter pad – in this case printed on paper and bound into a soft-back book. The name 'Anne' has been written on the cover; she may have been an agent but more probably was a FANY at one of the home radio stations. Note that the page has been cut across below the sixth line, leaving the sequence that starts 'GUZFB' to be used next.

Poly-alphabetic substitution ciphers

	A	B	C	D	E	F	G	H	I	J	K	L	M	N	O	P	Q	R	S	T	U	V	W	X	Y	Z
A	o	e	m	b	a	q	i	c	l	w	s	b	j	y	t	z	v	f	k	d	g	n	p	x	u	r
B	m	o	l	a	i	f	r	z	u	x	k	a	q	t	h	w	e	y	j	n	d	v	b	c	g	p
C	w	s	f	x	p	t	a	o	j	v	y	k	i	q	n	r	z	m	l	h	g	e	b	d	c	e
D	h	i	f	r	k	x	q	o	v	a	m	p	l	u	y	j	w	n	t	a	b	z	g	o	o	d
E	q	a	y	c	w	h	u	h	y	e	j	o	p	x	s	k	z	a	i	m	v	r	f	g	l	n
F	t	q	d	c	w	h	u	h	y	e	j	o	p	x	s	k	z	a	i	m	v	r	f	g	l	n
G	y	m	t	q	o	u	n	x	f	d	c	w	y	h	u	o	n	r	s	q	t	p	k	i	t	h
H	d	l	a	z	h	y	f	x	u	o	r	j	v	r	b	y	q	e	s	t	d	y	o	h	h	h
I	r	d	x	t	b	u	a	l	q	c	o	s	v	x	d	y	g	b	i	u	o	l	n	j	i	k
J	p	t	h	z	s	z	e	r	m	c	h	s	v	i	f	j	q	y	g	i	s	k	z	j	j	k
K	v	u	p	m	d	s	o	y	z	q	b	u	e	g	w	f	x	a	e	t	l	h	j	i	i	j
L	l	h	b	b	b	y	r	l	a	t	e	p	i	o	l	g	a	l	w	l	k	l	j	l	l	l
M	b	g	a	k	b	y	v	s	z	d	r	t	q	e	t	b	m	e	f	i	w	u	p	m	m	f
N	u	k	w	v	e	i	g	n	n	s	n	l	n	i	n	c	m	d	p	b	s	a	o	j	n	f
O	a	b	z	w	g	k	d	c	r	h	f	i	o	p	o	f	o	l	m	s	v	y	q	n	t	u
P	j	w	k	x	p	e	v	e	i	g	k	b	c	t	d	p	s	n	p	r	h	a	p	p	m	b
Q	e	f	v	g	z	q	n	i	e	o	u	p	y	p	s	u	q	h	l	u	o	w	q	p	m	b
R	i	v	s	d	l	t	w	r	o	j	w	e	g	u	e	k	r	e	k	e	x	p	f	r	r	a
S	s	e	r	b	b	j	s	m	s	m	n	b	t	n	a	o	p	h	s	w	s	y	u	s	s	t
T	f	j	g	i	x	r	c	e	l	l	w	w	i	k	u	t	q	p	t	d	y	u	u	m	u	o
U	u	u	e	w	f	f	y	g	c	i	z	n	c	o	u	v	h	x	u	f	u	u	m	u	u	o
V	k	r	q	n	t	l	m	p	c	y	o	g	i	i	h	d	l	o	x	v	f	q	c	t	w	y
W	c	v	w	o	j	j	w	u	w	r	k	d	a	e	z	o	y	o	r	c	e	w	w	w	w	y
X	x	u	x	p	x	d	w	g	b	b	b	n	x	f	j	k	m	r	x	y	s	o	t	a	o	x
Y	g	z	e	l	y	f	y	l	y	f	y	q	o	s	j	y	y	t	t	o	h	h	y	y	y	w
Z	x	y	o	j	q	b	s	s	z	m	r	l	u	w	z	f	z	g	p	z	v	d	z	l	z	e

An SOE poly-alphabetic substitution cipher printed on silk for easier concealment. (*http:// people.duke.edu/~ng46/collections/cryptology.htm*)

The poly-alphabetic substitution cipher shown above was another innovation introduced by Leo Marks. The table comprises twenty-six columns headed by the letters A to Z. The capital letters at the left in each column are the clear text, the lower-case letters are randomly produced cipher text, usually printed in red to enhance legibility. If you look across the row for plain-text 'E' (the most common letter in the English alphabet) you will see that it can encrypt as q, a, y, u, n, o, etc, thus making a statistical attack impossible.

This is how it is used: (1) Write out the message. In this case it is 'ENEMY TROOPS MOVING WEST'. (2) Below that, write the key repetitively. It can be a single word, but the longer the better. Let's assume, 'SHORTWAVE'. (3) Look up each letter in the cipher table and write that below. (4) Split into five-letter groups prior to transmission, it looks like this:

Cleartext	E	N	E	M	Y	T	R	O	O	P	S	M	O	V	I	N	G	W	E	S
Key	S	H	O	R	T	W	A	V	E	S	H	O	R	T	S	H	O	R	T	S
Ciphertext	R	Q	M	X	T	X	I	J	G	N	M	C	V	U	Y	U	C	F	R	M

The cipher text then becomes RQMXT XIJGN MCVUY UCFRM AOZRB. The last four letters are dummies to make up a five-letter group. If you try this yourself with your own message and key you will realize how quick and simple it is. After each message the key can be changed or the silk destroyed and replaced with another.

It is significant that when SOE switched to OTPs it was to protect communications between its bases in the UK only. Although OTPs have been proven mathematically to be 100 per cent secure (and produced fewer 'indecipherables'), the distribution of pads to agents in the field was the point at which they were most vulnerable. This was exacerbated by the fact that pads could not last forever and had to be replaced periodically. Also, the pads needed to be destroyed if the agent was in danger of being captured (although this would have been be a lot easier than making a TypeX machine disappear).

In spite of these issues, OTPs were used extensively by field agents in the latter years of the war.

The Playfair Cipher

This code was invented in 1854 and became a favourite of the British Foreign Office from the turn of the century. The advantage of this cipher is that the agent only needs to remember a single word instead of a whole poem. A reference card for Odd Sørli's Playfair Cipher is included in his UK National Archives file (see below). The card was kept on file with the de-coders at Grendon; Sørli had to memorize its contents.

It is assumed that the name at the top right (Howard) refers to the SOE decoder responsible for decrypting Sørli's radio messages from the field. His dispatches would have been in Norwegian (he didn't speak English), and so the Norwegian alphabet is used.

Odd Sørli's Playfair Cipher card (front).

The 5 x 5 letter grid in the bottom left corner of the card is fundamental to how the Playfair Cipher worked. The word Odd had to use to generate his key was TRØNDELAG. After writing this at the start of the grid as shown, he would then complete it with the other letters of the Norwegian alphabet: B, C, F, H, I, J, K, M, O, P, S, U, V, Y, Æ and Å.

Ignoring the spaces, the cipher text of his message would then be broken down into 'digrams' (two-letter groups) as follows:

TWO DESTROYERS SEEN IN BERGENFJORD YESTERDAY STOP NOW BUNKERING AND EXPECTED DEPART SOON

TW OD ES TR OY ER SX SE EN IN BE RG EN FJ OR DY ES TE RD AY ST OP NO WB UN KE RI NG AN DE XP EC TE DX DE PA RT SO ON

A null-X has been used to split double-S and double-D digrams. The code has been changed to LANZAROTE because the clear text is in English. (Repeated letters are omitted from the key-word.)

L	A	N	Z	R
O	T	E	A	B
D	F	G	H	IJ
K	M	P	Q	S
U	V	W	X	Y

Each digram of the clear text is now encrypted using a predetermined set of rules. For example, the letters of TW are on different rows and columns so they encrypt as the opposite letters of the rectangle it forms.

L	A	N	Z	R
O	*T*	*E*	A	B
D	F	G	H	IJ
K	M	P	Q	S
U	*V*	W	X	Y

In this instance, **TW** becomes *VE*. The next digram, **OD**, is in the same column so the letters below are chosen: *KD*.

L	A	N	Z	R
O	T	E	A	B
D	F	G	H	IJ
K	M	P	Q	S
U	V	W	X	Y

The third digram, ES, forms another rectangle:

L	A	N	Z	R
O	T	**E**	A	*B*
D	F	G	H	IJ
K	M	*P*	Q	S
U	V	W	X	Y

The clear-text ES becomes cipher-text BP … and so on through the message. There are four rules that apply to the substitution, and it can be seen that, with a little practice and a lot of care, an agent could soon become reasonably proficient.

The following image is the reverse of Odd Sørli's Playfair card.

A LANGT
B OP
C I
D DALEN
E STÅR
F DER
G ET
H HUS
I DER
J FÅR
K MAN
L ØL
M OG
N BRENNEVIN
O OG
P BRUS
Q DER
R FÅR
S MAN
T TA
U PÅ
V PIGERNES
W LÅR
X OG
Y DET
Z BÅDE
INDICATOR:-
ANY FIVE LETTERS.
1ST KEY 2ND KEY
NFLCB gives OGMDC
SECURITY CHECKS:-
TRUE:- 1st and last letters of indicator will be 10 away from each other on the alphabetic table.
BLUFF:- mistake at 10th, 20 etc.

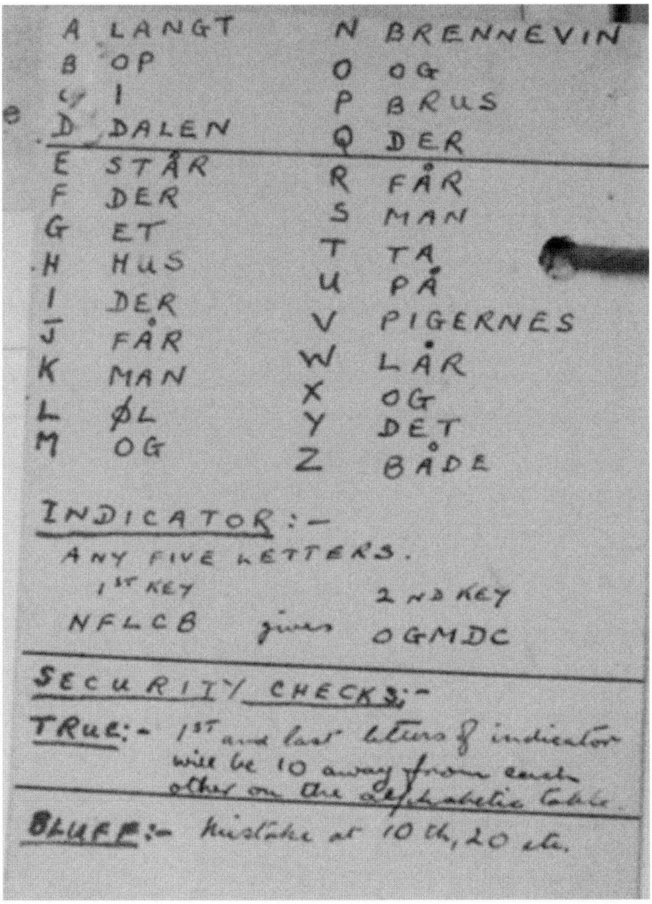

Odd Sørli's Playfair Cipher card (reverse).

At the top is a list of agreed abbreviations which enabled commonly used words to be sent as two letters: one indicating that an abbreviation is on its way, the second the abbreviation itself. But it also had another use. Repeated words and phrases can be used by cryptanalysts to crack codes so the Norwegian word '*og*' ('and') can be coded as 'O', 'M' or 'X'. In spite of the vulnerability of predictable content, German military radio operators were required to put the local weather conditions at the beginning of their messages, so Bletchley Park would start by looking out for words like REGEN,

SONNE and WOLKEN (rain, sun and clouds). Particularly stupid Enigma operators would end all their messages, 'HH' or even 'Heil Hitler'! These were called 'cribs' and were a great short cut to determining the day's settings for the machine.

Lower down the card is the heading 'Security Checks'. Under 'True' are the changes to be made to the coding if the agent wishes to reassure the receiver that it really is he/she originating the dispatch. The 'Bluff' is to be used if they have been captured and are sending the message under duress. In other words it is used to reassure the *Germans* that they are using the security check.

The Playfair Cipher could be broken if (a) there was enough text and (b) there was adequate statistical data on the frequency of digrams in the clear-text language. The latter is fairly easy to undertake today using a computer with access to text from the web, but doing it by hand in the early 1940s would have been an onerous task. The Germans must have had access to such data for English, but for Norwegian …? Playfair was nothing like as secure as Marks' OTPs (WOKs) or the more sophisticated variations of poem codes, but it was probably safe enough if used very infrequently for short messages.

Clever agents – for example Einar Skinnarland – would send dispatches in a mixture of English and Norwegian, a trick that is a nightmare for cryptanalysts.

Australian Coastwatcher Sub-Lt. Arthur Evans' decryption of the radio message alerting agents in the Solomon Islands to the loss of Lt. John F. Kennedy's motor torpedo boat PT-109.

Above is a remarkable message which was sent to Australian Coastwatchers (see Chapter 3) in the Solomon Islands soon after a Japanese destroyer, the *Amagiri*, collided with US Navy motor torpedo boat PT-109, causing it to explode and sink. Its commander, Lieutenant John F. Kennedy, and eleven crew members managed to swim to land – but no one knew where. Coastwatcher Sub-Lieutenant Arthur Evans had seen the explosion from his observation post high on Kolombangara, an island occupied by over 10,000 Japanese troops.

When the encrypted message came over the radio, he wrote down the twenty five-letter groups. After decrypting it he wrote the clear text below. By examining the five-letter groups you should be able to determine easily which *type* of encryption the Coastwatchers were using.

Successes and salutary lessons

There was constant pressure on agents in the field to get their coding procedures right; these usually took longer than the transmission itself, but failure to use them properly could render the intelligence useless. A team of about forty FANYs based at Station 53, Grendon Underwood, had the essential job of encoding messages prior to transmission and decoding those that had just arrived. Some of them were 'indecipherables', and in those cases they had to work out what mistake the agent had made and try to correct it – usually by bombarding the cipher text with alternate keys, sometimes as many as 20,000. If that didn't work, they would send the cipher text to Leo Marks, and he would try to break the message using cryptanalysis techniques.

Marks spent a lot of time staring at messages from Einar Skinnarland, who seemed incapable of sending a dispatch which *wasn't* indecipherable. But Skinnarland's traffic had a high priority because he was an engineer working inside the Norsk Hydro plant at Vermok. He had helped Norway to build the heavy water plant and was now helping SOE to destroy it.

The job of teaching code procedures to the agents trained to attack the Norsk Hydro heavy water facility also fell to Leo Marks. The group, code-named Operation GROUSE, was led by Jens-Anton Poulsson and included Knut Haugland, Claus Helberg and Arne Kjelstrup. Marks was hugely impressed when he first met them; they always turned up for classes on time and operated as a team. During one decoding exercise he noticed that Haugland had finished long before the others but was pretending to re-check his work, waiting for them to catch up. In his later assessment Marks graded three of the agents as 'excellent' and Haugland as 'quite brilliant'. Only one message from Haugland in the field appeared to be indecipherable; but later

Marks admitted it was *his* fault – he had misspelled a Norwegian word in the key.

Marks worked hard within the intelligence community to persuade the powers that be to change their codes to a system producing fewer indecipherables. One of the biggest problems was the prevailing – and dangerous – practice of home stations telling agents to re-transmit unreadable messages. While giving a motivational talk to the FANY decoders at Grendon, Marks said this:

> There's an indecipherable down there with your names on it. It's from a Belgian agent who's completely blown. He's sent us a message telling us his co-ordinates – that is, where he can be picked up. A Lysander is standing by to get him out. The message won't budge. At ten o'clock this evening he's due to come on the air and repeat it. If he does, those cars will close in. We will lose that man – just as a few weeks ago we lost a young Norwegian named Arne Vaerum, code-name Penguin. The SS shot him while he was retransmitting an indecipherable message.

8.5 A Suitable Ending

In 1942 the Political Warfare Executive (PWE) came up with an ingenious method to enable its propaganda agents to shorten their radio messages whilst simultaneously making them more difficult to decrypt. It involved the use of a dictionary – but not as a book code. PWE's explanation of the plan is shown opposite.

(*FO 898/73 UK
National Archives*)

APPENDIX III

METHOD OF SHORTENING W/T MESSAGES.

The aim of this method is to permit the maximum of information to be sent in the minimum of letters; the method may incidentally protect the code by making the message more difficult to unscramble.

For interpretation of the method, "Norsk Rettskrivnings- ordbok 1940" (Grundt Tanum) is needed. This is an uncompromising publication, and easy to obtain in Norway.

Three operations are involved before the message is transmitted:

    (a) Shortening sentences (i.e. conversion to journalists'
            "cablese").
    (b) Shortening words (for which "Norsk Rettskrivnings-
            ordbok is needed).
    (c) Coding.

Operation (a) is simply a matter of practice and the native wit of the man concerned.

Operation (b) is accomplished by going through Norsk Rettskrivningsordbok and striking out such parts of the words as can be removed without making the meaning doubtful. (The vocabulary is of course limited to that of Norsk Rettskrivnings- ordbok). The attached photostat (Appendix IIIa) of p.241 of N.R.

explains the system clearly. Take the word "krig"; this cannot be shortened. But the next word "Krigførende" can be shortened to "krigf", as there is no other word given which begins "krigf". And so on.

    The following words are represented by their initial letters:

        Norge, nordmenn, norsk

        England, engelskmenn, engelsk

        Amerika, etc.

        Russland, etc.

        Frankrike, etc.

        Tyskland, etc.

        Sverige, etc.

        Danmark, etc.

    A fullstop is represented by X.

    The attached photostat (Appendix IIIb) gives an example of a message shortened according to the method, and ready for coding.

By 'uncompromising publication' the writer means Norway's very large equivalent to the Oxford English Dictionary. In the example cited, letters are chopped off the end of the word to be used (in this instance words beginning '*krig*', 'war') until it makes a new word that is meaningless (see below). The recipient (also with a copy of *Norsk Rettskrivningsordbok*) reverses the process. And because the signal now includes many words not actually in the Norwegian language, the Funkabwehr will be challenged to decipher it. The worked example (not included here) shows a typical message in Norwegian. It is about 800 letters in length. After applying 'cablese' it reduces to 474, and then to 302 letters with the dictionary trick; that is a worthwhile shortening.

It is unknown whether PWE's system was ever used in the field.

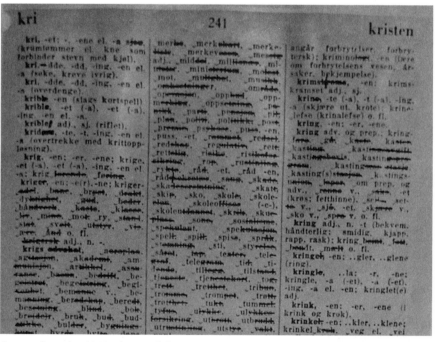

A page from the 1940 edition of the *Norsk Rettskrivningsordbok* showing words shortened until they become meaningless. '*Krigførende*' (belligerent) becomes '*krigf*'. (*FO 898/73 UK National Archives*)

Notes

Chapter 1
1. Charles H. Briscoe Phd, MAJOR HERBERT R. BRUCKER, SF PIONEER, Part III: SOE Training & 'Team HERMIT' into France, 2006. (*www.soc.mil/ARSOF_ History/articles/v3n1_bruckner_page_1.html*). Briscoe is the Command Historian.
2. Ibid.
3. Syllabus of Lectures at SOE Special Training School STS 103 (Camp X, Canada), early 1944. (*UK National Archives files HS 7/51, HS 7/52, HS 7/55, HS 7/56*)
4. Report from Operation DEHLIA "A"–"B" to Lt.-Cdr. Eric Welsh (SIS) from Alfred Henningsen, Eivind Viken and Atle Svardal, London, 24 November 1943 (in Norwegian). The instruction book is inside this file.
5. All SOE training schools had bars. It was important for directing staff to be able to assess the performance of recruits when under the influence of alcohol – the students, not the staff.
6. Robyn Walker, *The Women Who Spied For Britain*, Amberley Publishing, 2014.
7. (*UK National Archives*)

Chapter 2
1. Operation ERICA: Post-operation Report by Atle Svardal. Operation DEHLIA File. (*Norges Hjemmefrontmuseum: Norway's Resistance Museum*)
2. *Botnane og Årebrot grendalag*: www.botnane.no/2018/11/14/atle-svardal/
3. Operation DEHLIA File (*Norges Hjemmefrontmuseum*)
4. 2/Lt. Atle Svardal, Royal Norwegian Army, Record of Service to this Organization, Royal Navy Intelligence and the SIS, 25 September 1943.
5. William H. Garzke and Robert O. Dulin, *Battleships: Axis and Neutral Battleships in World War II*, Annapolis, Naval Institute Press, 1985.
6. Vera Henriksen, *Luftforsvarets historie – Fem år i utlegd* (History of the Air Force – Five years in history), Aschehoug, Oslo, 1996.
7. Ingrid Margrete Thorvaldsen, *Lokale krigsheltar får ny merksemd i den nye boka Nødrop fra Staveneset*, 25 August 2015. www.firda.no/nyhende/krigsheltar-heidra-i-ny-bok/s/1-51-7546571
8. Operation ERICA (10 January 1943 – 4 September 1943) by Atle Svardal. Report dated London 22 September 1943. Translation by SIS.
9. Ibid. See Chapter 8.1 for more about aerials.
10. Ibid.
11. Ibid.
12. Lorelou Desjardins, *A Frog in the Fjord* (https://afroginthefjord.com/2015/03/08/how-to-differentiate-the-norwegian-dialects/)
13. Operation ERICA (10 January 1943 – 4 September 1943) by Atle Svardal. Report dated London, 22 September 1943.

14. Ibid.
15. M. S. Goodman, *MI6's Atomic Man: The Rise and Fall of Commander Eric Welsh*, 2016. King's College London, King's Research Portal. https://kclpure.kcl.ac.uk/portal/files/53828217/The_Father_of_Atomic_Intelligence_.pdf.
16. Operation CYGNUS file. Letter N/874 dated 30 November 1943 from Welsh to Ås. Radio message quoted dated 28 November 1943. (*Norwegian archives*)
17. CYGNUS message N/997, 13 December 1943
18. CYGNUS message N/019, 16 December 1943
19. Petty Officer Dagfinn Ulriksen, Royal Norwegian Navy. Record of Service to this Organization, Secret Intelligence Service, undated copy.
20. Operation CYGNUS: Dagfinn Ulriksen and Ivar Møller, 1943–44. Secret Intelligence Service, undated report. (*Norwegian Archives*)
21. Petty Officer Dagfinn Ulriksen, Royal Norwegian Navy. Record of Service to this Organization, Secret Intelligence Service, undated copy.
22. Gaute Losnegård, *Wartime drama at the headland of Staveneset*. Fylkesarkivet i Sogn og Fjordane. https://resource.fylkesarkivet.no/article/9ce1e258-c56a-466c-a9dd-15b886df399.
23. Report from Operation DEHLIA "A" – "B" to Lt. Cdr. Eric Welsh (SIS) from Alfred Henningsen, Eivind Viken and Atle Svardal, London, 24 November 1943.
24. Botnane Og Årebrot Grendalag, www.botnane.no/2018/11/14/augevitneskildring-13-mars-1945/
25. Fredrick Persen, Report on Station ROSKA, www.firdaposten.no/atle-svardal/sigrun-solberg/roska/roska-rapporten/g/5-16-208183
26. Ibid.
27. 2/Lt. Atle Svardal, Royal Norwegian Army, Record of Service to this Organization. The Secret Intelligence Service (MI6), 25 September 1943.

Chapter 3
1. Eric Feldt, *The Coastwatchers*, Oxford University Press, New York, 1946.
2. Munro Leaf (illustr. Robert Lawson), *The Story of Ferdinand*, Faber & Faber, London, 2017, Grosset & Dunlap, New York 2011. Originally published in 1936, this book was banned in Spain and Germany for its 'pacifist' message.
3. Eric Feldt, *The Coastwatchers*, Oxford University Press, New York, 1946.
4. Walter Lord, *Lonely Vigil: Coastwatchers of the Solomons*, Bluejacket Books, Open Road Media, Kindle Edition, 1977, 2012.
5. Henry I. Shaw, *First Offensive: The Marine Campaign for Guadalcanal*, Marines in World War II Commemorative Series, 2015, via Project Gutenberg.
6. Letter from Sub-Lt. P. Mason RANVR to Commander E. A. Feldt RAN, SIO North Eastern Area, 26 March 1943.
7. Quoted in Walter Lloyd, *Lonely Vigil: Coastwatchers of the Solomons*, Open Road, New York, 1977.
8. Ibid. Note how huge the numbers are compared with the ships being watched by SIS radio agents in Norway.
9. Lt. W. J. Read, RANVR, Notes in Explanation of Accompanying Diagram of Bougainville, 26 April 1943.
10. Ibid.
11. Ibid.

12. *Bougainville Operations and the Battle of Cape St George, 3–25 November 1943*, Combat Narratives Solomon Islands Campaign, Volume XIII, Office of Naval Intelligence, U.S. Navy, Naval History and Heritage Command, Department of the Navy, 2019.
13. Ibid.

Chapter 4
1. Paul L. Kesaris (ed), *The Rote Kapelle: The CIA's History of Soviet Intelligence and Espionage Networks in Western Europe, 1936–1945*, CIA, 1979.
2. Ibid.
3. Paul L. Kesaris (ed), *The Rote Kapelle: The CIA's History of Soviet Intelligence and Espionage Networks in Western Europe, 1936–1945*, CIA, 1979.
4. Leopold Trepper, *The Great Game – Memoirs of a Master Spy*, Michael Joseph Ltd, first English edition 1977. Originally published in French.
5. Peter Wright, *Spycatcher*, William Heinemann Australia, 1987.
6. Wilhelm F. Flicke, (transl. Ray W. Pettengill), *War Secrets in the Ether Part III*, National Security Agency, Washington DC, 1953, declassified 2014.
7. 'Weimar Berlin: Berlin 1918–1933, neuralgic center of Europe. Arts, politics, literature, cinema, lifestyles.' An excellent website at: www.weimarberlin.com
8. Louis Thomas, *Alexander Radó*, Central Intelligence Agency, Center for the Study of Intelligence.
9. Alexander Radó and Marthe Rajchman, *Atlas of Today and Tomorrow*, Victor Gollancz Ltd, London 1938. This can still be found on the second-hand book market.
10. Ursula had a picaresque career, some of which was spent post-war in the UK acting as courier for the Soviet nuclear spy Klaus Fuchs. See: 'Ruth Werner: Communist spy who passed the west's atomic secrets to Moscow in the cause of fighting fascism' by Richard Norton-Taylor, *Guardian*, London, 11 Jul 2000, at www.theguardian.com/news/2000/jul/11/guardianobituaries.richardnortontaylor
11. Alias 'Jim', alias 'Alfred', alias 'Major Granatow', alias 'Alfred Feodorovich Capidus', alias 'Alexander Alexandrovich Dymov', alias 'John South', alias 'Albert Mueller', according to *The Rote Kapelle: The CIA's History of Soviet Intelligence and Espionage Networks in Western Europe, 1936–1945*, University Publications of America Inc. Washington, DC, 1979.
12. Alexander Foote, *Handbook for Spies*, 1949, Coachwhip Publications, Darke County, Ohio, 2011.
13. Wilhelm F. Flicke (transl. Ray W. Pettengill), *War Secrets in the Ether Part III*, National Security Agency, Washington DC, 1953, declassified 2014.
14. Leopold Trepper, *The Great Game – Memoirs of a Master Spy*, Michael Joseph Ltd, first English edition, 1977.
15. Ibid.
16. Alexander Foote, *Handbook for Spies*, 1949, Coachwhip Publications, Darke County, Ohio, 2011.
17. Guy de Téramond, *Le miracle du professeur Wolmar*, Édition du Monde illustré, Paris, 1910.
18. Leopold Trepper, *The Great Game – Memoirs of a Master Spy*, Michael Joseph Ltd, first English edition, 1977.
19. Editors of Time-Life Books, *The Shadow War*, Time-Life, Alexandria, Virginia, 1990.
20. The National Archives, KV 2/2068, Victor Sokolov, declassified 23 June 2005.
21. Leopold Trepper, *The Great Game – Memoirs of a Master Spy*, Michael Joseph Ltd, first English edition, 1977.

22. Wilhelm F. Flicke (transl. Ray W. Pettengill), *War Secrets in the Ether Part III*, National Security Agency, Washington DC, 1953, declassified 2014.
23. Malcolm Muggeridge, *Chronicles of Wasted Time Volume II: The Infernal Grove*, Collins, London, 1981.
24. Anthony Read and David Fisher, *Operation Lucy: Most Secret Spy Ring of the Second World War*, Coward, McCann & Geoghegan, New York, 1981.
25. Phillip Knightley, *The Second Oldest Profession: Spies and Spying in the Twentieth Century*, Norton, London, 1986.

Chapter 5
1. As quoted by M. R. D. Foot, *Resistance*, Eyre Methuen, London, 1977.
2. M. R. D. Foot, obituary of Sir Peter Tennant, *Independent*, London, 11 January 1997.
3. Andrew Croft, *A Talent for Adventure*, The Self-Publishing Association, 1991. This autobiography of Colonel Andrew Croft DSO OBE is highly recommended.
4. Peter Tennant, *Touchlines of War*, University of Hull Press, 1992.
5. Olav Krause Sætten, Report about the organizing of sabotage and guerrilla groups in the Trondheim District, Stockholm, 16 October 1942, UK National Archives.
6. Ibid.
7. Ibid.
8. Attachment to a letter from UK Foreign and Commonwealth Office SOE Adviser to Erik Gjems-Onstad MBE, 25 March 1983, Norwegian archives.
9. UK National Archives, HS 9/1114/3.
10. Odd Sørli, Report on work in Trondheim and Trøndelag, Stockholm, August 1943, UK National Archives.
11. Ibid.
12. Ibid.
13. UK Meteorological Office Monthly Weather Report MWR-1943.
14. Erik Gjems-Onstad, *LARK: Milorg i Trøndelag 1940–1945*, Midt-Norge Forlag, Stjørdal, 1990.
15. Ibid.
16. Erik Gjems-Onstad, Report on Operation Lark, Stockholm, 12 November 1943.
17. Ibid.
18. Ian Herrington, *The Special Operations Executive in Norway 1940–1945: Policy and Operations in the Strategic and Political Context*, PhD thesis, De Montfort University, 2004.
19. Erik Gjems-Onstad, Report on Operation Lark, Stockholm, 12 November 1943.
20. CIA Featured Story Archive, The Office of Strategic Services, Operation RYPE, www.cia.gov/news-information/featured-story-archive/2010-featured-story-archive/oss-operation-rype.html. Retrieved 18 October 2019.
21. Borge Langeland, Operation RYPE (March–June 1945). Retrieved from: www.cia.gov/news-information/featured-story-archive/2010-featured-storyarchive/oss-operation-rype.html
22. Ibid.
23. Borge Langeland, Operation RYPE (March–June 1945). Retrieved from: www.cia.gov/news-information/featured-story-archive/2010-featured-storyarchive/oss-operation-rype.html
24. CIA Featured Story Archive, The Office of Strategic Services, Operation RYPE, www.cia.gov/news-information/featured-story-archive/2010-featured-story-archive/oss-operation-rype.html. Retrieved 18 October 2019.

25. Ibid. The Norwegian courier was transferred to Sweden for treatment and survived.
26. Asbjørn Svarstad, 'Amerikanere vanæret tyske lik – i Norge (Americans disgraced German corpses – in Norway)', *Dagbladet*, 14 January 2012.
27. Ibid.
28. CIA Featured Story Archive, The Office of Strategic Services, Operation RYPE, www.cia.gov/news-information/featured-story-archive/2010-featured-story-archive/oss-operation-rype.html. Retrieved 18 October 2019.
29. Ian Herrington, *The Special Operations Executive in Norway 1940–1945: Policy and Operations in the Strategic and Political Context*, PhD thesis, De Montfort University, 2004.
30. Bane Nor, *Forgotten war heroes*, May 2015. www.banenor.no/Om-oss/arkiv-jernbaneverket/Jernbanemagasinet-arkiv/Nyheter/mai-2015/Jernbanens-folk-impressed-under-krigen/

Chapter 6

1. M.R.D. Foot, *SOE in France: An Account of the Work of the British Special Operations Executive in France 1940–1944*, Whitehall History Publishing in association with Frank Cass Publishers, London and Portland, Oregon, 2004. Originally published by HSMO, London, 1966–8.
2. Nancy Wake, *The White Mouse*, Sun Books, Melbourne, 1985, Macmillan Australia, 2011.
3. Obituary of Nancy Wake, *New York Times*, 14 August 2011.
4. Peter FitzSimons, *Nancy Wake, Australia's Greatest War Heroine*, Harper Collins Australia, 2001.
5. Robyn Walker, *The Women Who Spied for Britain*, Amberley Publishing, 2014.
6. David Stafford, obituary of Nancy Wake, *Guardian*, 8 August 2011.
7. Wikipedia: https://fr.wikipedia.org/wiki/Denis_Rake
8. Nigel Perrin, SOE Agent Profiles, https://nigelperrin.com/denisrake.htm
9. Vanessa Thorpe: 'Curtain rises on Gielgud's gay scandal', www.theguardian.com/stage/2008/feb/10/theatre.gayrights. The case was believed to have been a factor in the 1967 decriminalization of homosexual acts in the UK.
10. Nigel Perrin, *SOE Agent Profiles*, https://nigelperrin.com/denisrake.htm
11. Wikipedia: https://fr.wikipedia.org/wiki/Denis_Rake
12. Maurice Buckmaster, *They Fought Alone*, Odhams, 1958, Biteback Classics, 2014.
13. Robyn Walker, *The Women Who Spied for Britain*, Amberley Publishing, 2014.
14. Quoted in George C. Chalou, *The Secret War: The Office of Strategic Services in World War II*, Prentice Hall & IBD, 1992. Proceedings of a conference sponsored by and held at the National Archives in Washington, D. C., July 1991. Papers by veterans of the OSS, and scholars and archivists expert in the records of the OSS and WWII.
15. See Chapter 1.4 on How To Make A Radio Agent: Training.
16. From a letter he wrote to the website East Lothian at War, 13 October 1998: www.eastlothianatwar.co.uk/ELAW/SpecialOperationsExecutive.html
17. Max Hastings, *Das Reich: The March of the 2nd SS Panzer Division through France*, Holt, Rinehart and Winston, New York, 1981.
18. From a letter he wrote to the website East Lothian at War, 11 October 1998: www.eastlothianatwar.co.uk/ELAW/Special Operations Executive.html
19. Leo Marks, *Between Silk and Cyanide: A Codemaker's War 1941–1945*, Harper Collins, London, 1998–2000.

20. M. R. D. Foot, *SOE in France: An Account of the Work of the British Special Operations Executive in France 1940–1944*, Frank Cass Publishers, London, 1966–2004.
21. 'Sergeant John Sharp, radio operator who spent three months with the Maquis in occupied France for Operation Jedburgh', *Daily Telegraph* obituary, 30 September 2019.
22. Max Hastings, *Das Reich: The March of the 2nd SS Panzer Division through France*, Holt, Rinehart and Winston, New York, 1981.
23. Giles Milton, *Churchill's Ministry of Ungentlemanly Warfare*, John Murray, London, 2016.
24. Max Hasting, *Das Reich: The March of the 2nd SS Panzer Division through France*, Holt, Rinehart and Winston, New York, 1981.
25. David Nicolson, *Aristide: Warlord of the Resistance*, Leo Cooper, London, 1994. (Roger Landes' official biography)
26. TICOM/I-115. Further interrogation of Oberstleutnant Mettig of OKW/CHI on the German Wireless Security Service *(Funküberwachung)*, 17 September 1945.
27. Leo Marks, *Between Silk and Cyanide: A Codemaker's War 1941–1945*, Harper Collins, London, 1998–2000.
28. David Nicolson, *Aristide: Warlord of the Resistance*, Leo Cooper, London, 1994. (Roger Landes' official biography)
29. Ibid.
30. Dominique Lormier, *Bordeaux brûle-t-il? Ou la libération de la Gironde 1940–1945*, Dossiers d'Aquitaine, 1998. ('Is Bordeaux burning? Or the liberation of the Gironde'.)
31. David Nicolson, *Aristide: Warlord of the Resistance*, Leo Cooper, London, 1994. (Roger Landes' official biography)

Chapter 8
1. Eric Feldt, *The Coastwatchers*, Oxford University Press, New York 1946.
2. M. R. D. Foot, *SOE: An Outline History of the Special Operations Executive 1940–46*, Bodley Head, London, 2014. See p.127.
3. Benjamin Cowburn, *No Cloak, No Dagger: Allied Spycraft in Occupied France*, Frontline Books (an imprint of Pen & Sword Books), 2009, originally published by The Adventurers Club, London, 1960.
4. 'German Radio Intelligence', Lieutenant General Albert Praun, Chief of Army and Armed Forces Signal Communications (OKW) from 1944. This document is believed to have been written for the OSS after Praun's capture in 1946. Declassified 2014.
5. Dr Richard Novotny, Josef Hockauf and Dr Alexander Grachegg, *German D/F and intercepting system against illicit transmitters*, TICOM/I-148, Oslo, 8 August 1945.
6. Randy Rezabek, *TICOM Archive: Secret Intelligence in Nazi Germany*. www.ticomarchive.com. This is a very thorough source for TICOM materials.
7. Dr Richard Novotny, Josef Hockauf and Dr Alexander Grachegg, *German D/F and intercepting system against illicit transmitters*, TICOM/I-148, a German account of RDF operations against SIS and SOE radio agents in Norway, Oslo, 8 August 1945.
8. The National Archives, files HW41/401.
9. Bob King, *G3ASE: The Secret Activities of a Large Number of Radio Amateurs during World War Two*. http://cdmnet.org/RSS/SecretListeners/Bob's VI Article.pdf
10. Rhey T. Snodgrass and Victor F. Camp, *Radio Receiving for Beginners*, The MacMillan Company, New York, 1922.

11. *International Morse Code, Hand Sending*, Department of Defense, Dept. of the Army, Office of the Chief Signal Officer. www.youtube.com/watch?v=R-petiNdCIY

12. The DX Zone training apps: www.dxzone.com/catalog/Software/Morse_Code_Training/

13. For more about the history of cryptology, see David Kahn, *TheCodebreakers: The Story of Secret Writing* and Simon Singh, *The Code Book: The Secret History of Codes and Code-breaking* .

14. An excellent description of how these devices work can be found at Github: https://github.com/gchq/CyberChef/wiki/Enigma,-the-Bombe,-and-Typex. It was written by GCHQ, the successor to the Government Code & Cypher School at Bletchley Park.

15. Petty Officer Fred Jones, Royal Navy Radio Mechanic, quoted in *TypeX History/Development*: www.jproc.ca/crypto/typex.html

16. Operation CROW, October 1941–December 1942. PWE and SOE. HS 2/152. (*UK National Archives*)

17. This is rendered as 'Ring'd' in Tennyson's original, but it seems unlikely that agents were required to memorize such poetic abbreviations.

18. Text of poem from Wikipedia: Creative Commons CC BY-SA 4.0 International License.

19. Edward Lear, *The Owl and the Pussycat*, first published in 1871 as part of *Nonsense Songs, Stories, Botany, and Alphabets*.

20. *German Radio Intelligence*, Lieutenant-General Albert Praun, Chief of Army and Armed Forces Signal Communications (OKW), 1946. p.113.

Bibliography and Further Reading

Published sources

Buckmaster, Maurice, *They Fought Alone*, Odhams, 1958, Biteback Classics, 2014

Chalou, George C., *The Secret War: The Office of Strategic Services in World War II*, Prentice Hall & IBD, 1992

Connor, Ken, *Ghost Force: Secret History of the SAS*, Weidenfeld & Nicholson, London, 1998

Cowburn, Benjamin, *No Cloak, No Dagger: Allied Spycraft in Occupied France*, Frontline Books (an imprint of Pen & Sword Books), 2009. Originally published by The Adventurers Club, London, 1960.

Croft, Andrew, *A Talent for Adventure*, The Self-Publishing Association, 1991

Denham, Henry, *Inside the Nazi Ring: Naval Attaché in Sweden, 1940–45*, John Murray, London, 1984

Editors of Time-Life Books: *The Shadow War*, Time-Life, Alexandria, Virginia, 1990

Feldt, Eric, *The Coastwatchers*, Oxford University Press, New York, 1946

FitzSimons, Peter, *Nancy Wake, Australia's Greatest War Heroine*, Harper Collins Australia, 2001

Foot M.R.D., *SOE in France: An Account of the Work of the British Special Operations Executive in France 1940–1944*, Whitehall History Publishing in association with Frank Cass Publishers, London and Portland, Oregon, 2004. Originally published by HSMO, London, 1966–8.

Foot, M. R. D, *Resistance*, Eyre Methuen, London, 1977

Foote, Alexander, *Handbook for Spies*, Coachwhip Publications, Darke County, Ohio, 1949, 2011

Garnett, David, *The Secret History of PWE – Political Warfare Executive 1939–1945*, St Ermins Press, London, 2002

Garzke, William H. and Dulin, Robert O., *Battleships: Axis and Neutral Battleships in World War II*, Naval Institute Press, Annapolis, 1985

Gjems-Onstad, Erik, *LARK: Milorg i Trøndelag 1940–1945*, Midt-Norge Forlag, Stjørdal, 1990

Hastings, Max, *Das Reich: The March of the 2nd SS Panzer Division through France*, Holt, Rinehart & Winston, New York, 1981

Henriksen, Vera, *Luftforsvarets historie – fem år i utlegd* (History of the Air Force – five years in history), Aschehoug, Oslo 1996

Howe, Ellic, *The Black Game – British Subversive Operations against the Germans during the Second World War*, Michael Joseph, London, 1982

Jeffery, Keith, *The Secret History of MI6*, Penguin Press, London, 2010

Kahn, David, *The Codebreakers: The Story of Secret Writing*, Scribner, New York, 1997

Knightley, Phillip, *The Second Oldest Profession: Spies and Spying in the Twentieth Century*, Norton, London 1986

Lord, Walter, *Lonely Vigil: Coastwatchers of the Solomons*, Bluejacket Books, Open Road Media, 1977, 2012

Marks, Leo, *Between Silk and Cyanide: A Codemaker's War 1941–1945*, Harper Collins, London, 1998–2000

Milton, Giles, *Churchill's Ministry of Ungentlemanly Warfare*, John Murray, London, 2016

Muggeridge, Malcolm, *Chronicles of Wasted Time Volume II: The Infernal Grove*, Collins, London, 1981

Nater, Jenny, *Secret Duties of a Signals Interceptor: Working with Bletchley Park, the SDs and the OSS*, Pen & Sword Aviation, Barnsley, 2016

Nicolson, David, *Aristide: Warlord of the Resistance*, Leo Cooper, London, 1994 (Roger Landes' official biography)

Pidgeon, Geoffrey, *The Secret Wireless War: The Story of MI6 Communications 1939–1945*, Arundel Books, Richmond, 2008

Read, Anthony and Fisher, David, *Operation Lucy: Most Secret Spy Ring of the Second World War*, Coward, McCann & Geoghegan, New York 1981

Singh, Simon, *The Code Book: The Secret History of Codes and Code-breaking*, Fourth Estate, London, 2002

Snodgrass, Rhey T. and Camp, Victor F., *Radio Receiving for Beginners*, The MacMillan Company, New York, 1922

Tennant, Peter, *Touchlines of War*, The University of Hull Press, 1992

Trepper, Leopold, *The Great Game – Memoirs of a Master Spy*, Michael Joseph Ltd, 1977 (originally published in French)

Wake, Nancy, *The White Mouse*, Sun Books, Melbourne, 1985, Macmillan Australia, 2011

Walker, Robyn, *The Women Who Spied For Britain*, Amberley Publishing, 2014

Wright, Peter, *Spycatcher*, William Heinemann Australia, 1987

Available online

Flicke, Wilhelm F, *War Secrets in The Ether Part III* (transl. Ray W. Pettengill), National Security Agency, Washington DC, 1953, declassified 2014

Kesaris, Paul L. (ed), *The Rote Kapelle: The CIA's History of Soviet Intelligence and Espionage Networks in Western Europe, 1936–1945*. CIA, 1979

Praun, Lt. Gen. Albert (Chief of Army and Armed Forces Signal Communications from 1944), *German Radio Intelligence*. Declassified 2014, www.nsa.gov/Portals/70/documents/news-features/declassified-documents/friedman-documents/publications/FOLDER_240/41748999078819.pdf

Shaw, Henry I., *First Offensive: The Marine Campaign for Guadalcanal*, Marines in World War II Commemorative Series, 2015, via Project Gutenberg

Index